SURVIVOR RHETORIC

Negotiations and Narrativity in Abused Women's Language

Survivor Rhetoric

Negotiations and Narrativity in Abused Women's Language

Edited by
Christine Shearer-Cremean
and Carol L. Winkelmann

UNIVERSITY OF TORONTO PRESS
Toronto Buffalo London

© University of Toronto Press Incorporated 2004
Toronto Buffalo London
Printed in Canada

ISBN 0-8020-8973-9

Printed on acid-free paper

National Library of Canada Cataloguing in Publication

Survivor rhetoric : negotiations and narrativity in abused women's
  language / edited by Christine Shearer-Cremean and Carol L.
  Winkelmann.

Includes bibliographical references.
ISBN 0-8020-8973-9

1. Abused women – Language.   2. Abused women – Public opinion.
3. Narrative therapy.   4. Sociolinguistics.   I. Shearer-Cremean,
Christine   II. Winkelmann, Carol Lea

HV6626.S87 2004   362.88'083   C2004-902514-7

University of Toronto Press acknowledges the financial assistance to
its publishing program of the Canada Council for the Arts and the
Ontario Arts Council.

University of Toronto Press acknowledges the financial support for
its publishing activities of the Government of Canada through the
Book Publishing Industry Development Program (BPIDP).

Contents

Acknowledgments

The co-editors are grateful to the many people who helped them to complete this work. The women who have contributed to this volume are models for scholarly work in and for the community. Special thanks to Linda Parks from Miami University of Ohio, who provided hospitality and assistance in the early stages of this project.

Christine Shearer-Cremean would like to thank her husband, David N. Cremean, who has been an instrumental part of all her academic work; he has occupied the role of colleague, peer reader, friend, and beloved spouse. Her sister, Susan Stewart, has been both colleague and friend, providing support and encouragement throughout this project. Thanks to Timothy Martinez for reading and responding to work, and to Diane Bishop for her assistance in formatting the manuscript. Many thanks to department chair Ronnie Theisz, who graciously provided school funds for travel and support, and to Black Hills State University, which supplied research funds. Co-editor Carol Winkelmann has become friend and mentor throughout the duration of this project. Finally, Christine thanks her children, Samantha and Cormac, for keeping her grounded, continually reminding her why she teaches and writes.

Carol L. Winkelmann would like to thank her colleagues, Marie Giblin and Kandi Stinson, who listened to many stories about shelter life and encouraged her to write about shelter language and its many intricacies. She thanks her colleagues Paul Knitter, William Madges, and Sr. Rosie Miller OSF for their support and solidarity through the years as she has written about gender violence and as they accompany one another in the struggle to see justice for women in academia.

Christine Shearer-Cremean has been a wonderful colleague and co-editor. Other women have been generous with encouragement, including Carol's sister, Linda Gifford, and her friend Cathy Cornell. Finally, Carol is grateful to her spouse, John V. Ippoliti, and her son, Christopher R. McLaughlin, for their unending encouragement.

Christine and Carol also recognize the inspiration and energy they receive from the battered women with whom they have worked, and from other women – including friends, students, and community members – they have met in the struggle for human rights for women and girl children. May all social activists in the academy have such inspiration and support.

SURVIVOR RHETORIC

Introduction

CHRISTINE SHEARER-CREMEAN AND
CAROL L. WINKELMANN

Once everything is conceived in terms of language ... then the revolution
of the word is claimed to be inseparable from the revolution in the world ...
Patricia Waugh

How can we conceive of a revolutionary struggle which does not involve
a revolution in discourse?
Julia Kristeva

Violence against women has become increasingly recognized not only
as a legitimate field of academic study, but as a substantial human
rights issue calling for a holistic community response. American feminists have been arguing for over a decade that early responses to violence against women, such as the development of a network of safe
houses or shelters across the country, have not been sufficiently effective. Instead, they argue, the problem of physically and sexually assaulted women and girl children must be addressed across the
community because violence against women is based upon a complicated social, patriarchal network that permeates a variety of complex
discursive and social systems. Consequently, there has been a growing
coordinated community response to woman abuse within social service
agencies, the private sector, and the academic community. New conversations and conventions have developed in a multitude of locations,
including criminal justice, legal, clinical, religious, and academic communities. These conversations point both to increased public and insti-

tutional awareness of the woman abuse problem and to the need for more reflexivity on the part of interlocutors.

As they contribute to this project, academics and professionals, including feminists, have struggled to expand, resist, and reinvent the traditional gendered discourses of their professional fields. For example, feminist lawyers write against the patriarchal foundations of law and its implementation; feminist psychologists respond to the patriarchal nature of traditional therapeutic methods; and feminist literary theorists conduct ideologically contrary readings of texts in order to expose patriarchal assumptions and interpretations.

Researchers and women's advocates, however, have become increasingly challenged by recurrent, complex language issues as the topic of violence against women has become situated in various disciplines and discourses and as it has crossed boundaries through community, interdisciplinary, and even global conversations. Language makes apparent the socio-political realities that defy facile solutions, superficial resolutions, quick fixes, or instant progress, as traumatized women work for their own recovery and well-being or seek recourse and restitution for social injustice. For example, a two-week sensitivity training course for police who respond to domestic violence calls cannot adequately address the gender problems within the criminal justice system that women will face when they seek help from the police. Further, the problems are not simply a matter of sexism during police interviews with battered or raped women.

Discrimination against women is not limited, of course, to police departments and their training manuals, reporting procedures, shop talk, and so forth. The problem of gender violence is inherent, pervasive, and constitutive of patriarchal discourse as a whole throughout culture. The analysis of situated language use – for example, the analysis of the language of the criminal justice system – reveals the depth, breadth, and interlocking nature of cultural patterns that sustain the problem of violence against women. Women, including women traumatized from gender violence, who traverse community boundaries, run up against these patterns in everyday life, and they experience these patterns of sexism as obstacles even if they cannot precisely name or define them. Certainly, a profound, holistic, interdisciplinary, and cross-community response is necessary if the human rights of women are to be more fully implemented. Indeed, though this volume is concerned with the scholarship of Western feminists, we recognize that global dialogue is critical.

Of course, feminists and postmodernists have long flagged the centrality of the problem of language in progressive social change. Since the 1970s, feminism has exerted efforts to recognize difference, including language difference across race/ethnicity, class, age, sexual orientation, and so forth. And many feminists have been concerned about the problem of reconciling context-specific differences with universal political aims. In some Muslim societies, for example, the meaning of citizenship for women has subtle shadings that are dissimilar to and not easily reconcilable with the meaning of citizenship for women in Western democratic societies. The dialogue between feminists in these cultures has been challenging, but most promising. Indeed, postmodernism has relentlessly alerted us to the inherent language issues involved in any attempt to communicate. Postmodernism recognizes and asserts that language is not a vehicle for expressing the autonomous 'self'; instead, the self is mediated by a variety of community languages. This view does not displace body experiences or personal life history, but it recognizes the thoroughly social nature of language in both thought and communication. Language puts the 'self' together; indeed, the 'self' is a public, social, dialogic process, created and re-created in different forums, communities, and subcultures. Hence postmodernism, particularly in its strong varieties, tends towards perspectivism and cultural relativism. It highlights the incommensurability of language systems, prefers an understanding of language in terms of performance and rhetoric, and de-emphasizes notions of universal truth, aims, or progress. Incontrovertibly, then, both feminism and postmodernism challenge and influence mainstream academic conversations. Notions of language use from these two perspectives challenge simple articulations of the problem of violence against women or its quick eradication.

Independently, feminists in a variety of professional contexts have become increasingly convinced about the centrality of the social nature of language in formulating any conclusions or action agendas for combating violence against women. This anthology attempts to draw out some of language issues indicating the need for a more profound holistic approach to the problem of violence against women. It analyses survivor rhetoric as multi-layered, dialogic, situated, and re-situated discourse that defies categorical response. The contributors to the anthology regard language dissonances or conflict as a central, pervasive problem facing survivors as they encounter others – that is, individuals *and* institutions – in the community. For example, the contributors recognize problems such as an apparent 'disconnect' between an abuse survivor and the discourse systems (social service, legal, therapeutic, and so forth) she must negotiate in an attempt to re-establish her life. To various degrees, the contributors probe the dialectic nature of language use. Language, gender, healing, and empowerment are understood as created and re-created (or dismantled) each and every time the survivor (like every language user) engages in conversation. Simply stated, a commonality among the contributors is this conviction: Unless the researcher/advocate understands the continual reproduction of 'self' in relation to others through language, then she/he has an idealized, limited, ultimately inadequate model for both personal healing and social change. Language is a constitutive and dynamic element in the creation and re-creation of the self, other, and community. This view has important implications for understanding survivor rhetoric and thus dealing with the women who wield it.

To give an indication of how dynamic conceptions of language use inevitably disrupt conventional disciplinary 'truths,' we might consider psychology: a field of major influence on current concepts of trauma as articulated in the domestic violence and anti-rape movements. Some psychological constructions of the trauma narrative focus on its cohesiveness – as if healing from trauma can be accomplished via a series of discrete steps involving therapists and patients within the closed framework of a therapeutic relationship. Clearly, in a search for meaning, it is human nature to conceive of patterns, systems, or distinct linguistic architectures emerging from survivor narratives and, from the perspective of the therapist, there is functional 'truth' in this belief. A common agreement among psychologists is that, through the healing process, the survivor finds her own voice. In fact, the healing process *is* the reclamation of the survivor's voice. The survivor becomes able – by stages, and with the assistance of therapists or other helpful advocates – to move out of the patriarchal discourses that have impelled her to accept the traditional stereotyped roles for women and the ensuing, perhaps inevitable violence against them.

From a different perspective, however – a more socially influenced perspective – the healing process as described in many therapeutic and self-help schemas is, to various and sometimes unhelpful degrees, unidimensional. It is progressive, sometimes lockstep, even if recursiveness is recognized – that is, even if it is recognized that there will be some redundancy in the healing process as the survivor meets new challenges or reaches new levels of awareness. Healing is largely contained within a therapeutic relationship: that is, involving interactions between the therapist and the survivor, who then extends new and more appropriate concepts into her other relationships. Further, healing is ultimately the victim's responsibility, something she must do, evidence, perform, or enact. From a more social perspective, the healing process – as conceived within such a therapeutic framework – is stripped of its social context. In its description, it involves the interchange between therapist/advocate and the survivor until the survivor has recovered enough of her own voice to reconnect with the community in a healthier manner.

This is the basic psychological schema of even such influential writers as Judith L. Herman, therapist and author of the now classic *Trauma and Recovery*. Herman, concerned with survivors of incest and childhood trauma, charts three stages of recovery for patients. Clients must establish a sense of safety, reconstruct the trauma story, and restore the connection between themselves and their community. Herman does recognize that these healing stages are recursive: a client may revisit earlier stages as she moves through the healing process.

The first stage, however, is critical to attain before any other work can be accomplished. Beset with terror, the trauma victim needs to find a *sense of safety* from harm. With the therapist as facilitator, she must regain a sense of control over her body and her environment. Essentially, she must have a safe place to live and she must have supportive relationships. Next, the victim works with the therapist to restore a sense of power and control over her own life. So, secondly, the patient needs to engage in a process of *remembering and mourning*. She must give up the wordless, static nature of traumatic memory and replace it with testimony about her suffering. The therapist, as witness or ally, helps her to construct a new interpretation of the traumatic events – one that allows her to fully integrate the trauma into her life narrative. Thirdly, the trauma victim needs to *reconnect with the community*. Before this third stage, there is no full address of the social dimensions of trauma. The primary task was introspection. In this third stage, the survivor learns to look outward. She begins to fight for herself. For example, she might confront her family or challenge indifferent bystanders. She begins to build new relationships. In essence, she builds a new self, one that learns how to control fear and to move towards building new relationships of mutuality and intimacy. She may take on a 'survivor mission.' Indeed, a 'significant minority' sees the political or religious dimensions of their suffering and makes this a basis for social action (Herman 207). For Herman, social action can be educational, legal, or political involvement. It may be 'pursuing justice' through attempts to hold perpetrators accountable for crimes. She guardedly offers the idea that forgiveness involves the victimizer's confession, repentance, and restitution. To be clear, for Herman, recovery is never final or complete. But in the recovery process, empowerment and connection replace isolation and helplessness. Self-esteem is rebuilt. The survivor begins to learn to celebrate life.

Herman's tremendously influential work has redirected the course of trauma studies, reshaping in profound ways the study of violence against women. She searched for and found coherent patterns and meaning in the frequently stigmatized experience of women's trauma. Though some mental health professionals criticize aspects of her schema – for example, the difficulty of providing a sense of safety for the victim before providing a sense of solidarity, or the dubious merits of designating forgiveness as a last step of recovery – Herman has influenced a generation of scholars and therapists.

Another writer who has reshaped trauma studies is Elaine Scarry, literary studies scholar and philosopher. In *The Body in Pain*, Scarry offers an account of the structure of torture and war, but her approach to pain and suffering has found applicability across the disciplines. The prolonged, severe brutality indicative of many cases of domestic violence can be regarded as a species of torture. Although Scarry's approach is phenomenological, and thus less sequential or linear than other schemas, she works with a basic bipartite system: the *unmaking* and *making* of the self.

The infliction of torture is an inhuman act, Scarry argues, because it leads to the *unmaking* of human reality through grotesque, excruciating pain. Intense pain is world-destroying. The victim becomes all body as the psychological content of her mind – that which constitutes her self and her world – is obliterated. The ability to perceive physical facts in her mind is destroyed. In fact, the trauma of torture, the annihilating power of pain, leaves the victim unable to create meaning, demolishing language. The victim can only make inhuman groans and cries. Pain is the unmaking of her world. The torturer, on the other hand, experiences a growing sense of self that is based on the infliction of the victim's pain. The victim's shrinking world is his enlarging world. His power grows. He is voice and expanding self; the victim is expanding body and annihilated self. The agent of torture has no sense of responsibility outside of a sense of duty to inflict pain for some agency, for example, the regime he represents and its ideology. This frees him to objectify, deny, and destroy the victim. He makes her undoing his growth of agency, identity, and power.

Scarry's exploration of the unmaking of the world leads to an inquiry into the *making* of a victim's world when atrocity ends. The voice of the victim can be restored, particularly through the vehicle of the voice of a sympathetic other. If the pain is articulated, if it is brought into the world, it may be diminished and dissipated. A sympathetic voice can provide the hurt person with a self-extension. That is, the victim's pain can be expressed even when she cannot do it herself. One human being becomes the image of the hurt other. This is one way the voice can be recovered.

Again, Scarry does not delineate specific stages of recovery; rather, she undertakes a phenomenological exploration of the process. She notes two discernable stages of making: *making up* and *making real*. In the *unmaking* stage, the infliction of pain forces the victim into a state of pre-language because intense pain unmakes language, destroying the world by destroying linguistic reference to the world, by making the body the sole existent and its own enemy. The victim feels her body, not the weapon upon it. At the other end of the spectrum, however – its extreme – is imagination. When the victim is released from the grips of physical pain, she can engage in mental imagining. She can remember and reference the world. When her body is returned to a state of comfort, when it ceases to be an object of concern, she can extend her consciousness out into the world. The survivor is able to imagine objects and relations, that is, the world. She can *make up*.

In the *making real* process, the survivor endows the object of imagination with a material or verbal form. She opens into a wider frame – that of invention. She articulates her pain, for example. The survivor regains the ability to imagine and to create – to find, to make, and to endow with significance objects in the world through images, words, ideas, and so forth. She can self-express and self-extend. She can modify or adjust her relations to the objects that she can once again perceive. Thus, in the *making real* phase, the abuse survivor can offer personal, self-authored renditions of the traumatic event she suffered, renditions that may counter those of others. That is, in the best of circumstances, she can offer alternative representations of her abuse – including representations that challenge official representations. There may be a re-description of the traumatic event – in her terms. She is able to reconstruct her world.

Although Scarry is concerned about the inhumanity of political torture and especially the analogue between torture and nuclear war, her discussion is relevant to other types of pain, suffering, and trauma, including violence against women. As we have noted, conventional wisdom about healing from the sort of pain inflicted through domestic violence involves stages of silence, alienation, the rediscovery of voice, and the re-creating of identity and world. Scarry's account is subtle; yet, interestingly, her schema has been critiqued for its basic 'Christian existentialist morality.' Her account still involves notions of progress, improvement, and hope for permanent change. A postmodernist view of life and language – a view more and less represented in this anthology – critiques such absolute notions.

Generally, both Herman and Scarry see recovery from trauma as a progressive, staged process. Herman's pragmatic approach, devised to assist therapists, is more sequential than Scarry's abstract phenomenological approach. Yet both scholars basically view healing as a linear movement from a state of silence and alienation to one of rediscovering voice and human connection. These and similar schemas are functional, commonsensical, and descriptive, although – from our perspective – not sufficiently problematized.

The writers in this anthology do not seek to dispense with such assumptions: we all hope for permanent social change for women. Our contributors do not wish to minimize the contributions of these theorists as much as to problematize those contributions and thus widen the discussion. Hence contributors explore the complex, fragmented nature of trauma narrative. From a rhetorical (rather than therapeutic or phenomenological) perspective, our project asserts that – because of the dialogic nature of language – a unilinear, monodimensional healing process cannot and does not occur for abused women.

Take, for example, Herman's first stage of recovery: *establishing safety.* In a patriarchal culture, most abused women live without safety on several different levels. First of all, safety from male violence is not a guarantee for abused women, who may endure abuse, may not be able to escape it even if they leave, or may find it re-created in other relationships. Second, as long as women inhabit a patriarchal society, they are never fully safe. Even if they live with nonviolent partners, the threat of violence from other males is an ever-present reality. A feminist truism is that even the male privilege of nonviolent males is built upon the effects of the actions of violent males. Furthermore, in patriarchal discourse, women's narratives will always be called into question, doubted, made invisible – even by other women, who may be in denial that the reality of pervasive male violence against them even exists. Thus the female survivor of male violence may never experience the satisfaction of feeling safe or secure. How could she feel safe when her own voice will be always and everywhere vulnerable to uncertainties, shifts, gaps, and collisions of meaning? This is the reality of the process of language: meaning-making is dialogic, unstable, and forever open to disruption, interruption, and fragmentation.

Thus, in a real sense, abused women's shards of experience resist the fluent structural imposition of the healing narrative. Trauma narratives epitomize in a painful way the fragmentary and uncertain status of all narrative in a postmodern world. This is not to suggest it is not critical to 'tell one's story.' On the contrary, the atrocious stories of male violence against women must come to voice in order for women to secure their full human rights. However, inasmuch as the language process is inevitably dialectic, recursive, and unstable, it must be strategic to be effective. In order for women to construct healing, self-affirming trauma narratives, they cannot have false expectations about the efficacy of their own 'authentic' voice or trauma narrative. This is a basic contention of this anthology.

By examining carefully the situated language offered by abuse survivors, the writers in this volume complicate the notion or assumption that trauma narratives can unproblematically unfold within male-dominated discourse sites. The essayists look across diverse communities to examine the linguistic, political, legal, and social aspects of the rhetoric of survivors and their interlocutors. One resultant observation concerns the incommensurability of all interested languages about violence against women. These interested languages continually stratify and sometimes subvert women's language of abuse, their narratives of healing and recovery. Assuredly, this state of affairs will prevail with intensity while the dominant societal discourse is still patriarchal in nature or dealt with as unsituated or uninterested; yet, there are ways to strengthen the effects of women's narratives through a realistic understanding and assessment of the politics of language. The same argument may be made about the limitations of Eurocentric discourses regarding violence against women. This limitation is examined at length by Chandra Talpade Mohanty in *Feminism without Borders* in which she problematizes the tendency of Western feminists to falsely universalize or essentialize concerns about patriarchal discursive structures. The essayists in this volume limit their attention to Western linguistic, political, rhetorical, and psychological discourses, but they address diversity within Western discursive frameworks.

The writers in this collection attempt to keep alive an agenda for progressive social change by way of situated assessments within and across Western culture. The first two writers, Elana Newman and Carrie Baker, compose essays in which the problem of women's abuse narratives – when they are presented within a traditional, male-dominated discourse community – emerges clearly. Examined against a masculine epistemological framework, the woman's narrative is perceived as fragmented, disconnected, incoherent, invisible. The ability of a woman to synthesize her own narrative within the parameters of the dominant discourse is blocked or made irrelevant, and consequently her entire credibility is shattered. The incommensurability of these narratives becomes an identity issue for the abuse survivor, whose already unstable sense of self is further threatened. Newman and Baker identify and critique situations in which this phenomenon occurs. Given such linguistic constraints, these writers question whether abused women are sufficiently served by certain established critical discourses: the languages of law and psychology. These are two of the most pertinent discourses in the everyday experience of women who are trying to escape and recover from violence. Indeed, convention has it that therapy and restitution are essential to women's healing. These essays complicate facile or reformist remedies in the discourses of psychology and law.

Elana Newman, in 'Narrative, Gender, and Recovery from Childhood Sexual Abuse,' argues that the convergence of developmental, cultural, and psychological factors reduces the probability that most adult survivors of child sexual abuse will be able to create life-affirming, cohesive stories about themselves. Although psychologists emphasize the importance of survivors telling their story, few foreground such complications. Newman reviews several restrictions to the creation of trauma-related narratives, like neurobiological immaturity, self-imposed or imposed censorship, and the socio-cultural context of abuse. She combines theory, clinical evidence, and empirical evidence in presenting a child sexual abuse case to highlight the roles of gender and language in survivors' narratives about traumatic life experiences. Excerpts from an interview with the child sexual abuse survivor illustrate several points about the unique story-telling process that unfolds during the course of trauma-focused psychotherapy. Other researchers have addressed how traditional or mainstream counselling is inadequate to meet the recovering needs of child victims of sexual abuse (Mann; Agnew). Ultimately, Newman is concerned with the ways that narrative and gender interact to affect the recovery process, arguing that narratives in trauma-focused treatment of sexual abuse survivors need to be informed by a feminist perspective on power, sexuality, and language. A feminist therapeutic environment assists the survivor to more effectively create a coherent and enabling narrative in the face of complicating developmental and psycho-cultural factors.

Carrie N. Baker, in an essay entitled 'Speaking in Contradictions: Complex Agency of Battered Women Who Kill,' discusses how women accused of murdering their abusive partners have been encouraged by lawyers and advocates to use battered woman syndrome testimony in their legal defence. Such a strategy involves the creation of an abuse narrative in which the woman is seen as victimized by her partner to such an extent that she suffers from a psychological disability that prevents her from acting normally; the defence asserts that she develops a personality disorder. Many states have accepted some form of evidence on the battered woman syndrome as relevant to a woman's defence in these cases. Baker explores the assumptions about gender, identity, and agency underlying the Battered Woman Syndrome self-defence. She begins by describing the syndrome, including the cycle of violence and theory of learned helplessness. Then Baker explains feminist arguments that the law is male biased, particularly the law of self-defence, and describes reforms, including allowing evidence of the battered woman syndrome. In the third section, she addresses criticisms of the battered woman syndrome (self-defence) theory, including the claim that the theory lacks empirical support, has race and class biases, and relies on traditional stereotypes of women as passive victims. In the fourth section, she examines legal discourse to show the contradictory representations of battered women who kill their abusers. While battered woman syndrome testimony in theory supports the claim of self-defence, in many cases this evidence is used to argue (or is heard to support an argument) that the battered woman is mentally incapacitated, *not* that she is acting reasonably in the circumstances. In the final section she explores the complex agency of battered women. In terms of narrative theory, the expert witness becomes the narrator. The victim's voice is minimized through the agency of the psychologist/expert witness. In addition, the battered woman's syndrome focuses on the psyche of the defendant rather than the tumultuous, abusive environment or the social conditions that have created it. She concludes that neither the claim of self-defence nor the insanity defence captures the complex reality of battered women's lives because their actions are neither fully reasonable nor fully unreasonable, but a complex mixture of the two that the law, being categorical in nature, lacks the subtlety to recognize. Baker concludes by calling for the education of judges and juries about structural constraints against battered women. She argues that judges must be made to recognize gender inequality and society's failure to stop male violence against women, to enable them to understand why, for many battered women, killing might be the only way to survive.

Commonsensically, women *know* that their language and stories are often devalued when these are articulated to a male-dominated audience like the law or traditional psychology. Some theorists, although they understand the impact of gender, class, race/ethnicity, and sexual orientation, fail to adequately integrate these sociological factors into their theories and their practice. This happens in part because the models and schemas they devise are by nature merely templates that cannot completely accommodate particularities and difference. They create methodologies that mask the realities of language use and its essentially dialogic nature. Yet abuse survivors circulate within and among complex webs of discourse. Inevitably, survivors (like all language users) must engage with a multitude of discursive communities, many with different assumptions about gender, violence, and justice and different rules about language and genre, including narrative. For example, different religious, socio-political, and race/ethnic communities have different discursive assumptions and concepts, rules and regulations. Gay/lesbian/bisexual communities have different discursive conventions than heterosexual ones. Every time a survivor tells her abuse narrative within a particular web, it gets shaped and reshaped, it becomes differently inflected, as she interacts with various interlocutors with different conventions and rules. The consequences of this telling can be variously happy/unhappy, intentional/unintentional, anticipated/surprising, conscious/never recognized, conflictive/harmonious. The narrative changes, evolves, mutates.

The next group of anthology contributors, Batya Weinbaum and co-authors Cindy Holmes and Janice L. Ristock, begin to problematize the issue of situated and resituated abuse narratives. They explore the dynamism inherent in situated language use and its creation of new narrative forms. Healing narratives cannot simply be transposed from one context or location to another without the inherent dynamism of language creating new sets of discursive misalignments, disconnections, or contradictions with which to contend. These essayist begin to map out what actually happens when women bring their narratives to voice in new contexts.

Batya Weinbaum, in her study 'A Survivor within a Culture of Survivors: Untangling the Language of Sexual Abuse in Oral History Narrative Collected in a Politically Violent Situation,' considers what actually happens when a survivor shifts location or moves into new discourse communities. Weinbaum observes that certain religious, social, and political landscapes offer abused women a linguistic template upon which to resolve their own abuse, as they transition from victim to survivor and try to recover their self-esteem. Weinbaum traces the movement of a survivor, Dorit, as she converts from Catholicism to Judaism and, as part of her conversion experience, she moves from the United States to Israel. Domestic abuse survivors, like Dorit, may envision personal and political 'truths' as well as life stories on the basis of their own constructed narrative rhetoric rather than actual socio-political or historical facts. Dorit's experience as a physically abused woman informs – and, according to Weinbaum, misinforms – Dorit's politics, as she identifies with the Israeli right-wing political movement based primarily on her own trauma at the hands of an abusive husband. To elaborate: Dorit found logic, order, and a calling in Judaism, particularly because she still maintained a patriarchal conception of God. Judaism as a narrative construct, or architecture, permitted her to express feelings and a need for justice that Christianity seemed to restrict. She uncritically adopts an already existing religious discursive framework, Judaism, to cope with her tangled emotions about her abusive family and to find resolution. Then she transposes her tangled interpretation to the socio-political context of Israel. In the first instance, the transposition or wholesale adoption of the narrative structure of Judaism may be helpful; in the second instance, the transposition is detrimental to Dorit's growth. Weinbaum argues that Dorit is unable to perceive the Israeli-Palestinian political struggle clearly, as she is blinded by her own emotional identification with right-wing Israeli political and religious rhetoric. In fact, Weinbaum argues, the tense political situation in Israel and Dorit's active engagement in the anti-Arab cause permit Dorit to resolve her feelings as a formerly passive, abused woman. Weinbaum sees this phenomenon – as manifested in Dorit's narrative of her own abuse and conversion to Judaism – as being fairly common for recent immigrants to Israel possessing similar backgrounds. Further, Weinbaum suggests that in their desire to create a coherent narrative of their trauma, abused women may inaccurately assess socio-political dynamics because they do so primarily through the lens of their own abuse. Weinbaum's concern is that the various dominant feminist theories existing today do not adequately provide abused women with the linguistic strategies necessary to cope with a dominant, male logic/ language system. In Weinbaum's view, additional feminist research needs to address how some women naively seek other language landscapes to recover from the psychological effects of abuse. She also expresses concern that until we understand how our life experience shapes our perception of tense socio-political relations, we will be unable to calmly pursue peace.

In contrast to Weinbaum, who traces Dorit's literal change of geographical location, Cindy Holmes and Janice L. Ristock consider, in part, a shift in ideological location through their textual analysis in 'Exploring Discursive Constructions of Lesbian Abuse: Looking Inside and Out.' They examine the discursive constructions of lesbian abuse within feminist community-based educational booklets that are used to provide resources and help lesbians experiencing same-sex domestic violence. Also, they examine several American and Canadian 'backlash' writers who criticize feminist research on violence against women. These writers focus attention on lesbian abuse to attribute essentialism and anti-male sentiment to feminism. That is, they use lesbian battery to explode the notion of a lesbian utopia. Holmes and Ristock explore the assumptions made about violence, subjectivity, gender, race, and sexuality in these backlash writings and highlight some of their effects on and implications for the battered women's movement, particularly same-sex battering. Holmes' analysis explores the ways in which the educational booklets on lesbian abuse present a seemingly unified, coherent, or universal narrative on lesbian abuse that masks complexities, obscuring certain knowledges and subjectivities. For example, certain voices have been excluded: people who are bisexual or transgendered, women of colour, and those involved in situations of mutual abuse. Holmes and Ristock are interested in interrogating the way 'regimes of truth' (i.e., white middle-class feminist 'regimes of truth') obscure or delegitimize certain knowledges, subjects, and experiences through the process of legitimizing and normalizing others. Ristock examines constructions of abuse that focus on the topic of female perpetrators of violence and use lesbian abuse as an example to assert a discourse that shows women are 'just as bad' as men. Using a feminist, antiracist, postmodern lens, Holmes and Ristock discuss the ways power circulates in the production of knowledge on lesbian abuse. Their analysis of violence in same-sex relationships reveals these and other significant rhetorical problematics. For example, educational pamphlets draw on existing feminist theories of abuse in intimate heterosexual relationships to inform the analysis of violence in lesbian relationships. Such an analysis misses an interlocking model of oppression recognizing how women are currently positioned hierarchically to one another and how certain women have historically abused power over other women. In short, Holmes and Ristock attempt to make visible and problematize the way violence in same-sex relationships is constructed and reconstructed in different discursive and ideological contexts.

The final set of contributors, Cathy A. Colton, Brenda Daly, Christine Shearer-Cremean, and Carol L. Winkelmann, theorize postmodern rhetorics of violence against women. Cathy A. Colton, in 'Shattered Dreams: A Material Rhetorical Reading of Charlotte Fedders's Memoir of Domestic Abuse,' argues that rhetoric should be understood not only as a linguistic but also as a physical phenomenon. Thus, violence is also rhetoric, and the woman's battered body becomes the text. Colton uses the sensational domestic violence case of Charlotte Fedders, the ex-wife of a well-respected chief enforcement officer of the Securities and Exchange Commission. She argues that Charlotte Fedders's body becomes the site of an expanded understanding of rhetoric. Colton carefully builds her case by investigating and critiquing classical rhetorical theory and its notions of the art of the persuasion. Here persuasion is considered only as a mental or immaterial activity. As it has been classically understood, rhetoric is situated on the mind side of the body/mind dualism. However, by querying and re-imagining this classical model of rhetoric, Colton is able to assert that persuasion and coercion are intertwined and that they overlap in the act of seduction. The boundaries between mind/body are made ambiguous, blurred. To further support her reworking of rhetorical theory to entail violence, Colton uses Barry Brummett's theory of the social functions of rhetoric, including the exigent function, the quotidian function, and the implicative function, a methodology that allows Colton to further tease out the blurry boundaries between persuasion and physical coercion. The theoretical aspects of her argument are anchored in the story of the deteriorating relationship between Charlotte Fedders and her abusive spouse. Charlotte's body inscribes this deteriorating relationship. Rhetoric, asserts Colton, can be beaten into a woman. Another dimension is desire: Charlotte Fedders tries to live up to the tenets of her Catholic upbringing. She desires to be a good wife and clings tenaciously to the scripts of the good wife in order to please her husband. Thus, concludes Colton, desire and domination work together to repress women. Charlottte Fedders is finally able to leave her abusive husband by experimenting with alternative, more self-affirming scripts through participation in an egalitarian woman's book group and later through the writing of her memoir.

Thus, it is the tension between two types of discourses, destructive and self-affirming, that creates the opportunity for change. The destructive discourses experienced by Charlotte Fedders include the patriarchal language of her husband, with his physical and psychological torture. In addition, he withholds his language and thus denies her personhood because he will not engage with her dialogically. She turns to religious discourse. But, in this particular abusive context, the patriarchal symbolic structure of religious discourse fails her. It only emphasizes her failure as a wife. A doctor who encourages her to leave her spouse while she's pregnant might have provided a bridge into a healthier life, but Charlotte Fedders was not ready to accept and negotiate new concepts and actions offered by an alternative discursive script. She finally does choose and negotiate more self-affirming discursive frameworks, including that of a reading group of educated and sympathetic women. The group and the feminist literary texts they read provide an experience of community for Fedders. She becomes a rhetor in this collaborative and egalitarian community and, consequently, leaves behind the patriarchal and hierarchical discourses of her husband and church. Ultimately, Fedders writes a memoir of abuse that evolves over a period of time and is made possible through the experience of negotiating multiple and conflicting discourse communities. The tension between these communities encourages and motivates Fedders to position herself within more self-affirming discourses. Colton concludes by reiterating that violence is rhetoric and that material rhetoric can both force women to comply with their own domination or – if they understand its full functions – can free them from it. It is Colton's rejection of the mind/body duality and her ability to skilfully reveal the ambiguity of the boundaries between body and mind that characterize her as a postmodern rhetor. Furthermore, Colton understands the expanding of narrative imagination as a result of these encounters with a multitude of discourse communities.

Brenda Daly, in 'When the Daughter Tells Her Story: The Rhetorical Challenges of Disclosing Father-Daughter Incest,' challenges the now well-established view of psychiatrist Judith L. Herman. As the reader will recall, in *Trauma and Recovery* Herman posits that healing can only occur for sexual abuse survivors when they feel safe enough to tell their stories to affirmative listeners – a process also described by Colton in the previous essay. Daly argues that, given the difficulty of meeting these composing conditions – securing safety, telling stories, filling memory gaps with an affirmative therapist – storytelling or narrative may not suffice, in part because in addition to the problem of composition, there is the problem of the reception of the narrative by diverse, patriarchal discourse communities. The credibility of a narrative is determined by the receptivity of the audience. Thus, all survivors face major linguistic challenges when constructing credible narratives recounting sexual violation. For example, given the likelihood of a survivor's memory gaps, she must usually invent at least some details, but this very act of invention makes her vulnerable to accusations of dishonesty. To complicate matters, what is accepted as 'truth' in a therapist's office may not be accepted as credible in a court of law or may be attacked as lacking in both style and credibility by reviewers and literary critics. Frequently, those who wish to challenge a woman's 'truth' in these male-dominated rhetorical situations – therapeutic, legal, and literary – rely on attempts to discredit her ability to remember the violation. To illustrate this problem, Daly uses two father-daughter incest memoirs – Linda Katherine Cutting's *Memory Slips* (1997) and Kathryn Harrison's *The Kiss* (1997) – to examine issues of representation within a negative climate of reception. She concludes by underscoring the need to define recovery, not as the last act of an individual in therapy, but as collective political action. Even after the story is told, according to Daly, the recovery process is not yet complete because the survivor must then decide how to take action against the abuser. Some survivors choose to take the perpetrator to court, while others publish narratives disclosing the actions of the abuser. Unfortunately, given the current backlash against narratives of sexual violation – specifically, father-daughter incest narratives – this paper questions their adequacy as the final act of the recovery process. Therefore, Daly sees additional complications for sexual abuse survivors searching for their own voices because, in order to be effective, these women must control a number of complex factors, like the conditions of composition, the reception of the message, the institutional response, and the ensuing social action that should result.

In 'The Epistemology of Police Science and the Silencing of Battered Women,' Christine Shearer-Cremean argues that the rhetoric used by police officers in both their police reports and their interview protocols glosses over and subsumes abused women's narratives of pain and trauma. The epistemology of police science values only observable marks of abuse, thereby rendering the abused woman's body a physical text. If a woman is unable to represent her abuse in an empirically verifiable manner, like through bruising or blood, she is denied any other field upon which to articulate her physical suffering. The epistemology of police science does not recognize *language* describing physical pain as evidence. Shearer-Cremean emphasizes that police reports are not so much objective representations of crimes or 'calls,' but argumentative documents composed by officer/rhetors. The enthymemic nature of these documents (i.e., an officer took a particular course of action during a domestic violence call because particular physical facts were present) betrays certain epistemological assumptions that do not serve the interests of battered women. Shearer-Cremean analyses a police report of a domestic violence incident to demonstrate her thesis, discussing the 'empirical' nature of evidence and how an abused woman is situated within a legal context as a body-object. Last, using Elaine Scarry's *The Body in Pain*, she discusses the inability of women physically and emotionally tortured by their male partners to represent their suffering through language, and the legal implications of this problem.

In 'The Language of Healing: Generic Structure, Hybridization, and Meaning Shifts in the Recovery of Battered Women,' Carol L. Winkelmann offers findings from an ethnographic study of the language of battered women in a shelter in an economically depressed setting in the U.S. upper South. Her argument is that the mostly African American and white urban Appalachian shelter women attempt to survive abuse and to heal themselves by engaging in a similar series of rhetorical or linguistic strategies and dialogic communicative practices. Winkelmann's analysis is an attempt to reconcile the postmodern sense of the instability of language with the human need and nature to conceive of cohesive patterns emerging from sometimes related, sometimes disparate human experience. Despite the ever-shifting nature of language, human beings do strive to create structure and relationship in their search for meaning. Winkelmann examines how this process can be harnessed for strategic personal and social change. She shows how, during story-telling episodes with one another, survivors use hybrid language forms that lead to changes in the meaning of their utterances.

Hybrid language is the conjoined or shifting language forms derived from the dialogism of communication. While other essayists in this anthology highlight the problematic nature of meaning shifts as survivor rhetoric moves from context to context, Winkelmann shows how such meaning shifts can contribute to survivors' senses of recovery from the devastation of domestic violence. To illustrate hybridization and meaning shifts, Winkelmann focuses on the women's use of religious language. Like Aysan Sev'er in *Fleeing the House of Horrors*, a study of women's abuse narratives in a Canadian safe house, Winkelmann notes the significance of the way ethnocultural and religious factors figure into the experience of violence and survival strategies. Most of the women in Winkelmann's study were raised in conservative Holiness/Sanctified or fundamentalist/evangelical communities whose traditional religious concepts about gender roles and relations often fuel the family tensions and male aggression that leads to domestic violence. The women's language is suffused with the semantic shadings, metaphors, and concepts of this traditional religious socialization. Yet, because of the process of hybridization, they sometimes create their own semantic inflections or formulations that resist or subvert traditional meanings about gender roles and relations. The significance of Winkelmann's study is its attempt to reconcile a generic structure of healing – so functional within both therapeutic and feminist political contexts – with the inherent instability and dynamic movement of the language. Indeed, the language of healing makes apparent in a poignant and socially relevant way the manner in which all human discourse functions to greater and lesser degrees as the dynamic site of ideological action – sometimes even for the better.

Clearly, the writers in this collection attempt to keep alive an agenda for progressive social change – though only in the uncompromising light of the contingencies and complexities of language use in a postmodern world. They invite readers, as they consider these essays and as they create their own language about violence against women, to do likewise.

Works Cited

Agnew, Vijay. *In Search of a Safe Place: Abused Women and Culturally Sensitive Services*. Toronto: University of Toronto Press, 1998.
Herman, Judith Lewis. *Trauma and Recovery*. New York: Basic Books, 1992.

Mann, Ruth M. *Who Owns Domestic Abuse? The Local Politics of a Social Problem.*
   Toronto: University of Toronto Press, 2000.
Mohanty, Chandra Talpade. *Feminism without Borders: Decolonizing Theory,
   Practicing Solidarity.* Durham: Duke University Press, 2003.
Scarry, Elaine. *The Body in Pain: The Making and Unmaking of the World.* New
   York: Oxford University Press, 1985.
Sev'er, Aysan. *Fleeing the House of Horrors: Women Who Have Left Abusive
   Partners.* Toronto: University of Toronto Press, 2002.
Stoekl, Allan. 'Elaine Scarry's *The Body in Pain*, Paul Bove's Intellectuals in
   Power: The Pain of Being an Intellectual.' *Southern Humanities Review* 22
   (1988): 49–62.

Chapter 1

Narrative, Gender, and Recovery from Childhood Sexual Abuse

ELANA NEWMAN

Child sexual abuse is a prevalent and devastating form of sexual violence against females (e.g., Briere; Finkelhor et al.; Kendall-Tackett, Williams, and Finkelhor; U.S. Department of Health and Human Services).[1] Women with a history of childhood victimization have an increased lifetime risk of psychiatric disorders, medical illnesses, health risk behaviour, and health utilization as well as exposure to other potentially traumatic life events (e.g., Breslau et al.; Burnam et al.; Bushnell, Wells, and Oakley-Browne; Cicchetti and Stone; Golding; Koss and Heslet; Saunders et al.; Walker, Gelfand et al.; Walker, Unutzer, et al.). To help overcome these potential sequelae, many women with histories of sexual abuse seek psychotherapies that address the legacy of sexual exploitation. Most trauma-focused psychotherapies centre on the importance of telling one's story (Foa, Keane, and Friedman), although few emphasize the role of gender and language in creating reparative self-narratives. I review several factors that may restrict trauma-related narratives and suggest subsequent ways narrative and gender interact to affect the recovery process. I argue that story-telling in treatment must be informed by a feminist perspective, and I present a case example that illustrates this point.

The Effect of Child Sexual Abuse on Trauma-Related Narrative Capacity

One major developmental task during childhood is to master basic linguistic skills that are needed to put information into a narrative structure. Over time, children become linguistically able to temporally sequence such information as person, action, and place. Nelson theorizes that language is necessary to encode memories into a format that can later be extracted. Evidence in support of this theory suggests that adults may not be able to clearly describe nontraumatic experiences that occur prior to narrative skill acquisition (e.g., Winograd and Killinger). By extension, when a child whose language skills are just forming is sexually exploited, actual words may not be formed to catalogue this experience. The lack of a vocabulary may lead to subsequent encoding, retrieval, and narrative deficits for these events.

Another important developmental milestone is the emergence of a sense of self. The self provides an internal standpoint from which the child can position herself as a separate agent who interprets experiences and relates to others. Howe, Courage, and Peterson theorize that cohesive autobiographical narratives about trauma cannot form unless the child has acquired a cognitive sense of self. However, indescribable shards of the traumatic experiences may be incorporated into the evolving self-structures.

Specific aspects of child sexual abuse also can diminish or destroy a child's capacity to define the traumatic experience. Child sexual abuse requires a child to process intense emotional and physical sensations as well as complex cognitive information. The child, who is developing neurobiologically, often is not yet fully equipped to process complex information, let alone highly charged sensory-motor and cognitive information. When experiencing abuse, a child is confronted with contradictory messages regarding self versus other, attention versus neglect, pleasure versus pain, and good versus evil. This confluence of incongruent information can evoke intolerable affects, shatter intact basic assumptions, disrupt the child's evolving constructions of the world, and foster the development and maintenance of maladaptive belief structures and negative affects (Roth and Lebowitz; Roth and Newman, 'Role,' Process of Coping with 'Trauma'). For instance, sexual abuse communicates that the victim is an object used for someone else's sexual needs. Such meta-communications may become integrated into the child's evolving self-concept so that the survivor's identity is obscured and subsumed as an entity whose purpose is to serve others. Any subsequent lack of integration regarding abuse-related information may hinder the experience from being labelled. Alternatively, memories may become fractured, split off, and stored separately from language (van der Kolk and van der Hart).

The immediate external context of sexual abuse may further constrain the child's capacity for narrative. Typically, child sexual abuse occurs in a context of secrecy, with explicit or implicit threats of harm regarding disclosure (e.g., Browne). In these instances, language is absolutely prohibited. In other cases, abused children are told that despite any experienced pain or confusion, sexual contact is 'good for them' and what they secretly desire. Again, the child is manipulated to displace lived experience with the perpetrator's analysis of the event's meaning, and the child's voice and interpretation of the experience are substituted and silenced. Such censorship may hinder the experience from being internally acknowledged or catalogued; the victim may have to discount and minimize her feelings in order to prevent herself from feeling crazy or out of control. Furthermore, some developmentalists believe that linguistic representation of events among children primarily forms through social interaction. If language is learned and practiced in relation to others, it is quite probable that children will not have the linguistic discriminatory skill to describe or communicate external and internal situations in which they are not trained by parents (Nelson; Pillemer and White). Since abusive experiences often are not discussed with parents, the linguistic representation of abuse may be further suppressed.

Finally, the socio-cultural context of abuse further reduces the probability that narrative about abuse will be generated. Centuries of male-dominated culture have silenced children's and women's experience of sexual abuse, thereby reinforcing victims' disinclination to discuss their experiences with others (Armstrong; Brownmiller; Finkelhor et al.; Golden). Emerging from this history, rape myths have been constructed that deny rape's existence, deny male culpability, minimize the deleterious effect on women, and emphasize women's responsibility for male violence (e.g., Burt; Feild; Griffin; Malamuth). Such rape-supportive myths that hold women responsible for male violence continue to influence our attitudes towards women as victims, as well as attitudes that women victims have about themselves. In fact, some research supports the claim that early sexual abuse 'trains' a subset of abused women to embrace rape-supportive attitudes and stereotypical femininity (Briere, Smiljanich, and Henschel; Corne, Briere, and Essess). Finally, cultural messages that confound sexuality and violence may contribute, in part, to a survivor's hesitancy to speak out and name her experiences as abusive. Images found in pornography, music videos, romance novels, and magazines reinforce beliefs that violence is connected to sexual expression and that inequality needs to be addressed personally rather than structurally (e.g., Mills). Together, the socio-cultural and histori-cal milieux of sexual trauma create an environment in which survi-vors anticipate disbelief, shame, blame, alienation, or punishment from others.

In summary, a convergence of developmental, abuse-specific, proxi-mate, and socio-cultural forces reduces the probability that any one child will be able to identify her sexually exploitative experience in a coherent form to herself or others. These overlapping factors suggest there is a blurring between story-telling and identity formation among survivors of such sexual violence.

The Importance of Narrative in Healing

While tentative evidence suggests that abuse shatters narrative capac-ity, compelling scientific evidence illustrates that the creation and shar-ing of narrative about upsetting life events is reparative. Several studies indicate that communicating stories about traumatic life events can improve physical health outcomes (e.g., Browne; Greenberg and Stone; Pennebaker). For example, Pennebaker and Susman found that people who reported childhood sexual abuse were less likely to have health problems several years later if they had discussed the experiences with others in comparison to those who had not discussed these events. Similarly, students who had the opportunity to write or speak about traumatic life events had health gains and increased positive mood states compared to students who did not write about those events (e.g., Pennebaker and Beall; Pennebaker, Colder, and Sharp; Pennebaker, Kiecolt-Glaser, and Glaser). Comparable results lasting over fourteen months are experienced by Holocaust survivors (Pennebaker, Barger, and Tiebout). Finally, Harvey et al. have found that the degree to which female sexual trauma survivors engaged in diary writing, reflecting, and speaking about the sexual violation was positively associated with ratings of successful coping.

Clinicians specializing in trauma-focused treatment have addressed the importance of telling one's story in treatment, positing that translat-ing traumatic feelings and thoughts into language results in symptom reduction and improved health. However, therapists provide diverse explanations for this progress. Constructivist and cognitive behavioural therapists emphasize the role of creating adaptive meaning, integrating emotion into linguistic structures, or activating fear structures (e.g., Foa and Riggs; Harvey et al.; Lebowitz and Newman; McCann and Pearlman; Roth and Lebowitz; Roth and Newman, 'Process of Coping with Incest,' 'Role,' Process of Coping with 'Trauma'). Some dynamic clinicians posit that if a survivor can understand her life history and traumatic experiences, she can adaptively change her sense of self-esteem and self-identity (Herman). Finally, therapists who focus on the importance of writing stories about traumatic events believe that narrative transforms private images into public language, unites fragmented experiences, and reduces shame. Despite such diverse causal explanations, the consensus is that narrative is pivotal to trauma-focused psychotherapy (Feldman, Johnson, and Ollayos).

The Ways Gender Influences Reparative Narratives

Although narrative is the direct and indirect focus of many trauma-focused therapies, most treatments that address the long-term impact of sexual abuse have failed to account for the ways in which gender roles influence the construction of healing narrative. As described below, representation of gender influences story-telling in terms of content, process, and structure.

Healing narratives typically involve the search for meaning (Epstein; Frankl; Horowitz; Janoff-Bulman; McCann and Pearlman). As an individual searches for ways of understanding her sexually abusive experiences, ubiquitous cultural messages about women, gendered relationships, sexuality, and sexual violence are accessed (Lebowitz and Roth). For example, a child struggling to make sense of an abusive experience may encode partial or whole messages that indicate females are responsible for eliciting male violence, women are property, and sex is a commodity (Lebowitz and Roth). She may become trapped in a madonna/whore dichotomy, in which it is difficult to be both virginal and pure and also sexual (Ussher 14). The larger social context of inequities towards women (Hess and Ferree) serves to shape, reify, and etch such self-destructive messages into many survivors' self-constructions (Lebowitz and Roth). Finally, the constant barrage of misogynist messages in the culture may serve as constant cues to elicit memories, affect, and harmful behaviours in the survivor's life, thus intensifying the recovery process (Lebowitz and Roth). Constructing a health-promoting narrative not only requires encountering intense personal experiences, but also facing and contending with cultural representations.

The process of making meaning also requires that a victim/survivor acknowledge and integrate new affective and cognitive experiences, typically those that are culturally construed as 'masculine' experiences. Cultural constructions dichotomize gender, such that men are considered 'self-reliant, courageous, competent, and rational' whereas women are seen as 'dependent, sensual, and emotional.' Similarly, expression of anger is sanctioned among men but forbidden among women (Sheffield). Therefore, a female incest survivor may experience profound inhibition when she needs to experiment with a repertoire of feelings and cognitions that are gendered as masculine. Accessing 'male' emotions may not only deter any experimentation, but also evoke additional turmoil regarding women's place in the world. For example, accessing anger can only occur through identification with the perpetrator's viewpoint or generalized male aggression towards women. Rather than promote healing, implementing such male-gendered emotional constructs typically elicits confusion regarding masculinity and femininity, perpetration and victimization, and power and passivity. These expressions need to be carefully examined and challenged in a safe therapeutic environment.

In addition, gendered linguistic style may influence the process of story-telling within the therapeutic context. While the notion of 'women's language' often is hotly debated (e.g., Roman, Juhasz, and Miller) and shown to be situation specific, some scholars argue that women are socialized to use a deferential and affiliative style of language, especially in situations where they have less power. For example, women demonstrate more frequent use of heavily qualified statements, ask more questions of others, and interrupt less (Cameron; Lakoff). Furthermore, girls are socialized to avoid forceful, rough language (Lakoff). Given that survivors have been disempowered, the notion of paying attention to gendered linguistic style with respect to power seems meaningful in the therapeutic context. In fact, such a speaking style may alter survivors' self-narrative and the manner by which they explore and create stories within the therapeutic interaction.

Structurally, language itself may reflect and perpetuate cultural values and institutions, including patriarchal ones (e.g., Cameron, *Feminism*, 'Why'; Grossman and Tucker; Spender). Language is a social practice historically grounded in the male experience, and many linguistic representations and customs continue to influence the culture at large. For example, female sexuality and its expression have been constructed based on men's heterosexual experience and definition, with aggression and penetration as a key element (e.g., Dworkin; Rich, 'Compulsory,' *On Lies*). Furthermore, many terms for female sexuality and womanhood possess negative connotations that we may not consciously acknowledge (e.g., Adams and Ware). Definitions of sexual abuse and assault remain shaped by the male perception that only brutally forced acts of penetration constitute sexual maltreatment. Such definitions mirror cultural definitions and influence women's own perceptions of childhood sexual mistreatment. For instance, data from epidemiological studies illustrate that many women whose experiences meet legal definitions of rape do not answer affirmatively when asked if they were 'raped' (Koss). Definitions that reflect women's myriad of sexually exploitative experiences need to be integrated into survivors' autobiographical descriptions (Kelly).

The Need for Healing Narrative to Include Gender Concerns

To facilitate the creation of an empowering self-narrative, psychotherapy with incest survivors must, by necessity, address the broader social and political dimensions of abuse.[2] The survivor should be encouraged to examine existential, ideological, cultural, and religious issues that are relevant to her. She must be encouraged to be the expert of her experience while constructing and re-visioning her experiences of sexual violence in an atmosphere that permits her to consider alternative views and constructions, especially those that provide a counterpoint to the prevalent damaging patriarchal messages (Herman; Lebowitz). Thus, the therapist's function is not to teach clients feminist theories per se, but instead to encourage a client to derive her own healing self-construction through a dialectic process. This process is facilitated by encouraging a client to scrutinize and decide what is meaningful to her, rather than automatically interpreting the world based on unquestioned assumptions.

Sexual abuse silences women's linguistic and interpretative opportunity to define the sexually abusive experience for themselves, as described previously. Since such sexual abuse takes away a victim's capacity to label what is true for her, the first step of treatment is to permit the survivor to label and claim split-off aspects of experiences. This process occurs at the conceptual, linguistic, and relational level. Most directly, the survivor is encouraged to own, examine, and redefine her feelings and reactions in self-enhancing ways. The survivor is the expert and authority of her life, and she determines how little or how much the experience meant (Lebowitz). Linguistically, the therapist encourages the survivor to complete unfinished sentences, speak less deferentially, and create her own metaphors. A therapist attends to the manner in which pronouns, names, and verb tense may allow the client to temporarily distance her emotions from her experience as she grapples with the meaning of these events. Throughout treatment, the therapist monitors this language and, depending on the clients' needs and abilities at the time, encourages the client to experiment with less emotionally distancing terms. Interpersonally, the therapist communicates respect and autonomy towards the survivor by adapting an egalitarian therapeutic stance. Since sexual abuse represents a betrayal of power, the creation of a co-operative relationship that does not recapitulate exploitative asymmetry is a critical element in helping the survivor avow her own voice.

Another therapeutic goal involves creating a coherent, cohesive story in which appropriate and life-affirming meanings are derived to replace any debilitating self-cognitions. Life meanings must include an exploration of how sexual abuse affected one's gender identity and vice versa. For example, the emergent life story of a survivor attempting to make sense of incestuous experiences typically includes some recognition that the sexual exploitation of children is eroticized and glorified in the overall culture (Lebowitz and Roth). Claiming one's body, sexuality, and gender on one's own terms is another important aspect of this narrative. Disentangling the cultural messages from the experienced events can allow a survivor to create self-empowering meaning. This understanding often takes the form of a survivor relinquishing her sense of responsibility for initiating and sustaining abuse and instead appropriately blaming the perpetrator and the social context that condones sexual exploitation.

Jackie's Narrative over the Course of Treatment

'Jackie,'[3] a bright, articulate twenty-four-year-old college student, sought out trauma-focused group psychotherapy because she believed that both her uncle and father had sexually abused her. Although she had no cohesive memories, she had fragments that made her believe that focusing on the impact of child sexual abuse might help her overcome her psychological and interpersonal difficulties. Jackie had a long history of inpatient and outpatient interventions, and she had been diagnosed with manic depression, depression, borderline personality disorder, and cocaine and alcohol addiction, among other disorders. During her recent sobriety of approximately one and one-half years, she began to recognize that she had a variety of inexplicable reactions to the world. For example, she could not bear to see her body naked, avoided any TV show with sexual scenes or allusions in it, and felt dirty all the time.

Selected excerpts from conversations with Jackie are presented to illustrate my argument here (see Roth and Newman 1993 for a more detailed focus on Jackie's process of recovery with regard to helplessness). As part of a qualitative study on the process of coping (Newman), Jackie volunteered to talk with an interviewer and complete several self-report measures at three weeks, three months, six months, and nine months into treatment. Each interview was semistructured to elicit narrative about her views of the world, identity, emotions, and treatment. These interviews were tape recorded, transcribed, and coded. Although Jackie's evolving narrative was typical of other incest survivors interviewed, her words were selected since her experience represents the most dramatic linguistic and feminist transformation among the survivors interviewed.

Jackie did not name her abusive experiences until the interview at nine months. Prior to that time, she referred to her experiences of sexual coercion as the 'I word' rather than utter the word 'incest' aloud. Although she was aware that approaching the 'I word' was 'easier than accepting things I've always thought and felt about myself with no explanation,' the actual power of naming terrified her. She needed to distance herself temporarily from acknowledging her abusive history by using linguistic shorthand, while she simultaneously explored the possibility of her abuse. Interestingly, this fear of naming and the approach-avoidance of recognizing child sexual abuse are consistent with the history of sexual abuse and assault in American culture (e.g., Golden). At three months, Jackie accidentally said the word 'incest' aloud during an interview and described her reaction to hearing those words:

> I heard it ... It scared me ... it really made me feel bad ... [voice kind of shaky] It's, um, it's just gross. Powerful. Because I, 'cause that word has so many preconceived conno-, connotations to it, you know? It doesn't have the personal attachments and experiences I have to it. It's the thoughts of god it was that gross! It's taboo! It's stereotyped!

Her comments reflect her knowledge that naming is a powerful process that requires redefining and claiming one's own definition and not simply appropriating a culturally devalued and defined term. At nine months, after never saying 'incest,' Jackie naturally wove the words 'incest' into her discourse, using the word nine times. When asked how she understood the change in her language, she responded:

> I got panicking a couple of months that I wasn't going to remember anything. And, um, I became willing to go to any length and I was talking to my therapist and I was spelling things and describing things without saying them and I stopped and said, 'That's not good for me, is it?' And she said 'No, it's not.' I said, 'I should start saying the words.' And she said, 'Yeah.' And she told me I had to start saying all the words all the time, otherwise it was keeping me distant from it. So I got willing and I started saying them. I don't still say all the words, but I'm much better.

In this excerpt, Jackie understands how refusing to name her experience prevented her from claiming and transcending her experience. It is striking that as Jackie came to personally identify and name her experiences of sexual exploitation, she also began labelling her sexual body parts for the first time; defining her experiences as abusive and naming her corporeal self seemed to represent two interrelated processes. By intentionally using words such as 'incest,' 'breasts,' and 'vagina,' Jackie can begin to catalogue her experience and acknowledge her responses to her experiences in a manner that allows her to feel in control. By naming her experience, she actively counteracts not only the silence about her exploitation, but also re-evaluates the negative cultural constructions she has attached to her body and her experience. This cluster of changes suggests that Jackie's awareness of her oppression as a woman reverberated and affected her construction of herself as a sexual female. It also mirrors the unfortunate cultural milieu in which violence and sexuality are merged into a unitary category that results in sexual abuse becoming constructed as a sexual issue rather than a crime. Notably, as Jackie's language developed more specificity, it appeared that brutality and sexuality became more separate entities in her world.

As Jackie labelled her body parts, her own construction of her sexuality changed. For the first six months of treatment, Jackie experienced her sexuality as not belonging to her. Although she referred to numerous cultural messages about women being men's property, she was not cognizant that she had integrated discrepant fragmentary messages from her perpetrators and the culture into her self-construction. By the ninth month, she realized that her early sexual experiences had robbed her of the chance to define and embrace her own sexual self and that the culture had reinforced this initial construction. Although at nine months she had not yet reclaimed her body, she was well into the process of defining her female self. The following excerpt, at nine months, illustrates her perceptions of male-female relationships and sexuality. Jackie is explaining why she becomes enraged when she sees women in skimpy bathing suits:

> I think I got it into my head that when a women's body is looked at it's thought of in exploitative ways, [just like] the way I learned my uncle and my father and my grandfather think. So if [my boyfriend] sees a woman, and I think [that] he thinks what they [uncle, father, and grandfather] thought, when they saw a woman. Then *that* [boyfriend's thoughts] is out of line! And, um, I feel like they're [men are] actually powerless over their thoughts. And that they are just made that way and think those things and they can't help thinking those things, even if they are happily married to a woman. So it represents some of my warped perception of men and what they think. And it also represents that women have no choice. Well, some of them have a choice about what they wear ... But some of them might just have a body that's attractive and they can't help it. And men say things and look at her. She is being betrayed by them, robbed! I think it really affects me being robbed! ... I feel like I don't own my sexual body parts. Like they're ruined or contaminated. And they're not mine, but I have to carry them around with me.

In this excerpt, Jackie begins to disentangle her views about power and choice with respect to attractiveness and sexual desire. She is on the cusp of acknowledging the ways in which she has incorporated rape myths into her viewpoint, especially with respect to women's responsibility for men's dehumanizing responses to female sexuality. Furthermore, she recognizes, albeit fleetingly, how she has assumed the male gaze of objectifying women, and the ways this affects her own construction of her female body and attractiveness. As Jackie began to grapple with her identity as a sexual women, she also began to examine the dangerous power she believed her sexuality had on men. As Jackie described below, she believed her sexuality was the only tool she could use to gain authority in male-female relationships, but it also made her feel dirty and shameful.

> And, it's like I feel like I brought on what happened to me [the childhood sexual abuse] by being sexual. Any time a person tries to be manipulative,

sexually manipulative ... just even trying to attract somebody, ... that's bad because I feel I did that and got what I got. And if I see them do it, it's reminding me of what I didn't want to remind myself of, what I did. [pause] And I hate them at the same time for it. Because I hate people who do that, that horrible, disgusting thing, you know? ... But when I see somebody else acting like that, I feel threatened by the person because I feel like they're taking away attention from me. And the other side of it is, the attention I'm assuming is being given her, which is similar to what was given to me as a kid, is, um, is violating her! Raping her with her eyes, with their eyes, and stuff, um. And when I see a girl getting violated that way, I feel like I'm being violated ... So in public everyday kind of thing[s] I feel more violated, cheated, and stolen from than guilty ... And that feeling gets me so frustrated, my reaction is to want to take off all my clothes. Rip them off and throw myself out in the middle of the road and say fuck you to everybody. And the feeling I think is the frustration of the powerlessness. I tried so hard to control what parts of body I give, whether visually or physically, and not being able to do it with my father and the other people who were around, or with other people in the public when I assume they're violating me visually, um, and mentally ... I feel like I'm trying so hard to be in control and contain myself, keep myself private, and I'm being taken from.

This excerpt illustrates how Jackie is caught in a paradox where she both craves and loathes attention, but assumes that all male attention is sexualized and eroticized. She begins to articulate that she sees male attention as a finite resource in which women use their physical attractiveness to compete for attention from men, but this attention is always objectifying and dehumanizing. As she struggles with the notion of sex as a social commodity, she examines the tension she experienced as a child, with sexualized attention being the only way to fend off the neglect she experienced. Furthermore, in this excerpt, she is grappling with cultural rape myths in which females are responsible for eliciting male violence and their identity is to service men's needs. Finally, Jackie is expressing anger for the first time at her powerlessness, her inability to deny family members access to her body. Interestingly, her impulse to defiantly undress is a powerful protest, but also represents a way in which she is still trapped in viewing her own sexuality and body from an objectified male perspective.

Throughout treatment, Jackie moved from an ambivalent misogynist position to a position in which she embraced tenets of feminism, especially trust in women and pride in being female. During the first interview at three weeks, when she was asked to comment on her view of feminism or the women's movement, she replied:

> I find myself thinking the same kind of things I think they would think. And that scares me because those kind of people to me are like wasting their time, sticking their nose in everybody else's business. They can't change everybody else. People have to change if they want to change. All they can change is themselves and if [you] show by a good example, then it's going to happen by itself. So I just feel like they're a bunch of crybabies, that's the way I see it. And I think they're all gay.

Her attitude reflects the ways she has integrated cultural stereotypes and beliefs about feminists and incorporated a male hostility towards women. Although she is quite unaware of the way she is appropriating this animosity towards women and feminists, she is also experimenting with expressing a muted anger. Certainly, she has incorporated messages about feminists being 'dykes' and 'complainers,' but she simultaneously recognizes that she agrees with many feminist stances. Although this discrepancy worries her, she is not truly cognizant of the extent of the schism and its meaning to her. However, as she makes sense of her childhood sexual exploitation, she is automatically reworking her contradictory views and feelings towards womanhood. During her interview at nine months, she spontaneously stated:

> I've also started to accept being a woman and feel a part of that gender, you know? And uphold womanhood. This is really an important thing for me. And learn to love my little girl [referring to herself]. I don't like her sexual parts yet, but I feel part [of] or a pride in her gender though, *that* I never had before ... I don't feel so fake anymore. I feel more real. I used to be afraid if I wasn't perfect that everybody would know there was something really wrong with me. And now I can be a really whole person instead of a mannequin. It feels good.

It is salient that although Jackie is beginning to accept herself as a woman, she still needed to distance herself from the topic by using the third-person linguistic structure. Language tense functioned as a bridge that allowed Jackie to explore her feminist consciousness and sexuality without feeling wedded to any emerging stance.

Language was integrally related to her experience. As the content of

Jackie's narrative changed, her entire narrative style shifted. At each interview, she took increasingly more initiative in the direction of the interview, interrupted the interviewer more, and asked more direct questions of the interviewer. Her sentences became more declarative and no longer regularly ended in a tentative 'you know?' She described her emotions as she experienced the turmoil, rather than oscillating between feeling and describing. Her language became more complex and individualistic, not only in terms of affective and cognitive integration, but included more visual, auditory, olfactory, and kinesthetic descriptors.

Jackie's evolving narrative illustrates the importance of naming, struggling with gender issues, and forging female identity in the aftermath of childhood sexual abuse. Jackie's process of claiming herself could not have been accomplished without disentangling her view of herself as a woman, especially countering many stereotypical views of womanhood. She needed to examine her ideas about sexuality, attractiveness, her body, sexual desire, heterosexual relationships, and womanhood, and thereby determine what she actually believed and feared, as distinct from what she had been trained to believe and fear. Over time, her story-telling process changed in form and in content, as she blended issues of gender, sexual oppression, and self-identity by speaking and locating words and authority within herself. Jackie's use of language as a distancing technique worked to her advantage, as she could approach new topics while still temporarily distancing herself from the impact until she was prepared. Her story underscores the importance of facilitating recovery environments in which gender roles can be safely examined both in relation to and distinct from the experience of sexual exploitation.

Notes

1 Recently, sexual exploitation of boys has been acknowledged as an important societal problem. Although this article focuses on the influence of gender roles upon female survivors' narratives, such cultural representations also affect narratives among male survivors. For example, the following factors play a critical role in affecting how male sexual abuse survivors generate healing narratives: (a) homophobia, (b) assumptions that women never abuse boys, (c) assumptions regarding male desire for older women,

and (*d*) cultural prohibitions that prevent men from disclosing information about being powerless.
2 Although the author believes that the healing narrative process could occur in many contexts in which the survivor shares her story (i.e., self-help groups, autobiographical writing groups, consciousness-raising groups), this chapter confines the discussion to psychotherapy, since that is the field from which the data informing this perspective were derived.
3 'Jackie' is a pseudonym for this survivor.

Works Cited

Adams, K.L., and N.C. Ware. 'Sexism and the English Language: The Linguistic Implications of Being a Woman.' In *Women: A Feminist Perspective*, ed. J. Freeman, 470–84. 4th ed. Mountain View, CA: Mayfield, 1989.
Armstrong, Louise. *Rocking the Cradle of Sexual Politics: What Happened when Women Said Incest*. Reading, MA: Addison-Wesley.
Breslau, Naomi, Glen Davis, Patricia Andreski, and Edward Peterson. 'Traumatic Events and Posttraumatic Disorder in an Urban Population of Young Adults.' *Archives of General Psychiatry* 48 (1991): 216–22.
Briere, John. *Therapy for Adults Molested as Children*. New York: Springer, 1996.
Briere, John, Kathy Smiljanich, and Diane Henschel. 'Sexual Fantasies, Gender, and Molestation History.' *Child Abuse and Neglect* 18 (1994): 131–7.
Browne, Angela. 'The Victim's Experience: Pathways to Disclosure.' *Psychotherapy* 28 (1991): 150–6.
Brownmiller, Susan. *Against Our Will: Men, Women and Rape*. New York: Simon and Schuster, 1975.
Burnam, Audrey, Judith Stein, Jacqueline Golding, Judith Siegel, S. Sorenson, A. Forsythe, and C. Telles. 'Sexual Assault and Mental Disorders in Community Population.' *Journal of Consulting and Clinical Psychology* 56 (1988): 843–51.
Burt, Martha. 'Cultural Myths and Supports for Rape.' *Journal of Personality and Social Psychology* 38 (1980): 217–30.
Bushnell, John, J.E. Wells, and M. Oakley-Browne. 'Long Term Effects of Intra-Familial Sexual Abuse in Childhood.' *Acta Psychiatric Scandinavica* 85 (1993): 136–42.
Cameron, Deborah. *Feminism and Linguistic Theory*. London: Macmillan, 1985.
———. 'Why Is Language a Feminist Issue.' In *The Feminist Critique of Language: A Reader*, ed. Deborah Cameron, 1–30. New York: Routledge, 1990.

Cicchetti, Dante, and Sheree Stone. *Developmental Perspectives on Trauma: Theory, Research and Intervention*. Rochester: University of Rochester Press, 1997.

Corne, Shawn, John Briere, and Lillian Essess. 'Women's Attitudes and Fantasies about Rape as a Function of Early Exposure to Pornography.' *Journal of Interpersonal Violence* 4 (1992): 454–61.

Dworkin, Andrea. *Woman Hating*. New York: E.P Dutton, 1974.

Epstein, Seymour. 'The Self-Concept, the Traumatic Neurosis, and the Structure of Personality.' In *Perspectives on Personality*, ed. Daniel Ozer, John Healy, and R. Stewart. 63–98. Vol. 3. Greenwich, CT: JAI, 1991.

Feild, Hubert. 'Attitudes toward Rape: A Comparative Analysis of Police, Rapists, Crisis Counselors, and Citizens.' *Journal of Personality and Social Psychology* 36 (1978): 156–79.

Feldman, Scott, D.R. Johnson, and M. Ollayos. 'The Use of Writing in the Treatment of Posttraumatic Stress Disorders.' In *Handbook of Post-Traumatic Therapy*, ed. Mary Beth Williams and John Sommer. Westport, CT: Greenwood Press, 1994. 366–85.

Finkelhor, David, Gerald Hotaling, L.A. Lewis, and Christine Smith. 'Sexual Abuse and Its Relationship to Later Sexual Satisfaction, Marital Status, Religion, and Attitudes.' *Journal of Interpersonal Violence* 4 (1989): 279–99.

Foa, Edna, Terrance Keane, and Matthew Friedman. *Effective Treatments for PTSD*. New York: Guilford, 2000.

Foa, Edna, and David Riggs. 'Posttraumatic Stress Disorder and Rape.' In *Review of Psychiatry*, ed. John Oldham, Michelle Riba, and A. Tesman, 273–304. Vol. 12. Washington DC: American Psychiatric Association, 1993.

Frankl, Viktor. *Man's Search for Meaning: An Introduction to Logotherapy*. New York: Washington Square Press, 1963.

Golden, Linda. 'The Politics of Child Sexual Abuse: Notes from American History.' *Feminist Review* 28 (1988): 56–64.

Golding, Jacqueline. 'Sexual Assault History and Physical Health in Randomly Selected Los Angeles Women.' *Health Psychology* 13 (1994): 130–8.

Greenberg, Melanie, and Arthur Stone. 'Emotional Disclosure about Traumas and Its Relation to Health: Effects of Previous Disclosure and Trauma Severity.' *Journal of Personality and Social Psychology* 63 (1992): 75–84.

Griffin, Susan. 'Rape: The All American Crime.' *Ramparts* 10 (1971): 26–35.

Grossman, Aryn, and Joan Tucker. 'Gender Differences and Sexism in the Knowledge and Use of Slang.' *Sex Roles* 37 (1997): 101–10.

Harvey, John, Terri Orbuch, Kathleen Chwalisz, and Gail Garwood. 'Coping with Sexual Assault: The Roles of Account-Making and Confiding.' *Journal of Traumatic Stress* 4 (1991): 515–31.

Herman, Judith. *Trauma and Recovery.* New York: Basic Books, 1992.

Hess, Beth, and Myra M. Ferree, eds. *Analyzing Gender: A Handbook of Social Science Research.* Newbury Park, CA: Sage, 1997.

Horowitz, Mardi. *Stress Response Syndromes.* New York: Aronson, 1986.

Howe, Mark, Mary Courage, and Carole Peterson. 'How Can I Remember When "I" Wasn't There: Long-Term Retention of Traumatic Experiences and Emergence of the Cognitive Self.' *Consciousness and Cognition* 3 (1994): 327–55.

Janoff-Bulman, Ronnie. *Shattered Assumptions: Towards a New Psychology of Trauma.* New York: Free Press, 1992.

Kelly, Liz. 'What's in a Name? Defining Child Sexual Abuse.' *Feminist Review* 28 (1988): 65–73.

Kendall-Tackett, Kathleen, Linda Williams, and David Finkelhor. 'Impact of Sexual Abuse on Children: A Review and Synthesis of Recent Empirical Studies.' *Psychological Bulletin* 113 (1993): 164–80.

Koss, Mary. 'The Hidden Rape Victim: Personality, Attitudinal, and Situational Characteristics.' *Psychology of Women Quarterly* 9 (1985): 193–212.

Koss, Mary, and L. Heslet. 'Somatic Consequences of Violence against Women.' *Archives of Family Medicine* 1 (1992): 53–9.

Lakoff, Robin. 'Language and a Women's Place.' In Roman, Juhasz, and Miller, 280–91.

Lebowitz, Leslie. 'Treatment of Rape Trauma: Integrating Trauma-Focused Therapy with Feminism.' *Journal of Training and Practice in Professional Psychology* 7 (1993): 81–99.

Lebowitz, Leslie, and Elana Newman. 'The Role of Cognitive-Affective Themes in the Assessment and Treatment of Trauma Reactions.' *Clinical Psychology and Psychotherapy: An International Journal of Theory and Practice* 3 (1996): 196–207.

Lebowitz, Leslie, and Susan Roth. 'I Felt like a Slut: The Cultural Context and Women's Response to Being Raped.' *Journal of Traumatic Stress* 7 (1994): 363–90.

Malamuth, Neil. 'Rape Fantasies as a Function of Exposure to Violent Sexual Stimuli.' *Archives of Sexual Behavior* 10 (1981): 33–47.

McCann, I. Lisa, and Laurie Ann Pearlman. *Psychological Trauma and the Adult Survivor: Theory, Therapy, and Transformation.* New York: Brunner/Mazel, 1990.

Mills, Sara. *Feminist Stylistics.* New York: Routledge, 1995.

Newman, Elana. 'The Process of Recovery in Adult Female Survivors of Childhood Sexual Abuse: Schema Affect and Symptom Change.' Ph.D. diss., Duke University, 1992.

Nelson, Katherine. 'The Psychological and Social Origins of Autobiographical Memory.' *Psychological Science* 4 (1993): 7–14.

Pennebaker, James. 'Putting Stress into Words: Health, Linguistic and Therapeutic Implications.' *Behavior Research and Therapy* 31 (1993): 539–48.

Pennebaker, James, Steven Barger, and John Tiebout. 'Disclosure of Traumas and Health among Holocaust Survivors.' *Psychosomatic Medicine* 51 (1989): 577–89.

Pennebaker, James, and Sandra Beall. 'Confronting a Traumatic Event: Toward an Understanding of Inhibition and Disease.' *Journal of Abnormal Psychology* 95 (1986): 274–81.

Pennebaker, James, Michelle Colder, and Lisa Sharp. 'Accelerating the Coping Process.' *Journal of Personality and Social Psychology* 58 (1990): 528–37.

Pennebaker, James, Janice Kiecolt-Glaser, and Ronald Glaser. 'Disclosure of Traumas and Immune Function: Health Implications for Psychotherapy.' *Journal of Consulting and Clinical Psychology* 56 (1988): 239–45.

Pennebaker, James, and Joan Susman. 'Disclosure of Traumas and Psychosomatic Processes.' *Social Science and Medicine* (Special Issue on Stress and Coping in Relation to Health and Disease) 26 (1988): 327–32.

Pillemer, David, and Sheldon White. 'Childhood Events Recalled by Children and Adults.' *Advances in Child Development and Behavior* 21 (1989): 297–340.

Rich, Adrienne. 'Compulsory Heterosexuality and Lesbian Existence.' *Signs* 5 (1980): 631–60.

––––––. *On Lies, Secrets, and Silence.* New York: W.W. Norton, 1979.

Roman, Camille, Suzanne Juhasz, and Cristanne Miller, eds. *The Women and Language Debate: A Sourcebook.* New Brunswick, NJ: Rutgers University Press, 1994.

Roth, Susan, and Leslie Lebowitz. 'The Experiences of Sexual Trauma.' *Journal of Traumatic Stress* 4 (1988): 279–99.

Roth, Susan, and Elana Newman. 'The Process of Coping with Incest for Adult Survivors.' *Journal of Interpersonal Violence* 8 (1993): 366–77.

––––––. 'The Process of Coping with Trauma.' *Journal of Traumatic Stress* 4 (1991): 281–99.

––––––. 'The Role of Helplessness in the Recovery Process for Sexual Trauma Survivors.' *Canadian Journal of Behaviour Science* 24 (1992): 220–32.

Saunders, Benjamin, Lorenz Villeponteaux, Julie Lipovsky, Dean Kilpatrick, and L. Veronen. 'Child Sexual Assault as a Risk Factor for Mental Disorders among Women: A Community Survey.' *Journal of Interpersonal Violence* 7 (1992): 189–204.

Sheffield, Carole. 'Sexual Terrorism: The Social Control of Women.' In Hess and Ferree, 154–70.

Spender, Dale. *Man Made Language*. London: Routledge and Kegan Paul, 1980.

van der Kolk, Bessel, and Onno van der Hart. 'The Intrusive Past: The Flexibility of Memory and the Engraving of Trauma.' *American Imago* 48 (1991): 425–54.

U.S. Department of Health and Human Services, Administration for Children and Families, National Center on Child Abuse and Neglect. *The Third National Incidence Study of Child Abuse and Neglect (1993)*. Washington, DC: U.S. Government Printing Office, 1996.

Ussher, Jane. *The Psychology of the Female Body*. London: Routledge, 1989.

Walker, Edward, Ann Gelfand, Wayne Katon, Mary Koss, Michael Von Korff, David Bernstein, and Joan Russo. 'Adult Health Status of Women with Histories of Childhood Abuse and Neglect.' *American Journal of Medicine* 107 (1999): 332–9.

Walker, Edward, Wayne Katon, Janet Hansom, Jane Harrop-Griffiths, Lena Holm, M.L. Jones, Laura Hickok, and Ron Jemelka. 'Medical and Psychiatric Symptoms in Women with Childhood Sexual Abuse.' *Psychosomatic Medicine* 54 (1992): 658–64.

Walker, Edward, Jungen Unutzer, Carolyn Rutter, Ann Gelfand, Kathleen Saunders, Michael VonKorff, Mary Koss, and Wayne Katon. 'Costs of Health Care Use by Women HMO Members with a History of Childhood Abuse and Neglect.' *Archives of General Psychiatry* 56 (1999): 609–13.

Winograd, Eugene, and William Killinger. 'Relating Age at Encoding in Early Childhood to Adult Recall: Development of Flashbulb Memories.' *Journal of Experimental Psychology* 112 (1983): 413–22.

Chapter 2

Speaking in Contradictions: Complex Agency of Battered Women Who Kill

CARRIE N. BAKER

In the second wave of the women's movement, feminists criticized the legal system for male bias (MacKinnon 431). In particular, they criticized the law of self-defence for assuming the experiences and perspectives of men. To counteract this male bias in criminal trials involving battered women who killed their abusers, feminists advocated for the introduction of expert testimony on the battered woman syndrome in order to aid juries in understanding battered women's perspective. While feminists sought to 'assist women to speak in their own voices in the courtroom, and to describe the variety and complexity of their experience,' they advocated for the use of expert testimony on battering because they believed that 'battered women's voices either would not be understood or were not strong enough to be heard alone in a courtroom' (Schneider, *Battered Women*, 80). In their efforts to move beyond the male bias of the legal system, however, feminists made broad generalizations about the complex and varied experiences of battered women, often playing into traditional stereotypes of female passivity held by judges and juries. Battered women, on the other hand, have expressed a complex agency, encompassing both victimization and resistance. This chapter will show how these contradictions have played out over the last two decades in the legal treatment of battered women who kill.

I will begin by explaining the law of murder, self-defence, and insanity and the feminist arguments that the law of self-defence is male biased. Then I will describe the battered woman syndrome, including the cycle of violence and the theory of learned helplessness, and feminist arguments that courts should allow evidence of the battered woman syndrome in order to correct male bias in the law of self-defence. In the third section, I will explain subsequent feminist criticisms of the battered woman syndrome, including that the theory is inaccurate and lacks empirical support, that it has race and class biases, and that it relies on traditional stereotypes of women as passive victims. In the fourth section, I will explore the complex agency of battered women. I will first examine legal discourse to show the contradictory representations of battered women who kill their abusers. While the battered woman syndrome testimony in theory supports a claim of self-defence, in many cases this evidence is used to argue (or is heard to support an argument) that the battered woman is mentally incapacitated, *not* that she is acting reasonably in light of the circumstances. I will then argue that neither self-defence nor the insanity defence captures the complex reality of battered women's lives because their actions are neither fully reasonable nor fully unreasonable, but a complex mixture that the law, being categorical in nature, lacks the subtlety to recognize. I will conclude that feminists need to focus on educating judges and juries about the structural constraints on battered women, including gender inequality and society's failure to stop male violence against women, to enable them to understand why for many battered women killing might be the only way to survive.

The Feminist Critique of the Law of Self-Defence

Murder is generally defined as the unlawful killing of a human being with malice aforethought. Malice aforethought exists if the defendant intended to kill or to inflict great bodily injury, had a reckless indifference to an unjustifiably high risk to human life, or intended to commit a felony. Modern statutes often divide murder into degrees. First degree murder includes deliberate and premeditated killing. 'Deliberate' means that the defendant made the decision to kill in a cool and dispassionate manner. 'Premeditated' means that the defendant actually reflected on the idea of killing, if only for a very brief period. All other homicides are of the second degree, including intent-to-kill murder without deliberation and premeditation and intent-to-do-serious-bodily-injury murder, even if premeditated. Voluntary manslaughter is an intentional killing committed in response to provocation, otherwise described as killing in the heat of passion. Adequate provocation requires that a reasonable person would have been provoked (the provocation would arouse sudden and intense passion in the mind of an ordinary person such as to cause him or her to lose self-control), that the defendant was in fact provoked, that a reasonable person would not have cooled off in the time that elapsed between the provocation and the killing, and that the defendant in fact did not cool off. Involuntary manslaughter includes killing in a criminally negligent manner or during the course of committing a misdemeanour (LaFave and Scott).

In defending against a charge of murder or manslaughter, a defendant may plead self-defence or insanity. Traditional self-defence law allows a person to use deadly force in self-defence if the defender did not initiate an assault or provoke the other party, the defender was confronted with unlawful force (force that constitutes a crime or a tort), and the defender was threatened with immediate or imminent death or great bodily harm. The defendant must *reasonably* believe that she was faced with immediate or imminent death or great bodily harm if she does not respond with deadly force. The danger of harm must be a present one. Furthermore, a defendant may use only the degree of force necessary to repel an ongoing or threatened attack. In a minority of jurisdictions, the defender must retreat prior to using deadly force if a retreat can be made in complete safety (LaFave and Scott 456–8). Whereas self-defence is a justification for the use of deadly force, insanity is an excuse that negates the intent requirement for a homicide conviction. The insanity defence allows a defendant to avoid criminal liability by arguing that she did not have the necessary state of mind because of the existence of an abnormal mental condition at the time of the crime. The insanity defence authorizes the state to hold those who are not found criminally liable. The most common formulation of the insanity defence, developed by the American Law Institute, provides that a person is not responsible for criminal conduct if at the time of such conduct as a result of mental disease or defect she lacked substantial capacity either to appreciate the criminality (wrongfulness) of her conduct or to conform her conduct to the requirements of law. Some states also recognize the defence of 'diminished capacity,' under which the defendant may assert that as a result of a mental defect short of insanity, he or she did not have the required criminal intent (LaFave and Scott).

Feminists have argued that the law of self-defence is male biased. These arguments by advocates for battered women were part of a general critique by feminist legal theorists beginning in the early 1980s that questioned supposedly objective legal standards, such as the 'reasonable man' standard, as inherently embodying male perspectives and values (MacKinnon). Criticism of self-defence law has centred on the idea that the law of self-defence was traditionally formulated with two scenarios in mind: the case in which a person is suddenly attacked by a stranger or intruder and the case in which a fight or dispute between two equals 'gets out of hand' (Schuller and Vidmar 276). Advocates for battered women have argued that the battered woman's experience does not fit either of these typically male scenarios. The battered woman is faced with continual violence by an intimate partner, who is usually bigger and stronger than she is. Furthermore, according to many advocates, 'in the majority of cases the woman does not attack during a direct confrontation (i.e., during a beating), but rather at some point outside of a confrontation when no "imminent" threat may seem apparent to an outside observer (e.g., the husband was turning to leave, ... the husband was sleeping ...)' (Schuller and Vidmar; see also Maguigan 388 n. 22). One researcher found that in two-thirds of the one hundred cases he reviewed, the battered woman killed her batterer outside of a direct confrontation (Ewing 34).

Specifically, feminists have argued that the elements required to prove self-defence are male biased and discriminate against battered women. First, they have argued that the equal force rule discriminates against battered women because it assumes that the adversaries are of equal size and strength. Courts have often applied an equal force rule to prohibit a person from using a deadly weapon in self-defence unless one's attacker is using a deadly weapon (Gillespie 185; Kampmann 108; Walker, 'Battered Women Syndrome,' 1992; 325). Advocates of battered women have argued that this standard is male biased because the rigid application of this rule does not take into account size and strength differences between men and women or the fact that women are less likely than men to be trained in the use of violence. In fact, battered women often use a weapon against an unarmed man (Kampmann 109).

Second, advocates of battered women have argued that the requirement that one retreat before using deadly force discriminates against battered women because many juries confuse the concept of retreat and the question of why the woman stayed in the relationship (Gillespie 188; Kampmann 113).

Third, advocates of battered women have argued that the immediate danger rule reflects a male bias (Kampmann 111). According to the law of self-defence, a defendant must have a reasonable belief in either an immediate or an imminent threat of death or serious bodily injury. The immediacy requirement demands that the jury focus exclusively on the particular instant of the defendant's action. Cynthia Gillespie has argued that the immediacy requirement was developed to apply to the traditional male situation of a one-time confrontation between two strangers in a public place (185–6). The two-pronged rationale of the immediacy requirement was, first, that self-defence should only be permitted when there is no possibility of resorting to law enforcement for protection and, second, that self-defence should be permitted only when there is no possibility that the assailant will change his mind and retreat of his own accord. Gillespie has argued that neither rationale applies to 'a woman being threatened in her home by a mate who has carried out his past threats to harm her' (Gillespie 186; Crocker 126). To wait for an assault to begin is likely to place her in greater danger.

Feminists have advocated instead for the broader imminence standard, which allows the jury to consider the circumstances, including past events, surrounding the defendant's actions. In an 'imminence' jurisdiction, the jury is more likely to get an instruction that the evidence of the decedent's past violence towards the defendant as well as towards third persons should be considered as they evaluate the defendant's state of mind and the reasonableness of the defendant's perception that the decedent posed an imminent threat of death or serious bodily injury. Advocates for battered women have argued that a broader standard of imminence along with testimony as to the context of the battered woman's act can help the jury to understand the battered woman's perception of imminent danger. She may be reacting to past patterns of abuse (Kampmann 112) or she may be 'hypervigilant to cues of impending danger and accurately perceive the seriousness of the situation before another person who had not been repeatedly abused might recognize the danger' (Walker, 'Battered Women Syndrome 324).

Fourth, advocates of battered women have argued that the law's standard of reasonableness is male biased (Busch 18–19). In order to be acquitted, a defendant who uses self-defence must reasonably believe that she is faced with imminent death or great bodily harm if she does not respond with deadly force. Jurisdictions have varying interpretations of the reasonableness requirement. In 'objective' jurisdictions, the jury is told to measure the defendant's belief in the necessity of using defensive deadly force against a generic standard of reasonableness. In other jurisdictions, the jury is instructed to use a standard that includes the defendant's individual subjective point of view (Maguigan 409). Feminists have argued that reasonableness is actually determined from the perspective of a reasonable man because of the gender-biased attitudes of judges and juries in a society where women have been cast as unreasonable and irrational (Busch 20). One scholar has advocated a 'reasonably prudent battered woman standard' (Kinsports 416), a standard adopted by at least three jurisdictions (Maguigan 411 n. 111). Feminists have supported a subjective standard because it allows for the admissibility of information about the defendant's individual circumstances, including her history of abuse, which allows the jury to understand the social context in which the battered woman's act occurred.

Expert Testimony on the Battered Woman Syndrome

To remedy the male bias of self-defence law, advocates of battered women have sought to gain admissibility of expert testimony on the battered woman syndrome to aid juries in understanding why battered women kill. From the inception of the battered women's movement in the early 1970s, feminists have sought to uncover and understand domestic violence within a larger context of patriarchal social relations (Schechter 53–8). In the late 1970s, Lenore Walker developed the concept of the battered woman's syndrome based on a study of battered women (Walker, 'Battered Women Syndrome,' *Battered Woman Syndrome, Terrifying Love*). She initially interviewed a nonrandom sample of 110 predominantly white and middle-class battered women who had contacted social service agencies. She followed up this initial study with in-depth interviews of a more representative sample of 435 battered women (Schuller & Vidmar 274). On the basis of this research, Walker hypothesized that battered women experienced a repetitive cycle of violence that caused learned helplessness, which diminished women's ability to escape the battering.

According to Walker, the cycle of violence in battering relationships occurs in three stages: the tension-building phase; the explosion or acute battering incident; and the calm, loving respite. During the tension-building phase, several 'minor' battering incidents occur. The battered woman denies her anger, minimizes the incidents, and blames them on herself or on outside factors, not on the batterer. She accepts his abusiveness as legitimately directed towards her and believes that what she does will prevent his anger from escalating. During this phase, the woman attempts to calm the batterer by becoming nurturing, compliant, anticipating his every whim, or simply staying out of his way.

Knowing that his behaviour is wrong, the batterer fears that the battered woman may become so disgusted with him that she will leave. As a result, he becomes more oppressive, jealous, and possessive in the hope that his brutality will keep her captive. Over time, the battering incidents increase in frequency and severity, and the tension builds. The woman becomes more angry and stressed and is less able to control the situation.

An external situation will often upset the delicate balance of phase one and lead to phase two – an acute battering incident. The battering incident of phase two differs from those of phase one because it is uncontrolled and particularly severe. Walker characterized this phase as the uncontrollable discharge of the tensions that have built up during phase one. This phase usually lasts anywhere from two to twenty-four hours, but can go on for as long as a week or more. After the brutality of phase two, the batterer knows he has gone too far, and he tries to make it up to the battered woman. In the third phase, the batterer demonstrates extremely loving, kind, and contrite behaviour. The batterer apologizes, begs forgiveness, and promises that he will never hit her again. The battered woman convinces herself that the batterer will really change, and therefore stays in the relationship. According to Walker, if a woman remains in this situation through a second cycle, she is defined as a battered woman.

To explain why battered women stay in battering relationships, Walker used Martin Seligman's theory of learned helplessness (Walker, 'Battered Women and Learned,' 525; *The Battered Woman*, 45–54). According to that theory, animals who have learned that they cannot control a negative situation will no longer attempt to control it, even if later they experience a favourable outcome. Seligman based this theory on research with dogs. Seligman administered electrical shocks at random and varied intervals to caged dogs. At first the dogs attempted to escape the shocks. When nothing they did stopped the shocks, the dogs ceased any further voluntary activity and became compliant, passive, and submissive. When researchers provided an easy escape from the shocks, the dogs did not respond, even after being shown the way out. The dogs remained passive, refused to leave, and did not avoid the shocks. Only after the researchers repeatedly dragged the dogs to the exit did they learn to avoid the shocks voluntarily. The earlier in life that the dogs received this treatment, the longer it took to overcome the effects of learned helplessness. Walker argued that battered women stay in battering relationships because they learn to believe that they are helpless. The woman attempts to control the batterer's anger and stop the beatings during the first phase, but the battering incidents continue to occur and repeatedly escalate into phase two acute battering. As a result, the battered woman becomes depressed and feels helpless. No matter what she does, the battering continues. The batterer threatens to subject her to greater abuse if she attempts to leave or seek help. In conjunction with financial and emotional dependence on her batterer, the battered woman perceives that there is no escape and enters a state of psychological paralysis.

Advocates of battered women have argued that expert testimony on the battered woman syndrome is necessary to explain the effect of battering on the defendant's state of mind, to rebut myths and misconceptions about battered women, and to show why the woman's action was reasonable (Walker, 'Battered Women Syndrome,' 321). According to many advocates, the lay public harbours numerous misconceptions regarding the causes and effects of domestic violence. For example, many believe that battered women are masochistic, that battered women could leave the relationship if that is what they really wanted, that police can protect battered women, and that batterers are psychopathic personalities, are violent in all their relationships, and are unsuccessful and lack resources to cope with the world (Walker, *The Battered Woman*, 18–31). These common beliefs about battering lead juries to view battered women who kill as unreasonable and as responsible for the battering relationship. At an even deeper level, Elizabeth Schneider has argued, 'a woman who kills her husband is viewed as inherently unreasonable because she is violating the norm of appropriate behavior for women,' thus threatening 'deeply held stereotypes of appropriately submissive female conduct and of patriarchal authority' ('Describing,' 201–2). Overcoming these misconceptions is critical to a battered woman's claim of self-defence. Expert testimony on the battered woman syndrome provides jurors with 'an alternative perspective, or "social framework," for interpreting the woman's beliefs and actions – an interpretative social schema from which to view her actions as reasonable rather than aberrant' (Schuller and Vidmar 277). This testimony can answer questions that are inevitably in the minds of judges and jurors, such as why the battered woman didn't leave her home, why she may not have reported the battery to the police, and why she believed that the danger she faced on the particular occasion was life threatening. Furthermore, this evidence can 'educate the judge and jury about the common experiences of battered women, to explain the context in which an individual battered woman acted, so as to lend credibility and provide a context to her explanation of actions' (Schuller and Vidmar 61). Through this testimony, advocates of battered women have sought to convince judges and juries that a battered woman's decision to kill was reasonable self-defence.

Beginning in the early 1980s, courts began to accept the feminist arguments that traditional self-defence law was male biased, especially the concept of reasonableness (*State v. Wanrow*, 88 Wash. 2d 221, 1977; *Terry v. State*, 467 So. 2d 76, Fla. Dist. Ct. App. 1985; *People v. Minnis*, 118 Ill. App. 3d 345, 1983; *State v. Anaya*, 438 A.2d 892, Me. 1981; *State v. Allery*, 101 Wash. 2d 591, 1984), and courts began to allow testimony of the battered woman syndrome. For example, in the landmark case of *State v. Kelly* (478 A.2d 364, N.J. 1984), the New Jersey Supreme Court set a precedent by admitting expert testimony in cases involving battered women who kill their abusers. The court held that the expert testimony might aid juries in determining whether, under the circumstances, a reasonable person would have believed there was imminent danger to her life. The Supreme Court of Canada accepted the use of expert testimony on the battered woman self-defence in the case of *R. v. Lavelleé* ([1990] 1 S.C.R. 852). In that case, the court argued that battering alters what is 'reasonable' so that juries should consider the 'history, circumstances and perceptions' of the appellant in light of expert testimony on the battered woman syndrome. The expert testimony allows the jurors to overcome stereoptyes and myths about battered women in order to determine what the accused reasonably perceived, given her situation and experience. However, many courts have refused in practice to admit expert testimony on battering and many women have not been able to meet the standards of self-defence law. Women who killed their abusers frequently have been found guilty and often have received long sentences (Busch 22). As the battered woman syndrome gained broader circulation and acceptance, a feminist critique emerged that challenged both the accuracy and the usefulness of Walker's theory.

Critiques of the Battered Woman Syndrome Self-Defence

Critics claim that the battered woman syndrome theory is flawed for its inaccuracy and lack of empirical support, for its race and class biases, and for its reliance on stereotypes of passivity and victimization (Gagne). Numerous critics of the battered woman syndrome have pointed to weaknesses in Walker's research and her theory of the battered woman syndrome, and they have questioned common notions about the circumstances in which battered women kill. For example, Walker's original research sample was nonrandom, primarily white and middle class, and lacked a control group (Schuller and Vidmar 280). In addition, there is little empirical support for the cycle-of-violence theory (Faigman 627–8). Schuller and Vidmar point out that not all couples go through the cycle of violence as articulated in the model, nor is there a universal time frame for the cycle (280). Walker found that only 65 per cent of cases involved a tension-building stage prior to the battering, and in only 58 per cent of the cases did a period of loving contrition follow the battering incident (Walker 96–7).

Walker's application of the theory of learned helplessness to battered women is also flawed. Schuller and Vidmar argue that there is little support for learned helplessness in Walker's research data. In fact, the majority of battered women engage in a variety of responses in an attempt to end the abuse, which is not consistent with learned helplessness (Faigman 628–30). In addition, the theory of learned helplessness is inconsistent with the battered woman's act of killing her batterer. From 1976 to 1987, 60 per cent of deaths by intimates were males killing females, but 40 per cent were females killing males (Koss 72). Recent research indicates that women in assaultive relationships show a high degree of resourcefulness and persistence in their responses to their violent situations (Koss 85). For example, they often seek help and repeatedly attempt to escape battering relationships (Busch 43–4). In addition to weaknesses in Walker's research and theory, ideas about when battered women kill are in dispute. Holly Maguigan has challenged the 'compelling stereotype' that battered women attack in nonconfrontational situations. Based on empirical work in other disciplines and a review of appellate opinions, Maguigan argues that the majority of battered women kill during confrontations (388–401).

In addition, the battered woman syndrome theory has race and class as well as heterosexual biases (Bricker; Stubbs and Tolmie). Walker notes that in her work with battered women who kill in self-defence, black women were twice as likely to have been convicted of murder and sentenced to longer periods in prison than those who were white or from other minority groups ('Battered Women Syndrome,' 329–30; 'Response,' 224). Women who are poor and less educated as well as lesbian women suffer a similar bias in the courts (Bricker 1379). The battered woman syndrome does not 'work' for poor and minority women because the standard is based upon the experiences of white, middle-class women. Sharon Allard argues that battered woman syndrome testimony incorporates a stereotype of a 'good,' 'normal' battered woman and that black women, inevitably classified by jurors as 'other' because they do not fit the mould, do not benefit from testimony that reinforces this white-identified stereotype (Allard 193–8). Delores Donovan and Stephanie Wildman criticize the traditional definition of reasonableness on the ground that it excludes 'not only women, but also members of other minority groups with distinct socioeconomic characteristics setting them apart from mainstream middle-class America' (436–7). In one case, a white jury convicted a black defendant who did not fit the stereotype of the typical battered woman: she was physically large and was expressionless on the witness stand, unable to communicate the fear she felt the night of the stabbing (Bochnak 197). Allard calls for the creation of a battered woman model that incorporates race and class factors in an 'intersectional analysis' (193–8). Such a model would incorporate the social and economic constraints imposed by race and class.

The battered woman syndrome theory has created a powerful new stereotype that is hard for many women to fulfil. Expert testimony on the battered woman syndrome was meant to overcome jurors' stereotypes about battered women, but has in fact created a new standard against which women are judged: a passive 'battered woman' model of self-defence, which is the opposite of the traditional 'male' model of self-defence (Schneider 1986 200). As a result, the battered woman self-defence may merely replace 'jurors' misconceptions about battered women ... by another stereotype – the "typical" battered woman' (Schuller and Vidmar 287), thereby 'invit[ing] courts to prevent the fair trials of women who are not "good" battered women' (Maguigan 444–5). For example, Walker has noted that women who demonstrate anger, either by the way they kill their batterers or in their courtroom behaviour, are less likely to be found as having used justifiable force ('Response,' 224). This new stereotype portrays women as powerless and passive victims and men as violent aggressive brutes, a portrayal that replicates 'old stereotypes of incapacity in a new form' (Schneider, 'Describing,' 198) and reinforces traditional, essentialized, binary notions of female and male identity. According to Schneider, 'judicial opinions suggest that lawyers who have submitted expert testimony have had this testimony focus primarily on the passive, victimized aspects of battered women's experience, their "learned helplessness," rather than circumstances which might explain the homicide as a woman's necessary choice to save her own life' and a reasonable response to a life-threaten-ing situation (198 n. 17). More fundamentally, the use of expert testi-mony undercuts the battered woman's voice because of the implicit assumption that 'an expert, a professional, someone not a battered woman, is needed to translate the experiences of a large number of women in this society' (218). Schneider has warned against the risk that experts will become not just a complement to but a substitute for women's voices.

The battered woman syndrome theory has also perpetuated common stereotypes about female incapacity by characterizing battered women as mentally ill. Walker's description of the experiences of battered women as a *syndrome* suggests that battered women are mentally ill. According to Schneider, 'the term "battered woman syndrome" has been heard to communicate an implicit but powerful view that battered women are all the same, that they are suffering from a psychological disability and that this disability prevents them from acting "normally"' ('Describing,' 207). Criticizing the usage of the word 'syndrome' to describe battered women, Donald Downs argues that domestic vio-lence victims' sense and perception of danger must be seen as an alternative form of reasonableness. Walker has recognized the danger of 'misdiagnos[ing] and over-clinicalizing' the victims of abuse. She acknowledges the danger of using the 'battered woman syndrome di-agnostic category' for 'women who are responding naturally to poten-tial or actual abuse' because they may be misclassified as being mentally ill. According to Walker, '[m]any battered women themselves fear that the batterers' taunt that no one will believe them because they are crazy will come true' ('Battered Women Syndrome,' 329). She argues that her research does not support the idea that women who are abused develop a personality disorder ('Response,' 223). However, the presence of testi-mony on the battered woman syndrome has been found to be associ-ated with increased perceptions of diminished capacity on the part of the woman ('Battered Women Syndrome,' 320). Another danger is that an attorney's use of expert testimony on the battered woman syndrome focuses the jury's attention on the psyche of the defendant rather than on her environment (Johann and Osanka 99–156, describing 'mental assessment approaches' to litigating cases).

While advocates of the battered woman syndrome surely do not mean to perpetuate sexist stereotypes, this may be an unintended effect of using the battered woman syndrome theory in defence of women. Schneider argues that the battered woman syndrome encapsulates 'stereotypes of individual incapacity and inferiority which lawyers and judges may respond to precisely because they correspond to stereotypes of women which the lawyers and judges already hold' (*Battered Women*, 85). In an analysis of the first case to accept expert testimony on the battered woman syndrome, the New Jersey Supreme Court case of *State v. Kelly*, Schneider found that the court, while admitting expert testimony on the battered woman syndrome, emphasized the relevance of this evidence to an evaluation of the battered woman's psychological 'weakness' rather than to whether she acted 'competently, assertively and rationally in light of the alternatives' (79). According to Schneider, courts have treated battered woman syndrome evidence as relevant to an impaired mental state defence rather than a defence based on the reasonable apprehension of imminent danger because 'courts are more likely to hear and respond to a perception of women as damaged than as reasonable' (89). They find it 'easier to focus on those aspects of the testimony which characterize the woman as passive and helpless (i.e., her inability to leave) rather than active and violent but reasonable' (79).

Instead of focusing on the woman's victimization and psychosis as the term 'battered woman's syndrome' suggests, expert testimony on battering should focus primarily on the external circumstances in which a battered woman finds herself. For example, expert testimony should include society's failure to prevent male violence, in particular the failure of police and medical professionals to address domestic violence effectively (Busch 70–71). Expert testimony should also address how gender inequality has shaped the behaviour of both the abused woman and the batterer (Posch). Women's economic constraints as well as the influence of race and sexuality should be addressed if this information helps to explain the battered woman's actions. By moving beyond the battered woman syndrome, expert testimony on battering can account more accurately for the experiences of a broader range of battered women.

The Complex Agency of Battered Woman Who Kill

The legal discourse involving battered women who kill reveals these contradictory representations of battered women as both agents and victims. Despite feminists' efforts to use expert testimony on the battered woman syndrome to show the reasonableness of the battered woman's decision to kill, defence counsel have represented or have been heard to represent battered woman as lacking agency, often because of mental incapacity. When women who kill their batterers use the battered woman syndrome defence, they are often arguing, in a sense, 'I had no choice, he made me do it.' The discourse surrounding the battered women syndrome theory shows these contradictory tendencies.

For example, in the case of *State v. Felton* (329 N.W.2d 161, Wis. 1983), the battered woman was represented both as a reasonable actor and as both mentally incapacitated. The court described the battered defendant's testimony as follows: 'she stated that she debated what to do, and she testified that she knew there was no other way out without Robert killing her or the children.' The court, however, describes the clinical psychologist as testifying that 'Rita functioned automatically to survive ... her aggressive response was not in fact consciously thought out.' Whereas the defendant testified that she debated about what to do, the expert testified that she acted 'automatically.' At the postconviction hearing, the expert psychologist's testimony further removed agency from the defendant: she testified that the battering 'was the provocation which caused Rita to be deaf to the voice of reason and *to act from that impelling force* rather than from wickedness, cruelty, or recklessness' and that 'Rita had a severe personality disorder and *did not have the substantial capacity* to appreciate the wrongfulness of her acts and was *unable* to conform her conduct to the requirements of the law' (Johann and Osanka 271). Rita's defence was clearly based on incapacity, not on the reasonableness of her use of self-defence, despite her description of herself as acting based on reasoned debate.

The negation of the battered defendant's agency is often reflected in the commonplace testimony of battered women that they have no memory of the moment when they killed their abuser or that the killing was an accident. The defendant in *State v. Felton* remembered feeling the trigger, but not firing the shot (Johann and Osanka 270). In another case, the defendant testified that 'before I knew it, the gun just went off.' She had shot her husband three times in the back and twice in the back of his head (Johann and Osanka 299, *State v. Necaise*, 466 So.2d 660, La. App. 5 Cir. 1985). In the case of *State v. Koss* (551 N.E.2d 970, Ohio 1990), the court described the defendant's testimony as follows:

> She could not remember anything from the time her husband hit her to the time when she heard a 'noise,' which she believed was gurgling blood. When asked upon cross-examination if she caused the death of Michael, purposely or not, appellant answered that she had 'no idea.' She testified

that 'I purposely did not kill Michael Koss,' and '[i]f I killed him, it was an accident.' (971)

One woman stated that she didn't know her pistol fired (Johann and Osanka 309, *Clenney v. State*, 344 S.E.2d 216, Ga. 1986). Leslie Almond testified that she did not remember picking up a knife or defending herself, Rachel Olsen testified that she did not remember stabbing her husband, and Carol Gardner had no memory of shooting her husband (Bochnak 157, 122, 201). Another woman who killed her husband by running him over with a car and then stabbing him states, 'I just drove out and I didn't really see him until my car stalled and he was just lying there. I looked in the mirror and it looked like he was trying to get up. I got out ... I don't remember picking up the knife but I must have, and ... I started stabbing him' (Bauschard 82). In many cases, the killing is characterized as an accident, again removing agency from the battered woman. One court stated that 'the decedent then jumped up and the revolver went off' (Bauschard 307, *People v. Powell*, 424 N.Y.S.2d 626, 1980), seeming to transfer agency from the battered woman who pulled the trigger and placing agency in the decedent. The language of another case – 'the gun discharged during an argument' – seems to transfer agency from the woman to the gun she was holding (Johann and Osanka 314, *U.S. v. McIntire*, 461 F.2d 1092, 5th Cir. 1972). In these cases, the defendant's lack of memory removes her agency.

The tension between the battered woman's act of killing her batterer and the characterization of the battered woman as a victim creates an inherent dilemma for the defense of battered women who kill. Postmodern feminist legal scholar Mary Joe Frug has argued that feminism should be informed by the postmodern attention to multiplicity and resistance to a sole definition of women. Legal scholar Jennifer Wicke argues that members of subordinate groups should be wary of postmodernism and its critique of the unified, coherent subject because 'legal rules grant rights or privileges only when those who seek legal protection are able to exhibit a coherent subjectivity' (Frug 19). Frug, however, responds that the coherent subject is actually a critical obstacle to legal protection for members of subordinated groups:

> Law requires all legal claimants to assume a particular posture – a partial identity – in seeking judicial assistance; we must leave aside much of the multiplicity and complexity of our lives in order to engage in legal discourse. Injustice occurs ... when legal rules structure these particular

postures in such a way that subordinate groups cannot squeeze into them at all. In these situations, legal rules need to expand the narrow and rigid character of the subject position they impose as a condition of admission to the legal arena. (22)

The battered woman syndrome is an attempt to create a coherent subjectivity for battered women in a system that privileges male subjectivity. However, the theory has instead created a subjectivity that has obscured the complex agency of battered women's lives and excluded the experiences of many women.

The battered woman syndrome exemplifies the strengths and weaknesses of viewing women as a group distinct from men. According to Schneider, a basic assumption made by advocates of the syndrome is that women act in self-defence under different circumstances and in different ways than men ('Describing,' 213). Expert testimony on the battered woman syndrome has been central to acquittal for many battered women who strike back against their abusers. However, the theory makes broad generalizations about the complex and varied experiences of battered women. Any reasonableness standard, even a 'reasonable battered woman standard,' puts some women's experiences at the margin. Not surprisingly, those women are often women of colour and poor women. Holly Maguigan asks 'how to resolve the tension between group and individual standpoint in the context of a criminal trial, whose purpose is the assessment of individual culpability. If there is a separate standard of reasonableness, to what degree does the definition of the group require conformity to the definition by the individual defendant on trial?' (443). The battered woman syndrome theory gives voice to the experience of many women, but simultaneously silences other women.

The battered woman syndrome also oversimplifies the experiences of battered women, who manifest what Mark Hobart calls 'complex agency.' According to Hobart, 'a person may be more or less willingly part agent, part instrument, part patient in relationships, and at different times ... Agency and patiency are situational, overlapping, ironic and under-determined' (96). The battered woman who kills is a victim of abuse but also resists her abuser. She is an instrument insofar as the batterer controls her actions, she is an agent insofar as she controls her actions, and she is a patient insofar as she is battered. Her motivation may be varied and complex before, during, and after the homicide. Hobart distinguishes three types of motivation – desire, self-interest, and duty – and argues that motives may be mixed. The battered woman may be motivated by self-interest – her survival, in which case she acts in self-defense; she may be motivated by duty – to protect her children from abuse or perhaps death at the hands of the batterer; and she may be motivated by desire – anger towards or hatred of her abuser. The battered woman may be motivated not only by the conduct of her batterer, but by memories of previous batterers or child abuse. These motivations may ebb and flow, shifting and changing over time.

When a battered woman on trial for murder uses the battered woman syndrome theory in her defence, the meaning of the theory may shift throughout the trial. At times she may use the theory or the theory may be heard as an assertion of agency in the sense of meaning 'killing my batterer was a reasonable action under the circumstances,' to support a theory of self-defence. At other times, the theory may be a denial of agency, an assertion of victimization and weakness, as if the woman were saying, 'I had no choice, he made me do it.' As Hobart says, 'the reasons for action may be partly uncertain or under-determined and open to alternative explanations by the participants themselves' (91). Yet throughout this process, each time a woman denies her agency (or is heard to do so), the underlying irony is that she does so to justify the *act* of killing, an extreme assertion of agency. The battered woman also asserts her agency by appealing to judges' and jurors' stereotyped notions of female weakness in order to achieve her goal of freedom. If she is freed, the woman has exercised agency through the assertion of non-agency; she becomes a victor by asserting victimization.

The agency of battered women is both resistance and complicity, their subjectivity is 'multiple and contradictory' (Moore 49, 66). Henrietta Moore asks, 'How is it possible for people to both consent to and dissent from the dominant representations of gender when they are encoded in the material world all around them?' (75). The battered woman consents to the dominant representation of gender insofar as she tolerates abuse and appeals to notions of victimization as an excuse for killing her batterer. However, she dissents from those representations insofar as she fights back against her abuser, kills him, and then claims that what she did was reasonable self-defence. 'If one cannot resist by placing oneself outside dominant structures and discourses, one can none the less displace oneself within them. Individuals can refuse the construction deviously or ironically, they can refer to it endlessly, but do so against its purpose, against the grain' (Moore 82). The battered woman refuses gender construction ironically in that she acts 'against the grain' of the feminine sex role by killing her abuser, but then claiming victimization.

The agency of battered women is also complex because 'decisions and responsibility for action involve more than one party in deliberation or action' (Hobart 91). At each stage of the process, various actors are involved in shaping the meaning of the battered woman's act of homicide. Before the homicide, the woman's motivations are shaped most clearly by the batterer, but also by police action or inaction, other family members (e.g., endangered children), and the availability of resources in the community to deal with battering. At the scene of the homicide, the batterer's actions are critical to whether a woman can successfully assert self-defence later at her trial. After the homicide, the meaning of the battered woman's act is influenced by police at the homicide scene, the state's decision to prosecute, her attorney's theory of defence, the judge's decision to allow expert testimony, the expert witnesses' testimony, and the jury's verdict.

Recognition of complex agency is at the heart of the critique of battered woman syndrome theory. The dilemma, according to Schneider, is how to 'describe *both* victimization and agency in women's lives': 'expert testimony which emphasizes or is heard to emphasize only battered women's helplessness or victimization is necessarily partial and incomplete because it does not address the crucial issue of the woman's action or her agency in a prosecution for homicide – namely, why the battered woman acted.' Schneider notes that the woman has acted but she has also been acted upon: 'it is not fair to say that she has been "self-acting" or really an agent, in the sense of free agent. Yet there is a sense in which the notion of victimization in its extreme form seems to deny any agency, the possibility of individual action, or the fact of action altogether.' Schneider also notes that 'the notion of agency carries with it assumptions of liberal visions of autonomy, individual action, individual control and mobility that are also inadequate and incomplete.' She recognizes the importance of group identity for an understanding of individual experience: the battered woman syndrome suggests that 'psychological and social factors are interrelated and that individual experience is necessarily shaped by group identity.' However, she argues that advocates for battered women must 'allow for change by transcending static stereotypes. Feminist legal work must *both* describe *and* allow for change ... must take account of battered women's experiences in being acted upon *and* acting' ('Describing,' 95). Feminists must recognize women's agency, but also recognize the constraints under which battered women live (*Battered Women*, 84).

Conclusion

By the early 1990s, domestic violence had been 'discovered' by society. A 1996 study revealed that expert testimony on battering and its effects had been admitted to some extent by courts in every state and by sixteen of the nineteen federal courts that had addressed the issue, and that twelve states had enacted legislation supporting the admissibility of expert testimony on battering (National Institute of Justice 33). Courts and politicians came to judge the actions of battered women who killed 'through the lens of the battered woman syndrome' (Busch 23). Researchers in the 1990s have also built upon the battered woman syndrome theory by using trauma theory to understand the effects of battering on women. For example, they have argued that battered women suffer from post-traumatic stress syndrome ('Battered Women Syndrome,' 327), a diagnostic category listed in the *Diagnostic and Statistical Manual of Mental Disorders IV* (American Psychiatric Association). Recent research has confirmed this contention (Busch 74–8). Use of this research to explain the actions of battered women, however, is subject to the same feminist critique as the battered woman syndrome – that these theories pathologize women rather than looking to the structural constraints shaping women's behaviour such as society's tolerance of male violence.

In the last few years, however, as a result of the feminist critique of the battered woman syndrome and the dramatic increase in social science research into domestic violence, much of which has called the battered woman syndrome into question, some courts have started to move beyond the concept of the battered woman syndrome, especially the notion of learned helplessness, and have begun to allow a wider range of expert testimony on battering. Policy makers are beginning to see that the concept of battered woman syndrome is too narrow and ambiguous and that the experiences of battered women cannot be characterized by a single construct. These weaknesses are reflected in the fact that the introduction of expert testimony on domestic violence in court has often not lead to acquittals. In a 1996 study of the appeals of 152 battered women convicted in state court, 70 per cent of the convictions that were affirmed on appeal by higher courts had used or recognized expert testimony (National Institute of Justice iv). While feminist legal reforms, including the introduction of expert testimony on battering, have led to acquittal for many battered women who kill, many others are convicted and serve long sentences.

Some cases of battered women who kill, such as those involving confrontational circumstances, fit within the traditional definition of self-defence: the woman's actions are clearly a reasonable response to a life-threatening attack. In other cases, the acts of battered woman are so unreasonable that they just as clearly qualify for the insanity defence. However, between these two poles are many cases where the actions of battered women are both reasonable and unreasonable. Insights gained by studying the identity and agency of battered women are useful in understanding the ambiguity of battered women's actions, an ambiguity that the law has failed to capture. The law is categorical: it asks only whether the action was reasonable or unreasonable. Human agency, on the other hand, is more complex than this simple polarity. Advocates of battered women have attempted to stretch self-defence doctrine to include the situations of battered women who kill. But the resulting generalizations about battered women have created a new category that erases the complexity of their experiences and, ironically, reinforces the larger structure that perpetuates battering. Framing male violence against women in terms of the battered woman syndrome has reinforced the prevailing gender ideology that undermines the long-term goal of empowering women.

Hope lies in raising the awareness of judges and juries about the social conditions in which battering occurs, including the 'unresponsiveness of police or health professionals' and the 'broader social context of economic resources, family, children, or religion, which constrained the [battered women's] choices' (Scheider, *Battered Women*, 80). While the law requires a determination one way or another – innocence or guilt – juries have broad powers to interpret facts, creating a tremendous capacity to accommodate ambiguity. Therefore, the key is to focus on educating judges, juries, and society at large not only about battering and its effect on women's lives, but about society's failure to stop male violence against women and about how gender inequity in society constrains women's choices.

Works Cited

Allard, Sharon A. 'Rethinking Battered Woman Syndrome: A Black Feminist Perspective.' *UCLA Women's Law Journal* 1 (1991): 191–207.
American Psychiatric Association. *Diagnostic and Statistical Manual of Mental*

Disorders. 4th ed. Washington DC: American Psychiatric Association, 2000.

Bauschard, Louise. *Voices Set Free: Battered Women Speak from Prison*. St Louis, MO: Women's Self Help Center, 1986.

Bochnak, Elizabeth. *Women's Self-Defense Cases: Theory and Practice*. Charlottesville, VA: Michie, 1981.

Bricker, Denise. 'Fatal Defense: An Analysis of Battered Woman's Syndrome Expert Testimony for Gay Men and Lesbians Who Kill Abusive Partners.' *Brooklyn Law Review* 58 (Winter 1993): 1379–1437.

Busch, Amy. *Finding Their Voices: Listening to Battered Woman Who've Killed*. Commack, NY: Kroshka, 1999.

Crocker, Phyllis L. 'The Meaning of Equality for Battered Women Who Kill Men in Self-Defense.' *Harvard Women's Law Journal* 8 (1985): 121–53.

Donovan, Dolores A., and Stephanie M. Wildman. 'Is the Reasonable Man Obsolete? A Critical Perspective on Self-Defense and Provocation.' *Loyola Law Review* 14 (1981): 435–68.

Downs, Donald Alexander. *More than Victims: Battered Women, the Syndrome Society, and the Law*. Chicago: University of Chicago Press, 1996.

Ewing, Charles Patrick. *Battered Women Who Kill: Psychological Self-Defense as Legal Justification*. Lexington, MA: Lexington Books, 1987.

Faigman, David L. 'The Battered Woman Syndrome and Self-Defense: A Legal and Empirical Dissent.' *Virginia Law Review* 72 (1986): 619–47.

Frug, Mary Joe. *Postmodern Legal Feminism*. New York: Routledge, 1992.

Gagne, Patricia. *Battered Women's Justice: The Movement for Clemency and the Politics of Self-Defense*. New York: Twayne, 1998.

Gillespie, Cynthia Gillespie. *Justifiable Homicide: Battered Women, Self-Defense, and the Law*. Columbus: Ohio State University Press, 1989.

Hobart, Mark. 'The Patience of Plants: A Note on Agency in Bali.' *Review of Indonesian and Malaysian Affairs* 24 (1990): 90–135.

Johann, Sara Lee, and Frank Osanka. *Representing ... Battered Women Who Kill*. Springfield, IL: Charles C. Thomas, 1989.

Kampmann, Mary. 'The Legal Victimization of Battered Women.' *Women's Rights Law Reporter* 15 (1993): 101–13.

Kinsports, Kit. 'Defending Battered Women's Self-Defense Claims.' *Oregon Law Review* 67 (1987): 393–465.

Koss, Mary P., et al. *No Safe Haven: Male Violence against Women at Home, Work, and in the Community*. Washington DC: American Psychological Association, 1994.

LaFave, Wayne R., and Austin W. Scott, Jr. *Criminal Law*. 2nd ed. St. Paul, MN: West, 1986.

MacKinnon, Catharine. 'Feminism, Marxism, Method, and the State: Toward Feminist Jurisprudence.' In *Feminist Legal Theory: Foundations*, ed. D. Kelly Weisberg, 427–36. Philadelphia: Temple University Press, 1993.

Maguigan, Holly. 'Battered Women and Self-Defense: Myths and Misconceptions in Current Reform.' *University of Pennsylvania Law Review* 140 (1991): 379–486.

Moore, Henrietta L. *A Passion for Difference*. Bloomington, IN: Indiana University Press, 1994.

National Institute of Justice. *The Validity and Use of Evidence concerning Battering and Its Effects in Criminal Trials*. Washington DC: National Institute of Justice, 1996.

Posch, Pamela. 'The Negative Effects of Expert Testimony on the Battered Woman's Syndrome.' *American University Journal of Gender, Social Policy, and Law* 6 (Spring 1988): 485–503.

Schechter, Susan. *Women and Male Violence: The Visions and Struggles of the Battered Women's Movement*. Boston: South End, 1982.

Schneider, Elizabeth M. *Battered Women and Feminist Lawmaking*. New Haven, CT: Yale University Press, 2000.

———. 'Describing and Changing: Women's Self-Defense Work and the Problem of Expert Testimony on Battering.' *Women's Rights Law Reporter* 9 (Fall 1986): 195–222.

Schuller, Regina A., and Neil Vidmar. 'Battered Woman Syndrome Evidence in the Courtroom.' *Law and Human Behavior* 16 (1992): 273–91.

Stubbs, Julie, and Julie Tolmie. 'Race, Gender, and Battered Woman Syndrome.' *Canadian Journal of Women and the Law* 8 (1995): 122–58.

Walker, Lenore E. *The Battered Woman*. New York: Harper & Row, 1979.

———. *The Battered Woman Syndrome*. New York: Springer, 1984.

———. 'Battered Women and Learned Helplessness.' *Victimology* 2 (1977–78): 525–34.

———. 'Battered Women Syndrome and Self-Defense.' *Notre Dame Journal of Law, Ethics, and Public Policy* 6 (1992): 321–34.

———. 'A Response to Elizabeth M. Schneider's "Describing and Changing: Women's Self-Defense Work and the Problem of Expert Testimony on Battering."' *Women's Rights Law Reporter* 9 (1986): 223–5.

———. *Terrifying Love: Why Battered Women Kill and How Society Responds*. New York: Harper & Row, 1989.

Chapter 3

A Survivor within a Culture of Survivors: Untangling the Language of Sexual Abuse in Oral History Narrative Collected in a Politically Violent Situation

BATYA WEINBAUM

Confusion between how something is narrated (the narrative truth) and what happened historically (the historical truth) is a hazard in the psychoanalytic profession.[1] Given the range of possibilities existing between the truth and falseness of representations of the past, and the fact that the fundamental feature of human intelligence is having 'the capacity to reconstruct events and to create new meanings and whole narratives out of memory fragments,' this problem is of particular concern (Haaken 1081–2). All we really collect is an individual person's account of an event as rendered into a shared present, which in itself becomes yet another event. This confusion between the present account and the past event can be an issue in feminist ethnographic research, even when other cultural forces and models might be operative or perhaps dominant, such as the complexities inherent in the formation of women's language. Boundary-blurring in both instances should interest those attempting to build on theories of the unconscious and politics in cultural studies, especially for those who, following Louis Althusser, have used psychoanalysis for studying ideology and the transformation of the subject.

Neither subject nor object is necessarily free from projection. Ultimately, sense making or meaning making exists in the present, not in the dimly remembered or highly charged past. However, this chapter primarily explores how the survivor of domestic and child abuse often needs to dramatize while relating life history, forging a truth held together by the force of narrative rhetoric and metaphor rather than by fact.[2] This observation conflates the idea that, as a group, women have a connected worldview and tend to express themselves in the same kind of language. I will focus on a close reading of one woman's language, which reveals how she dealt with her own victimization by becoming desensitized towards other people's suffering. Unfortunately, her narrative and metaphors were replicated in other life stories I have collected in my fieldwork, from which I also draw, as indicated throughout in the notes. These detectable patterns made me suspect that regaining one's own sense of power and self-worth by imagining the right to claim power over others might in fact be a common rehabilitative need – not only for sufferers of domestic abuse, but also for sufferers of national and ethnic dislocations and defeat, as indicated in the emergence of National Socialism in Germany after that country's defeat in the First World War, as well as other world-historical cases.

British Marxist feminism has used French theory to rethink Marx's theory of ideology in terms of women's representation, including linguistic representation. This Marxist feminism looked specifically at women's language connected language, knowledge, and power, which led to looking at language as a system of signs that must be read as a consequence of social construction and as a mechanism for re-evaluation and change. The psychoanalytic method was used to locate starting points to define this trajectory. Psychoanalytic criticism began to articulate a problem inherent in all feminist criticism, the linking of the social with total individual and personal feelings (54). Many feminist theorists have moved to reclaim Freudian processes, if not all of his specific conclusions,[3] although Freud's conclusions concerning female survivors of childhood sexual abuse have been anathema to those involved in trauma research. Such scepticism is not surprising given his career, in which he first asserted that symptoms, known as 'hysteria,' were the result of sexual abuse and then retracted the assertion under the social pressures of the times (Herman 10–20; Jacobs, *Victimized Daughter*, 7–9; Manlowe 11–14; Waite 5–6).

Even though he was a psychoanalyst writing in the Freudian tradition, Frantz Fanon's process-driven explorations of colonialism and nationalism in *The Wretched of the Earth* intrigued me as I attempted to untangle the language of sexual abuse in descriptions of contemporary politically violent situations. Although I interviewed many others who showed the effect of trauma on personal identity, on which much work has been done,[4] here my method is to analyse a spoken account from an oral history study done in 1989–92[5] of one interviewee in Palestine/Israel on a micro-textual level. In writing up this interview, I draw upon my own empathy as a survivor, with empathy defined as 'the process through which one's experienced sense of basic connection and similarity to other humans is established' (Jordan et al. 69).[6] On a linguistic level, using my empathetic connection to listen and respond, and seeing a partial mirroring of myself in my respondent, I detected much behind the flow of this abused woman's associations. Primarily, I noticed how she connected her personal experience of violence to the frame of current events during the Palestinian *Intifada* (I am referring to the first uprising of 1987 that continued, abated, and then re-emerged in 2000). She used the language of the diagnostic category post-traumatic stress disorder (PTSD) to narrate her own story, as well as the story of the Jews, as a struggle for the creation and maintenance of underlying integrity. Thus, she spontaneously combined the stories of survivors of child and domestic abuse, war, political terrorism, and the Holocaust under a single motivating trend.[7] Sexual abuse produces trauma by shattering a precarious sense of female identity and creating a feeling of vulnerability (Haaken 1082). Dorit's languages coincided with the language of those in the country in which she has chosen to live who have been traumatized by other means.

My micro-analysis of an oral history transcript of a female Jewish convert who joins the Israeli right and is also a subject of survivor culture[8] reveals how she crosses Israeli society's discursive boundaries, between the personal and the public spheres. I suggest that a narrative process of pain, suffering, trauma, recovery, and survival on a micro-level, which Brison states is so important in the aftermath of violence for trauma survivors ('Survival Course,' 'Uses'), can fuel expansion of the growing Israeli right-wing on a societal level. Such a need to dramatize through the telling of life stories seems to be especially strong among women reaching out to grasp religious ideology, particularly recent converts.[9] Hence, those engaged in further ethnographic studies can additionally benefit by detailed analyses of abused women's language, by paying close attention to representations of violence in the personal realm that connect with memory and narration of violence in the political arena.

However useful the insights derived from minute examination of battered women's negotiation of language might be, one cannot readily make leaps that are unmediated by other factors, like personal experience and the political agency of the subject. For example, some subjects might move from victimization in one realm to transcendence, transformation, and compassion towards the immediate oppressor and others;

some may even move from personal abuse to political activity to eradicate the cause of systemic oppression.

The ability of victims/survivors to work politically to overcome systemic oppression needs to be accompanied by their opportunity to obtain treatment and care in a woman-run, woman-only environment. This was discovered by the women in Zenica in Central Bosnia (Cockburn 174–5). With supportive grassroots feminist structures, women can more easily come to other political conclusions besides fascism, and can start to redirect anger at legitimate social causes. But it seems that this process won't happen spontaneously on its own – women need to find that 'women can do everything' (188). Free feminist space to imagine other routes for recovery needs to be available (185), rather than spaces organized by traditional patriarchal religions.

Background and Purpose of the Study

The interviewee/subject who converts something from sensual experience into language through her story-telling (i.e., into symbol) can be in an experiential cycle of her learning, engaging in a conversation with a purpose. First, the subject presents a wish to be appreciatively understood by the interviewer (Weinbaum, 'Shifting Gears'). Thus, a story told is neither true nor unmediated, but only adulterated retrospection; once a story can be communicated, the narrator has already selected facts and converted them for presentation in a particular symbolic order, therefore creating a story resonating with pre-selected emphasis. The subject chooses what to disclose; those choices forge, tarnish, and otherwise spin the narrative.

With this in mind, I discuss the narrative, identity, fragmentation, and discourse style of a woman survivor of domestic battering and childhood abuse I will call 'Dorit.' A former U.S. citizen, Dorit is a tall, vivacious, attractive blond woman struggling for self-respect, who presents herself as a right-wing, recent convert to Judaism and immigrant to Israel. Dorit's narrative indicates how her need to survive personal domestic violence motivated her conversion to Judaism from Catholicism.

In psychoanalytic terms, this conversion can be understood as the subject's acting out a need to believe in an ideal father, to re-establish her violated basic needs of trust and security. As Jacobs discovered (in stories collected elsewhere), this need appears strongly in abused daughters (*Victimized Daugther*, 34). In numerous cases, spiritual realms have been evoked as a lens for survivors to filter their trauma; Dorit is only one example of the phenomenon (*Victimized Daughter*, 41). Her story illustrates the conclusions of other researchers, who point out that often survivors' empowerment processes must include untangling internalized messages and meanings in the patriarchal constructs of Christianity (Manlowe x–xi).

Dorit reports rejecting the Catholicism that allowed abuse and battering by her brother and husband. She recalls the religious and cultural denigration of women in Catholicism as the basis upon which her silent suffering of abuse and violence had been legitimated, also common in other survivors' reports (*Jacobs*, *Victimized Daughter*, 49–50). By rejecting what she perceived as the religious basis of her denigration, Dorit found a way to re-establish trust and security. Like other survivors, she developed an ideal self.[11] The ideal reconstructed self was defined and mirrored first by rabbis and teachers and then by the symbol of (for her) a new God, which became a receptive, interpretative framework in which she could give meaning to her victimization.[12] She then projected, transferring this understanding onto the Jewish people and Israelis, who 'took her in,' offering the protection she failed to get previously in familial sites. This conversion and subsequent immigration to recover from abuse separated her from her past, helped her enter a liminal state, and resulted in her incorporation into a new social order. What she got from her *aliyah* process was similar to what other survivors have gotten from participation in 12 Step groups, establishing and creating a new set of connections within a community of peers providing a context of relationships in a liminal sphere (Manlowe 102). In undergoing *aliyah*, Dorit rebuilt the bases of human connection, such as trust, autonomy, identity, and intimacy, that had been destroyed by abuse, as others do through self-help groups (Herman 133). Like the 12 Step groups do for others, the *aliyah* support worked to reshape and reform Dorit's personal identity and the collective to which she belonged. This subtext to her *aliyah* then formed her perception of the political situation in Israel, providing the supportive interpreting framework in which she understood both her own victimization and society.

However, because she was a newcomer, Dorit's need led to a reinforcement of the blind spots she already had about the actual historical situation. In deciphering her narrative, I saw connections between her past abuse and battering as a child and as a wife and her experience of the current violently threatening situation, particularly at the outbreak of the *Intifada*. For example, according to Jacobs (*Victimized Daughter*, 37), many survivors identify with victims of the Holocaust as a way for their fear of the perpetuator to merge with the fear of anti-Semitism and

Nazism. This fear, prevalent in the Jewish community and in Israel, becomes a way to project a generalized fear of danger, to legitimate a so-called paranoid, over-reactive 'trembling' constantly vigilant state, often recognizable among survivors. Referred to as 'hyperarousal,' such a state, the first symptom of post-traumatic stress, consists of the human system of self-preservation, accomplished by going into 'permanent alert' (Herman 35).

Victims of chronic abuse stay in this hyperaroused state. They are continually hypervigiliant, anxious and agitated, with a chronic apprehension of imminent doom. They seem prone to increased activity, agitation, pacing, screaming, and crying upon any symbolic or actual danger (Herman 86). Victims start easily, react irritably to small provocations, but often pass as 'normal' within Dorit's country of choice, Israel, to which many other survivors with the same symptoms, even if derived from other events, immigrate. Thus, by moving to Israel, where threats of danger occur daily and one regularly interacts with survivors of other traumas, Dorit relocated to an environment where she might live out her possible 'addiction' to trauma. Therapists have noted this habit to be a contributing factor to revictimization (Waite 29). It is easier to access a generalized, socially acceptable fear than to face the fear aroused by a specific rapist, abuser, or perpetuator (Jacobs, *Victimized Daughter*, 37–8).

Perhaps in making this move, Dorit was even attempting re-enactment, an attempt to master the traumatic experience, which psychiatrists often regard as a sign of a stage of recovery. In other words, it is common for survivors to deliberately seek out circumstances to try to actively re-engage their fears (Herman 197). Mary Douglas has argued that the body is both a complex structure and a symbol for other complex structures, and a model that can serve for any bounded system (115). Thus, what Dorit did in the process of regaining her own boundaries was to find an appropriate larger social milieu in which to fight for re-establishment of threatened, precarious boundaries. To cleanse herself, she argued for the cleansing of a larger social body, Israel. Thus, one can analyze the interconnections she made between sexual violence and danger, and violence and danger in a warring situation.[13]

Methodology

In this study I conducted thirty-five interviews between 1989 and 1992. Of this larger group of women, not all shared the experience of abuse.

The four women who identified that they had[10] each utilized abuse metaphors to explain the basis for her move to ardent nationalism. All the right-wing women suggested interest in a nationalistic 'cleansing' of Arabs from 'Jewish land,' as they felt that Arabs did not behave as polite 'guests' within it. Yet, no left-wing women used these metaphors and associations from their own experience of abuse to explain their political conceptions of how both ethnic groups – Palestinian and Jew – could work together towards peaceful co-operation.

Dorit was one of the thirty-five women from diverse backgrounds in Palestine/Israel I interviewed between 1989 and 1992. I collected forty hours of tape during this period. I first met Dorit in a casual exchange in an art gallery of Sephardic ritual objects in Jerusalem, and then interviewed her in my hotel room. At the time, I was based in an inexpensive hotel in a religious section of West Jerusalem near the Green Line.[14] The interviews were open ended, structured with prompts frequently drawn from the week's news to encourage the respondent to discuss the current political situation.

I had evolved this method of soliciting narratives of women's political involvement in Israel when I made an initial trip there in 1989, with an assignment to write something for an anthology for a small independent publisher. I used an open-ended projective slate of questions, developed in the field, tuned to the particulars of the immediate political situation, and worked backwards from there to larger world views and ideological beliefs. I asked for Dorit's responses, for example, to current events in the news such as the reaction of the ultra-orthodox to the Olympic team that had visited the Old City, in order to situate her life story (as I did with others) in the larger framework of contemporaneous media discourse.

After listening to the tape, which I did after Dorit left, I returned to interview her further. The second interview after initial contact was in Dorit's home, in a fairly expensive rental apartment in West Jerusalem, which she shared with two other working women. The third and final interview was in the lobby of the King David Hotel, in which locale Dorit reported that she often met her boss, for whom she worked as a private secretary. There in an environment quite luxurious and seemingly quite comfortable to her, I let her examine the transcript and share her responses even though the draft I presented was rough. Her choice of environment was wise, as she could provide herself with vivid, visual, sensual details for constant distraction when her difficult feelings and past memories would come up as she read.[15] In an environment of potted plants, music, and sweets, she was protected by sufficient anchorage in the present: if old feelings threatened to overwhelm her, she could hold onto something safe in the immediate present environment.

During July 1989, the month in which I initially worked with Dorit, I had first visited a kibbutz where I had worked at the age of nineteen. I also made contact with women's centres, located research sites, and attended Women in Black and Women at the Wall demonstrations. At all stages of the research, I searched for the lived experiential realities of the women's lives, rather than for objective facts. My search seemed to be part of the recent struggle for the rights of the disenfranchised, which has called women, minorities, and representatives of third world cultures since so much has been distorted or let out in traditional history (Rosenwald and Ochberg 3). My intention was to record how each woman sensed and experienced her own history, and to understand what each woman felt about the history she expressed.

In other research, I have analysed how my questions and stance as an observer changed in response to the answers I received during interactions and interviews.[16] Additionally, I have explored ways in which the women spoke their stories, the metaphoric use of the language of war, and images they drew upon using language of the family. Some Israeli Jews' denial of the harsh realities for some Palestinians seemed to stem from trauma. I explored the ungrounded use of history as a way to regain bearings after the upheaval of immigration, the impact of imagined audience, and the intervening factors preventing all women from bonding on the maternal nexus to work together across class, race, ethnicity, and nationalism. I discovered that these latter factors included the effects of the media, religion, the *aliyah* process of taking out citizenship and moving to Israel, and socialization through education.

The language Dorit used in describing her first-hand experience of the *Intifada* and violence in general in Israel most directly reflected her experience of battering in marriage, although she had mentioned childhood abuse as well. Whichever event established her root metaphor, its reflection provided a strong emotional coherence. She tried, like other women, to make sense of her experiences in marriage and childhood. Rather than valuing and protecting her, the institutions of childhood and marriage apparently had devalued and demeaned her. As survivors do, she sought a resolution of her personal trauma by feeling called upon to engage the whole world (Herman 207). She articulated the political, religious dimension of her personal tragedy and made it the basis for social action. This gave her a way to transcend her personal atrocity, as she redeemed her trauma by making it a source of a larger, survivor mission. Once she understood victimization, she focused on truth-telling in a way that helped other victims overcome their problems, a common denominator of all social action (Herman 208).

I am aware of the difficulties of drawing generalizations from a particular case. However, a sense of trauma of some sort or another is the motivating force for the majority of immigrants to Israel.[17] This would include, for example, immigrants who moved there as a result of the Holocaust or who fled pogroms and religious persecution in the Soviet Union.[18] Thus, I noticed linguistic patterns indicating trauma in transcripts of at least two other subjects on which I performed micro-analysis. Still other immigrants came after intense personal shake-up, including a single mother with a baby abandoned by her 'disappeared' comrade in the Chilean coup, and a single mother whose husband had died, leaving her a widow in Argentina. Trauma also motivated the *aliyah* of a woman raped in the Moroccan crisis and of a woman horrified at the French anti-Semitism revealed around cases in the media after the Second World War.[19]

Nonetheless, listening constructively as I worked with Dorit became difficult for me. I began to see the point made in an earlier interview by a left-wing activist in Women in Black, a weekly anti-occupation street ritual sustained for several years by Israeli women that I was also researching (Weinbaum, 'Challenges'). Fanon (203–51) had pointed out in his psychological studies of war and mental disorders that anxieties and neuroses continued well after rapes and attacks; the Women in Black activist, Katya Frischer, had noted that dealing with some people in Israel was like dealing with rape crisis victims. Frischer, who had been working for recognition of nonrecognized Arab villages in Israel and later went on to law school, developed her point analogously. She argued that those who have been raped live in re-enacted fear of men, and similarly, that Jews in Israel whom Arabs have attacked live in continual restimulated fear of attack by Arabs.

Political Landscape as Ground for Acting Out Frustrations and Needs

For Dorit, the *Intifada* was an arena for her to reorient according to her own needs and frustrations. Reluctantly, gradually, I decided that her needs were not based on the immediate situation, but on the social order in which her personal problems had first developed. Difficulty emerged even with my awareness of ideology criticism[20] in the field, as I struggled with what Barrie Thorne has called the 'problematic balance, a dialectic between insider and outsider' as one participates in and yet observes the same world (73). I became increasingly aware that Dorit's way of retelling political events actually contained more interesting subtexts, one being how she made the transition from victim to survivor, a subtext shared by others in the study. Another was how the socialization process of her moving to Israel and taking out citizenship had created cultivated expression of a fearless, ancestral defiant pride, a tough will and refusal to compromise that Fanon associates with nationalism (64).

Such a process also became implicit in other stories. Some subjects asserted that the ideology of self-defence apparently applied to Jews, who had a traumatic history from which to recover. However, these same subjects did not extend to Palestinians the identical ideology of standing up for one's rights. The subjects dismissed and even demeaned the present suffering of Palestinians, suffering they regarded as practically fictional, behaving much as the colonial French regime did in attempting to convince Algerians, through torture and brainwashing, that neither an Algerian nationalism nor an Algerian people existed (Fanon 233). I listened analytically for the difference between historical truth and narrative truth. Guiding metaphors emerged as Dorit associated experience, such as claims she made that the Palestinian kids were dazed, 'like kids that were on drugs' when they protested by stone-throwing during the *Intifada* (462). These metaphors were shockingly outrageous if one is not working with a mundane, literal, one-dimensional view of reality, i.e., a 'truth' that does not radically confront one's own, albeit limited, version of reality. The view that the stone-throwers must have been on drugs conveyed shortcomings in Dorit's own understanding. The idea that there might be legitimate reasons for a genuine uprising was clearly beyond her comprehension. This insight was useful for understanding the context of acceptable justification of the ideological underpinnings of those right-wing Jews in present-day Palestine/Israel. I found I could understand 'the process within which experience is prevented from informing belief' (Earnest 253).

Dorit held on to Judaism to bring her closer to the truth. She had recently undergone the *aliyah* process. This U.S. convert had in her forties turned to Judaism as she left her violent, abusive husband in southern California. She found that Judaism gave her precepts with which she could stand up to her husband. Her process was strikingly similar to the way frustration complexes were described as an emerging expression of the unconscious in the Mau-Mau revolt (Fanon 245). Dorit had experienced her Catholic indoctrination as emphasizing 'turning the other cheek, never defending yourself, never raising your voice, always being calm' (Weinbaum, *D'ot*, 274).[21] She perceived that Catholicism had made her an 'emotional mess' suffering extreme guilt, and brought her to thinking she 'was the ruination of the world,' as if suffering was going to make her 'holy and close to God' (274). As Dorit herself articulated it, 'In my Catholicism and in my Christianity there was a real ideology about laying down your life for your enemy ... and what it did for me was make me into sort of a doormat person' (ibid., 267).

Through adoption of what she understood as Judaism, she overcame the ingrained submissiveness based on her Catholic upbringing. As she said, 'In Judaism, I found a profound sense of order, it's logical. It says justice, justice, you will pursue justice. It doesn't say let people beat you up and you will be ok and you will be holy' (ibid., 268). Her sense of Judaism's confrontational honesty had brought her to the religion. However, Jews might recognize this as a grandiose projection onto Judaism, whose followers have also learned through years of suffering to 'lay low' and 'turn the other cheek,' such as converting and taking oaths to Christianity during the Inquisition just to stay alive. Nonetheless, Dorit had clung to this glorified aspect of Judaism throughout the terrifying experience of facing her husband in court. Judaism helped her to detach from her victim status.

The call to justice that she felt in Judaism enabled her to hold on to her self-respect. As a woman beginning to rebel against her own victim status, she found in Judaism the theoretical underpinnings to explain the 'bad' status quo. She also found the ability to detail the necessary steps to liberate herself from her suffering.

When Dorit's ex-husband pinned her against the wall, hit her, pounded her up against the wall he had pinned her to, and told her he was going to divorce her and kill her, she experienced such fear that she remembers she could barely speak (*D'ot* 274). She reported experiencing herself as an emotional wreck, 'a zombie' (274),[22] out of which state she could not lead herself, given the promulgation of the morbid dependency of the Christian self-sacrificing ideal (Manlowe 64). In turning to Judaism, in her later interpretation, she seized hold of a different gestalt of behaviour than the rightness of violence against women supported by the idea that women must be dominated and led. She moved out of

the Christian ideal that the survivor's suffering must have divine purpose, which many abuse survivors take from religious language to give
spiritual meaning to their post-traumatic stress syndromes; sometimes
they even conceptualize themselves as suffering, martyred saints and
virgins (Herman 106, Manlowe 79). Thus, this choice to reject Christianity and to turn towards Judaism empowered Dorit and allowed her to
move from victim, to conscious victim, to action. Such a process motivated her to change, despite recent scholars locating a history of patriarchal spirit in Judaism that leads it to support domestic violence against
women (Graetz 12–13):

> When I started moving in Jewish circles and I told some of this to a Jewish
> lady, she said, if my husband ever treated me like that he had better not
> close his eyes. I had never heard a woman speak with such strength. In
> Christianity there is this sweet and soft stuff. If you married him, you
> have to stick it out ... And the further I moved into it, it gave me an awful
> lot of strength until finally when I came to University of Judaism, in Los
> Angeles. I was talking to Rabbi Rhimbaum. I said to him something about
> forgiveness. What I don't understand is Jews have a hard time forgiving.
> He said, it is not that we have a hard time forgiving. It is just that we don't
> want it to happen again. So we keep talking about it to make sure it
> doesn't happen again, because in the Torah, it says remember and ob-
> serve. So I told him a little something about my husband. He said you've
> got to do something about it because it is called a sin of omission. In law, it
> is also an act of omission. I took my husband to court and through
> Judaism I won. Because, I wrote up my own order to show cause and I
> told them that in Christianity I was always taught just to forgive and
> forget, but that my ex-husband ... took the kids, he stole the money, and he
> threatened my life. As a Jew I am called to justice. And my call to justice is
> not to let this person get away with that kind of abominable behavior and
> robbery. The judge saw it. No matter what my ex-husband tried ... it didn't
> work. You know what I took with me when I went to the final trial was my
> little Hebrew prayer book. It got me through ... I was so terrified of him
> that when I sat in the witness stand to give testimony, and he looked at me
> through those knitted dark eyes, I kept seeing him pound, pound, pound
> against the wall. It scared me ... I took off my glasses so I couldn't see him
> and I spoke from the heart. I think that is what did it. I spoke from the
> heart. (Weinbaum, D'ot 275–7)

Thus, like other survivors from devout, patriarchal, Christian backgrounds, for Dorit 'rethinking religious rhetoric and institutions is paramount for overcoming valorization of female self-abnegation' (Manlowe 84). Dorit's move to Israel, with the heightened, honoured status of an immigrant, helped her find the new, grounded connectedness that psychohistorian Robert Lifton describes as necessary to overcome the interruption of personal continuity in one's lifeline once trauma has occurred, severing relationships and breaking trust and faith in the previously known.[23]

Toby Epstein Jayartne and Abigail J. Stewart have noted the important feminist research principles of understanding emotions, understandings, and actions in the subject's own terms. They stress that translating experience into predefined categories might have the effect of silencing voice (85). Yet, I began to experience my own suspicions of the feminist derivation of understanding, insight, and knowledge from emotion (Griffiths 95). The determination of Dorit's logic, with which I could not agree, was based on an abused woman's feelings, feelings I felt I should support. Yet as I subtly negotiated interview tactics, direction, and space in this long, intense period of interviewing and re-interviewing many women of different perspectives in a short time frame, I began to question whether feminists are right to trust feelings as a basis for research and theory.

For example, Dorit came to the interview armed with documents as intellectual tools, the way she had similarly gone to court to seek justice with her Hebrew prayer book. She came to the interview knowing I was interested in women's opinions on current events, and that my intent was to seek her views of the present Israel/Palestinian politics. Early in the interview, she handed me an interview with Arafat published in *Playboy*. This interview documented his assistance from Arab oil as well as his budget of $220 million to 'administer political and social programs.' She was also reading James Adams' *Financing of Terror* and Samuel Katz's *Battleground: Fact and Fantasy in Palestine*. She was brimming with information, eager to discuss her conversion from Roman Catholicism. She was also, as she put it, an eyewitness to the outbreak of the *Intifada* in East Jerusalem. Throughout her interview, I got a sense of how someone coming from a battering experience of violence could draw strength from a nationalistic spirit calling for self-defence. Initially, in descriptions of her eyewitness to the *Intifada*, she described how the young men throwing stones had the same kind of 'hazed daze' that she used to see when her 'mother would go off ... in that fanatic anger,' or that her husband possessed. She insisted, 'That is what I saw,' when giving descriptions of actions by the Palestinians in comparison to descriptions of actions of her previous batterers (*D'ot* 262). I particularly picked up on this because other right-wing women had evidenced the same trend in previous interviews, one of whom had experienced rape in the Moroccan revolt and eagerly projected her hate and fear for her original abusers onto all Arabs and Palestinians in her immediate vicinity. Both these subjects radiated charismatic energy as they described what it was like to live daily with the threat of violence rippling throughout society.

After listening to her narrative of conversion, I asked Dorit if she saw the Jews as being beaten by the Arabs and as earning the right to defend themselves. Her response was an enthusiastic 'Yes, that is right.' This idea gave further force to her assemblage of compelling, if not completely persuasive, explanations and interpretations of the behaviour of current Israeli Jews:

> I see them as strong. Seeing them strong yet I am hearing the world come against them, the same way that the world was coming against me. Oh let them have it. Let them have it. Let me tell you, if you let them have it, they will take everything from you and they will bury you twenty feet under the ground and they will sit on your grave and they won't give a damn. That is exactly where they wanted me. That was after my brother stole my Mercedes. My kids were gone, the house was gone, everything was gone. You cannot stand there, being a pacifist and saying, Oh, I love you. I forgive you. Oh yes. They think you are a fool. They will just keep taking more and more. So when I hear somebody say 'drive them to the sea,' I take that literally. I don't think it is a light-hearted joke. I think they mean exactly that. I don't think they would bat an eyelash about it. (Weinbaum, *D'ot*, 276–7)

Using ethnographic principles to see through the eyes of those embedded in a daily situation in which one is not living oneself, I could see how the response above showed that she took and ingested my interpretation. ('I see them as strong.') Then, she associated. She began from her own specific survival act as the context, providing her with the root metaphor that cognitively organized 'sense' or meaning in her present reality. By going from the present 'see' to the continual 'seeing' in 'seeing them as strong,' she showed an active process in her mind that brought her to the next association, 'hearing the world come against them, the same way the world was coming against me.'

At this point, the reference of 'they' or 'them' shifted from the Jews to those intimates whom she experienced as coming against her, including ex-husband and brother. Thus Dorit's historic events became active in the present, the root metaphors for her contextualizations. The 'them' subsequently shifted to include the Palestinians ('Let them have it'), in a phrase that communicated first the desire to inflict violence upon a collective object and then, in repetition, intense satirical derision of co-operating with one's own dispossession. Another subject I interviewed also criticized this notion in a subsequent interview, using the metaphor of negotiating what one gives up in dividing properties during divorce. That is, we can come to understand in a literary sense that the act of women 'making sense' in the narrative of a collected oral history text is beyond true or false. Rather, the speaker creates the sense historically in the active present, whether or not she receives a projection or transference in the psychoanalytic sense by the individual researcher.[24]

As I listened to Dorit's story-telling, it became important to distance myself from the metaphorical power of persuasion in her rhetoric. I had to at least recognize the limitations of her metaphors, although the images themselves might have seemed to have some virtues in clarifying understandings. As the anti-violence movement once drew upon the language of combat to describe victimization of women within the 'war zone' of the patriarchal family (Haaken 1078), here she utilized her female victimization in the patriarchal family to create sustained metaphors to understand warring political dynamics in Israeli culture.

These patterns exhibited in a close textual analysis of Dorit's interview were reflected in other interviewees who had disclosed their experience of previous trauma. Another subject came to the interview clutching at the ideology of the 'right to possess.' Having been dispossessed personally at an early age when anti-Jewish feelings arose during the revolt in Morocco, she clung to her prayer book during the interview to find personal strength, exhibiting the same self-protection through projection that I observed in Dorit.[25] Others also generalized into an unlocatable 'they,' asserting what are popular myths in Israel: 'What they would like us to do is chop ourselves up like salami bits, and the Arabs would have the right of return. They would fill our country up with billions of Arabs' (Weinbaum, *D'ot*, 62). The latter speaker had recently immigrated just previously and did not have her home completed at the time of the interview. Nonetheless, she successfully reversed what some Palestinians must have themselves experienced: that the Jews were filling up their country with 'billions' of people. Furthermore, according to this woman's analysis, the actions of the unspecified 'they' would lead to 'the Arabs' to having the right of return. This assertion is clearly a distortion. Only a small sector of the entire Arab population of the Mideast or the world was requesting the right to return, and the number does not reach into the 'billions.'

From Personal Trauma to Self-Recovery through Politicized Nationalistic Reaction

The more I worked with Dorit's interview transcript, the more I began to examine her free association with images. I could see that her language interwove personal trauma with the trauma of war. As was pointed out previously, some survivors (in the earlier case, specifically of the Holocaust) wish to make all future enactments of a similar phenomenon cease to occur (Greenspan). As a battered, abused woman, Dorit had experienced an onslaught nearing obliteration; she then declared that all Jews, a group to which she now considered herself to belong, must fight back against obliteration. She utilized Holocaust imagery of 'the ashes,' for example, into which she might disintegrate if she gave up her ideological beliefs.

After revealing earlier in her narrative her personal confusion and state of distress after domestic battering, Dorit went on to cite an article that Hitler had written in the 1940s. He had stated that the weapons he used against Jews in Europe would be mental confusion, distortions, inconsistency of the heart, 'like your heart and your mind are two different things' (Weinbaum, D'ot 280), and panic. Dorit felt that what he chose as his weapons were still with Israelis – especially panic. She maintained that Jews have a self-hating, suicidal mentality, and asked, 'What are you going to do with your physical self if you give it all up? Swim in the ocean, I guess,' referring to a possible outcome of another Israeli popular myth, that the Arabs want to 'throw them into the sea' (281). She considered what she viewed as the Jewish tendency to 'give it all up' as a survival of defeatism, the legacy of Hitler.

Yet at the same time, her stories contained elements similar to those of the survivor stories analyzed by Henry Greenspan: self-recrimination, guilt, rage, despair, and flailing, grandiose attempts to give communicable form to what was in reality incomprehensible (Greenspan 145). These elements were shared by the narratives of other right-wing women reclaiming Judaism whom I interviewed. I found Greenspan's insight relevant, that stories of survivors are stories 'of individual hearts that only hint at a world in which all cries were silenced' (145). I examined the stories of battered women and survivors of abuse with Greenspan's forms of narrative analysis, generalizing 'trauma' and broadening 'survivor' to mean a survivor of personally jarring experiences that could not be understood on a cognitive level as being just and fair, either to the individual or within the world.

Dorit, like Greenspan's subjects, who had survived the trauma of the Holocaust, exhibited a need to 'make a story' in which she desired to negate her earlier personal annihilation. Likewise, she exhibited the same guilt, rage, and despair about the here and now, her guilt as a survivor stemming from surviving both Catholicism and domestic battering.

Greenspan characterized the stories of survivors as having the ability to speak eloquently about a passionately proposed future in which the possibility of catastrophe ceases. Curiously, Dorit manifested this pattern, in speaking enthusiastically of a utopia where Jews could come together to right a wrong, give themselves credit for their success, and build a joyous future. For Dorit, as for others, a certain drama existed in this life-as-text rendition. This drama also came from her fight against usurpation. In Dorit's case, the fight seemed to be against the battering by her husband, the violation by her own family that certainly exacerbated matters, and the devastation of her divorce. Further, her narrative process, like those of the survivors of other catastrophes, entailed sweeping texts, icons, and facts into highly idealistic categories. She presented a totalistic historical view by projecting a need to cleanse her own slate, thus quieting the screams inside to overcome her own interior disintegration. A tight weave of current and historical reality held past pain and horror in check. In this picture, no ambivalence seemed to occur. She deftly projected all the guilt, blame, and responsibility onto the other side, as evidenced in the one-sidedness of her stories, in which all Israelis and Jews were victims and all Palestinians and Arabs were demons.

Thus, as story-teller and narrator Dorit told both her life story and the present Israeli political history in a way that excluded what, for her, remained impolitic to include. A story may tell us one thing officially, Rosenwald and Ochberg conclude, but at the same time 'point our attention to another undeclared truth without which it rings false' (11). As these scholars argue, a life story is more than just a recital of events. Rather, a life story is an organization of experience 'relating the elements of experience to each other and the present telling' (8).

Consequently, Dorit's rendition of her eyewitness view of the outbreak of the *Intifada* in East Jerusalem could be read as a narrative of her self-recovery. I could empathetically intuit and recognize parts of this from my personal experience of telling stories dramatically as part of overcoming my own childhood experience of violence.[26] The person Dorit was on that day as she witnessed the outbreak of the *Intifada*, and later as she told me her story, was the person she had been years in becoming. She recounted:

> When I came to make *aliyah* in 1987, I lived up in the Old City. I went back to the convent and stayed there until I completed my method of *aliyah*. It was the beginning of the *Intifada*. I got there on November 28, which was America's Thanksgiving Day. The *Intifada* began December 9. I remember the date because I was walking from the King David Hotel down into the Old City. I was with a Jewish friend and we didn't even get out to the gate and he says, 'Let's get out of here. Let's get out of here now.' I think that a lot of people who have lived here perceive the danger before it ever happens ... He knew something was up. Sure enough. Later on that day there were riots and things that were happening. He said they might be having trouble here and sure enough that was the day it had started. I was supposed to go East Jerusalem and every morning I would have to get up and walk past the tear gas and the soldiers, the IDF [Israeli Defense Force], the UN and the Arabs, the stones and everything to go to my job. It was something like living through the sixties – I would have imagined at Berkeley or at Kent State University. Because the feeling of animosity was very, very thick. They were yelling 'Kill the Jews' from the mosque. (Weinbaum, *D'ot*, 269)

In the beginning of Dorit's scary narrative about the outbreak of the *Intifada*, she perceived the events according to American categories, along American calendars. She situated the event in her own historically specific *aliyah*, marked by relation to an American holiday. She perceived current events in Israel through the lens of specific periods of import in American history – 'like the sixties,' as she imagined would have happened in Berkeley or Kent State. Not surprisingly, like the majority of political actors in the social movements of the 1960s, she did not relate to the opponents in terms of negotiations, gradual progress, reform, or improvement via compromise. Rather, Dorit thought in terms of sharp dichotomies, such as them/us, 'the desirable and the intolerable, victory and defeat, now or never' (Offe 830).

She also related what she identified as a generalized survivor's 'sixth

sense' and what psychotherapists call 'hypervigilance,' or a premonition of danger in advance that survivors of abuse often have developed
as a way of coping (Manlowe 10).[27] In Israel, such hypersensitivity was
a shared feeling among many, according to Dorit. She seemed to like
being in a country where this sense of living in anticipated danger was a
shared psychic phenomenon, as even extremely painful and life-threatening situations mean something entirely different when they are shared
by the general community (Waite 31). Such a shared state presumably
re-enacted her pre-existing psychic structure of surviving while poised
on the verge of catastrophe, achieved by other survivors of childhood
violence by different means such as joining the circus, going into prosti-
tution, taking great personal risks, and otherwise finding ways to live
dangerously. Survivors of childhood violence frequently live their adult
lives in risky situations to recreate the feeling of living on the brink. By
choosing to live in Israel and thus continuing to live in a sense of
danger, she integrated her history and autobiographical memory with
the history of others who had also survived trauma, perhaps choosing
also to escape the devastating sense of social isolation that so often
magnifies trauma (Waite 31). Thus she could survive while at the same
time maintaining her self-defining sense of being a victim, a situation
other survivors have not so easily resolved (32).

Because I had just come from interviewing a Palestinian woman from
the PLO who said that her group advocated peaceful coexistence, I
asked Dorit to specify who the 'they' was as used in her phrase 'they
were yelling "kill the Jews ..."' She avoided a direct response and
continued to extend the concept of 'they' in an unspecified manner:

> *They* were just trying to stir up the people. And the people, especially in
> the Old City, are very easily stirred up. It doesn't take much to get
> involved in mob violence. It doesn't take anything. This is of course what
> *they* wanted. *They* want people just to jump on. It doesn't matter the
> reason why, just do it. (Weinbaum, *D'ot*, 270) (emphasis mine)

This extension of 'they' into utter amorphousness makes attribution of
senseless, irrational violence with an unspecified 'reason' an easy next
step. Then she continued to ground her narrative in reference to her
own timeline of 'sense,' in her *aliyah* experience. She anchored her
experience of the event in her own categories of known reality:

> I took a job as a house person, taking care of a child, because I was running
> out of money. I still hadn't made my *aliyah* process yet [i.e., gotten a

government stipend]. I had just come back. I was still in the Old City. This girl came into the youth hostel, which is just yards away from the temple mount. The temple mount is very close. She comes in and says, 'Nobody move. Nobody get out of here. The soldiers have declared this a day of danger and no one is to go out.' Somehow it struck me as very funny. I had heard of Valentine's Day, Christmas Day and of course every other kind of day but I had never heard of a day of danger,[28] so I laughed. I said, 'This I gotta see.' So this little French friend of mine, Giselle and I, we went up to the terraces. When you get up high on the terraces, you see what used to be Pontius Pilate's place. He used to get up there and look down and see what the Jews were up to. So that is the same thing I did. We went up there to see what the Arabs and Jews were up to. (270)

Dorit's response to the collective danger and to the spectre of possible displacement seemed to provide her with relief regarding her own experience of individual danger. Drawing a parallel between her own and Pilate's removal to a safe place in order to get an aerial view, she lessens the danger as well as situating herself in ancient history. Dorit reaches back in history to get her bearings, as women inhabiting different nationalistic warring settings often do, including women in Ireland, Central Europe, and Palestine/Israel. Cockburn points out that 'it is when present events make collective identity politically important that we reach for history, spanning the gap between present and past with stories that stress "people," nation and land' (3). The problem is, as she also warns us, that the concepts of people, nation, and land are slippery ones.[29]

In the models Dorit used to tell her story, in accordance with models of intelligibility specific to the culture in which she was participating, she drew from the particular religious education open to her as she clung to her prayer book to organize daily practices and belief. Consonant with the forces attempting to stabilize the given organization of her society and culture, her story complied with the general cultural model enacted in Israel. Hence, her stories passed as 'sensible' and even self-evident to her. However, her justifications might alarm those operating with other cultural models.

Yet these misunderstandings of self and others do not hinge on false beliefs, as Earnest argues (383). Rather, institutional practices bear directly upon them. In Dorit's case, the institutions would include media, *aliyah*, and religious education, all of which impart a heightened sense of self as member of an exalted group: Jews acting upon an external environment. These forces are great enough to cause individuals, in the stress of scrambling for survival with the added burden of personal recovery, to lose their ability to revise existing categories for interpretation of ongoing social reality.

Conclusion

By listening to Dorit's narrative and to the narratives of other abused women describing their own observations and experience, as well as comparing these stories to data of abused women collected elsewhere, I saw a pattern. Recent arrivals to Israel who immigrate based on trauma seem to find, in the continued reliving of danger, a vast theatre in which to reverse their own role as helpless, passive victim at earlier points in their individual life stories.[30]

Narrative criticism provides a base to argue that subjects continually re-invent histories to serve their own contemporary psychological and political aims. They grasp at straws, reaching back to find a shelter in ancient history. This, coupled with the personal charge of the recent immigrant's own relived and slightly rescripted dramatizations, provides a powerful springboard. When circulated among their narrators in social reality, the stories establish a basis for cohering right-wing positions, which then motivate further actions of recent arrivals. These in turn have an influence in electoral politics, since each citizen gets a vote after a brief waiting period. But individual acts of protest and group acts of outrage can also emerge.

In terms of significance for feminist theory, at this juncture, what would my close study of Dorit's narrative and those of others like her reveal? Line-by-line analysis reveals no 'women's connectedness' automatically giving women a source of resistance to dominant logic, as some feminists (e.g., Irigaray, Chodorow, Gilligan) argue.[31] The claim to 'women's identity' outside of specific life histories that lead to certain ideological conclusions, whether logical or not, obscures the narratives of some women – especially those who experience disconnection as a result of abuse, battering, or rape. Under closer scrutiny, these claims seem to evaporate, clearing the way for the emergence of more grounded social research and theory, as it becomes evident that there might be a close relationship between a woman's experience of surviving abuse and her wider worldview. This seems particularly so when analysing religious views in light of war and national conflict.

Indeed, this is the goal of true ethnography – to represent the irreducibility of human experience' (Willis and Trondman 5). Thus, this linguistic analysis contributes to the field of feminist ethnography by its heightened awareness that if one has three witnesses to the same event or series of events, one has to decide, as a researcher, which version to privilege as reality. One purpose of my exploration was to understand this individual experience – of both the interviewee and the interviewer – but also to gain understanding of the psychological underpinnings of what is known as the Israeli right wing by a close examination of language and rhetoric. Another purpose was to explore the relationship between war, gender, and personal/cultural aspects of conflict in a multicultural environment in which many bring their own case histories to a particular historical experience, blocking the road to peaceful co-operation; these impediments cannot always be swept aside by the utopian, emotional hope that women, as women, will always be for co-operation on the basis of a shared female nature. This will not be the case as long as some women have the additional burden of overcoming and surviving personally shattering abusive situations. I hope this exploration of some motivations for the turn to the right in Israeli society, as revealed through close examination of survivor language, contributes to establishing the basis for more peaceful conflict resolution and for more peaceful living, giving each woman the space for her own right to recovery, or the right to be understood as being in the process of recovery, no matter what her route or experience may be. Here we have gained a richer picture through language of some women's lives, and in particular how survivors of abuse, through seeking mirrors of themselves in those overcoming a weakened sense of national identity, may temporarily at least pull themselves up, unconsciously blurring subjectivity and objectivity, sliding signifieds and signifiers, mixing meanings and metaphors until such a time as they regain wholeness and get back on their feet. To understand this process is not to excuse fascism or supercharged nationalism with all the blinders they represent; awareness of the ability of the right wing to manipulate some women's apparent needs can in the long run only benefit more progressive factors.[32]

Notes

1 While the focus here is on one oral history narrative, see also Weinbaum, 'The Relationship between Gender Identity and Nationalism' and 'Shifting Gears,' in which I explore similar dimensions. Spence discusses the differential use of these terms in his book on meaning and interpretation in psychoanalysis.

2 Her responses to childhood abuse led to revictimization in adulthood, a
   pattern Jacobs finds to be common among survivors (*Victimized Daughter*,
   70), as does Herman (111). (For further discussion of this phenomenon, see
   also Finkelhor et al., Russell, *Secret Trauma*, and Wyatt.) Thus, while most
   of the stories the subject narrates have more to do with domestic battering
   leading to conversion to Judaism and subsequent Jewish nationalism, she
   also disclosed a personal history of abuse by her brother. Since early abuse
   sets the stage for later abuse, even though I did not focus on the childhood
   aspects of her narrative, the stage setting in terms of language and perception was still there.
3 See, for example, Chodorow and Dinnerstein, in the United States;
   Kristeva from France; and Mitchell from England.
4 See, for example, Brison, 'Surviving Sexual Violence.'
5 This interview was conducted in *Mea Shearim*, an ultra-religious Jewish
   neighbourhood in West Jerusalem, in the early part of 1990 as part of my
   larger study, *Searching for Peace on Hostile Grounds* (forthcoming).
6 Empathy is furthermore often described as 'the ability to feel what others
   feel, to experience the emotional state of the other such that one becomes
   sensitive and responsive to the other's needs' (Jacobs, 'Victimized Daughters,' 130). Although empathy is typically described as an aspect of personality, I feel such a quality is also necessary to conduct insightful ethnographic research in the field. For more on empathy, see Tavris and Offe.
7 Recovery literature often invokes the Holocaust (see Hermann, Bass and
   Davis, Jacobs, *Victimized Daughter*) in a similar vein, and psychiatrists have
   begun to merge the boundaries of traumas survival in terms of symptoms
   exhibited as they begin to describe related symptoms shown by both
   incest survivors and combat veterans (Jacobs, *Victimized Daughter*, 9;
   Haaken 1079). Critics charge that invoking the Holocaust to dramatize the
   private, otherwise unacknowledged pain of survivors might trivialize
   both the nature and the magnitude of suffering by oppressed groups
   (Haaken 1079).
8 Survivor culture in this sense refers to the way women feel proud to have
   survived the trauma of brutal treatment, rather than remaining traumatized and shamed; see Brison, 'Survival Course.' For a discussion of the
   sexual abuse recovery movement, situated as part of the 'adult child'
   movement that critiques the dysfunctional American family, see Haaken
   (1071–3).
9 For discussion of the need to dramatize in relating life histories given in
   psychoanalysis, see Spence.
10 In other random sample interviews conducted elsewhere that focused on

experience of sexual violence and sexual exploitation (which was not the focus of my questions), of nine hundred women interviewed, one in four had experienced rape and one of three sexual abuse in childhood (Hermann 30, Russell 1984). Therefore, it is likely that more women than those who expressed so had actually had similar experiences, which they did not choose to share. Nonetheless, my interviews with left-wing women as a whole did not contain such language and metaphors. See, for example, Weinbaum, 'Radicalizing Impact' and 'Impact of Children.'

11 In other words, Dorit's construction of an alternative identity through an idealized self to overcome the trauma was as a convert, a devout follower of a new religion; for others, it has been through excelling in sports, academic, performance, the arts (Jacobs, *Victimized Daughter*, 52–3). All of these routes are persistent attempts at psychological reparation, common for survivors of abuse, who begin reconstructing their identity over and over again (Waite 21).

12 Again Jacobs has noted that looking to God for this reason is common among abuse survivors elsewhere (*Victimized Daughter*, 42).

13 For more analysis of such interconnections, see Schott 178–9.

14 The Green Line refers to the 1967 border of Israel before that country expanded as a result of the war.

15 See Foa and Kozak on how fear memoirs are accessed when a subject is presented with current information. Reading her own words about her past and seeing my reflections about her stories must have had the capacity to stir old things up. Consciously or unconsciously aware of this possibility, Dorit had chosen an environment in which she could pamper herself if need be. See also Hermann (178) about the importance of a strong anchor in the present if one is going to explore previous negative times. Dorit might have sensed that new memories might be brought up and recovered as she experienced the full impact of the facts she already knew, which she had reported to me. This is when new recollections of previously repressed trauma usually emerge (Hermann 184), as I discovered in other interviews.

16 For further discussion, see Weinbaum, 'A Story Involving Participants.' In an additional article I explored how my respondents often surprised me with their answers to my questions. I took particular interest in how American feminist theories of the possibility of bonding through motherhood were contradicted by pro-natalist ideology, which has traditionally been explored less with regard to Israeli women than to their Palestinian counterparts. In other words, nationalism and the need to reproduce children of one's own group far surpassed the basis for bonding on the

shared experience of mothering, which I recognized was more of a Western feminist point of view. See Weinbaum, 'The American Feminist Concept.' Relevant as well was the fact of my own Reform assimilated Jewish
upbringing, in the Midwest, far from the centres of struggle for Jewish
identity. My process in the field is further explored in 'Searching for
Peace.'

17 I, like Manlowe, use 'trauma' to mean 'a violating experience that has
long-term emotional, physical, and spiritual consequences that may have
immediate or delayed effects' (5). Encompassing social problems such as
war, anti-Semitism, and the Holocaust, the term can be applied to any
experience that causes intense, sometimes repressed memories that can
endure for a lifetime (6). See Brison for discussion of the pros and cons of
competing approaches to the definition of 'trauma' ('The Uses of Narrative,' 200–1).

18 See, for example, the story of Ana Golden, 'Israel is Our Country,' in
Weinbaum, D'ot, in which she recounts her parents' decision to leave
Switzerland as a result of anti-Semitic events in the schools (58–61).

19 See my 'Utopian and Dystopian Moments' (forthcoming), 'Relationship,'
and D'ot as well as my forthcoming Searching for Peace on Hostile Grounds.

20 'Ideology criticism' refers to the process by which belief is stronger than
perception and continues in the face of facts to the contrary of one's belief.
In other words, if I believe women are liberated, I will look at women
being portrayed as having professional careers and going back for higher
education on television to confirm my belief. Even if somebody shows me
facts to the contrary, such as the lack of childcare at professional conferences or the university, the trivialization of those career women on television shows, the fall in the percentage of women in tenure jobs on campus,
or the growing pay gap between men and women, my ideology or belief
will fail to adjust in response to the mere presentation of such fact. Ideology criticism such as Earnest makes is the critical analysis of how beliefs
hold sway in spite of evidence provided in contradiction to staunchly held
views.

21 A Catholic reader of this manuscript at an earlier stage pointed out that
Dorit's is only a fundamentalist interpretation of Catholicism. Catholicism
and the many forms it takes are very complex, as I have analyzed further
elsewhere, for example, in my studies of Mexican culture (Weinbaum,
Islands). Nonetheless, others have explored the misogynous themes to be
found in general in Christian culture, to which Dorit might also have been
responding. See, for example, Manlowe, who argues convincingly that
any of the qualities that make a good Christian are the same qualities that

make a female 'feminine.' Manlowe includes self-sacrifice for love, submission to an all-powerful male, reliance on external authority for direction, distrust of the authority of one's own experience, and belief in a redeeming male saviour (60). Also key is the stress on the value of obedience (69).

22 I am assuming that by this phrase Dorit refers to the 'emotional numbing' that, researchers have found, traumatized victims use to block off the effect of overwhelming events; see Haaken (1070) and Waite (21). Manlowe defines the state as 'psychic numbing,' the diminished capacity of victims to feel (6). Waite describes this experience as a sudden psychic death, a complete alienation from self and others that renders the survivor inactive from depletion of meaning and vitality. Primitive minds describe this state as soul-loss (Ellenberger). Studies of abuse survivors have described abuse as 'soul murder' (Shengold). Thus, it seems apropos that Dorit chose to move to action again through reclaiming – through pursuit of a new religion – her lost soul.

23 This reflection is from a transcript made in spring 1992 in New York (Manlowe 6, 179). See also Lifton.

24 These ideas of root metaphor and historical moment in the active present are from Pepper (232).

25 For more discussion of this second subject, see Weinbaum, 'Relationship.'

26 For a discussion of the extended effects of incest and how these might intertwine with fieldwork, see Ronai.

27 According to Lani Ravin, an American-born Jew who lived sixteen years in Israel, in this situation it was likely not intuition or a 'sixth sense' but hypervigilance or hyperarousal – as mentioned earlier, a state of permanent alert – that would heighten awareness of a phenomenon, leading to insights that might be interpreted as 'premonition.' Perhaps Dorit's companion was taking note of little tell-tale signs of disruption of normal order signalling danger, signs of which non-Israelis might not be aware. For example, on Yom Kippur, at the outbreak of the Yom Kippur War, vehicles were on the road, which Israelis knew was not supposed to occur. Israelis might notice breaks in everyday routine, such as Arabs not being in line to get their work assignments, the streets being too quiet, too many Arabs on the streets, or no Arabs on the streets; or, if stores are shut, this might mean that Arabs had gotten a directive not to work because of a strike (personal communication, March 1998).

28 The phrase that struck her as humorous might have been a mistranslation, as the army can declare an 'emergency situation' (Ravin, personal communication).

29 For the Jews of Kiryat Arba, for example, the spot where King David established his first royal throne seven years before he conquered Jerusalem led to the creation of a fortified settlement under the leadership of Rabbi Moshe Levinger, symbolizing a 'Jewish roller-coaster ride through history' replete with majestic temples, the Wailing Wall, Exile, and the Promised Return. See Friedman (3).

30 This pattern was also recognizable in the stories of other subjects, such as those recorded in my article 'Shifting Gears in Life History Research.' The suggestion that Israel's turn to the political right is based on the short-sightedness of traumatized recent immigrants was first made by Tova Adiv, whom I interviewed in Kibbutz Gan Schmuel in spring 1990 and whose interview 'Voicing Our Pain' is contained in *D'ot* (51–7). Tova is a pre-state sabra and had been collecting and voicing her own observations for several years.

31 See also Belenky et al. and Miller, who argue that women understand the world differently, in connected and intuitive ways.

32 See, for example, Power's analysis of right-wing women in Chile.

Works Cited

Adams, James. *Financing of Terror*. New York: Simon, 1986.

Bass, Ellen, and Laura Davis. *The Courage to Heal: A Guide for Women Survivors of Child Sexual Abuse*. New York: Harper, 1994.

Belenky, Mary, et al. *Women's Way of Knowing: The Development of Self, Voice and Mind*. New York: Basic Books, 1986.

Brison, Susan J. 'Survival Course.' *New York Times Magazine*, 21 March 1993; 20.

———. 'Surviving Sexual Violence.' *Journal of Social Philosophy* 24.1 (1993): 5–22.

———. 'The Uses of Narrative in the Aftermath of Violence.' In *On Feminist Ethics and Politics*, ed. Claudia Card, 200–25. Lawrence: University of Kansas Press, 1999.

Chodorow, Nancy. *The Reproduction of Mothering: Psychoanalysis and the Sociology of Gender*. Berkeley: University of California Press, 1978.

Cockburn, Cynthia. *The Space between Us: Negotiating Gender and National Identities in Conflict*. London: Zed, 1998.

Dinnerstein, Dorothy. *The Mermaid and the Minatour: Sexual Arrangements and Human Malaise*. New York: Harper, 1977.

Douglas, Mary. *Purity and Danger*. London: Routledge, 1966.

Earnest, William R. 'Ideology Criticism and Life History Research.' In Rosenwald and Ochberg, 250–64.

Ellenberger, H.F. *The Discovery of the Unconscious*. New York: Bass, 1970.

Fanon, Frantz. *The Wretched of the Earth*. Trans. Constance Farrington. New York: Grove, 1966.

Finkelhor, David with Sharon Araji. *A Sourcebook on Childhood Sexual Abuse*. Beverly Hills, CA: Sage, 1986.

Foa, Edna, and Michael Kozak. 'Emotional Processing of Fear: Exposure to Corrective Information.' *Psychological Studies* 99.1 (1986): 20–35.

Friedman, Robert L. *Zealous for Zion: Inside Israel's West Bank Settlement Movement*. New Brunswick, NJ: Rutgers University Press, 1992.

Graetz, Naomi. *Silence Is Deadly: Judaism Confronts Wifebeating*. Northvale, NJ: Aronson, 1998.

Greenspan, Henry. 'Lives as Texts: Symptoms as Modes of Recounting in the Life Histories of Holocaust Survivors.' In Rosenwald and Ochberg, 145–64.

Griffiths, Morwenna. *Feminisms and the Self: The Web of Identity*. London: Routledge, 1995.

Haaken, Janice. 'The Recovery of Memory, Fantasy, and Desire: Feminist Approaches to Sexual Abuse and Psychic Trauma.' *Signs* 21.4 (1996): 1069–94.

Herman, Judith Lewis. *Trauma and Recovery*. New York: Basic, 1992.

Jacobs, Janet Liebman. *Victimized Daughter: Incest and the Development of the Female Self*. New York: Routledge, 1994.

———. 'Victimized Daughters: Sexual Violence and the Empathic Female Self. *Signs* 19.1 (1993): 126–45.

Jayaratne, Toby Epstein, and Abigail J. Stewart. 'Quantitative and Qualitative Methods in the Social Sciences: Current Feminist Issues and Practical Strategies.' In *Beyond Methodology: Feminist Scholarship as Lived*. Research, ed. Mary Margaret Fonow and Judith A. Cook, 85–106. Bloomington: Indiana University Press, 1991.

Jordan, Judith V., Alexandra G. Kaplan, Jean Baker Miller, Irene Stiver, and Janet L. Surrey. *Women's Growth in Connection: Writings from the Stone Center*. New York: Guilford, 1994.

Katz, Samuel. *Battleground: Fact and Fantasy in Palestine*. New York: Shapolsky, 1986.

Kristeva, J. *Desire in Language: A Semiotic Approach to Literature and Art*. Oxford: Basil, 1980.

Lifton, R.J. *Life in Death: Survivors of Hiroshima*. New York: Random, 1967.

Manlowe, Jennifer L. *Faith Born of Seduction: Sexual Trauma, Body Image, and Religion*. New York: New York University Press, 1995.

Miller, Jean Baker. *Toward a New Psychology of Women.* Boston: Beacon, 1976.

Mitchell, J. *Psychoanalysis and Feminism.* Harmondsworth: Penguin, 1974.

Offe, Claus. 'New Social Movements: Challenging the Boundaries of Institutional Politics.' *Social Research* 52.4 (1985): 816–68.

Pepper, Stephen C. *World Hypothesis: A Study in Evidence.* Berkeley: University of California Prress, 1942.

'Playboy Interview: Yasir Arafat.' *Playboy* (September 1988): 51–66.

Power, Margaret. *Right-Wing Women in Chile: Feminine Power and the Struggle Against Allende 1964–1973.* University Park: Pennsylvania State University Press, 2002.

Ronai, Carol Rambo. 'Multiple Reflections of Child Sex Abuse: An Argument for a Layered Account.' *Journal of Contemporary Ethnography* 23.4 (1995): 395–426.

Rosenwald, George, and Richard Ochberg, eds. *Storied Lives: The Cultural Politics of Self-Understanding.* New Haven: Yale University Press, 1992.

Russell, Diana E.H. *The Secret Trauma: Incest in the Lives of Girls and Women.* New York: Basic, 1986.

———. *Sexual Exploitation: Rape, Child Sexual Abuse, and Sexual Harassment.* Beverly Hills, CA: Sage, 1984.

Schott, Robin May. 'Philosophical Reflections on War Rape.' In *On Feminist Ethics and Politics,* ed. Claudia Card, 173–199. Lawrence: University of Kansas Press, 1999.

Shengold, L. *Soul Murder: The Effects of Childhood Abuse and Deprivation.* New York: Ballantine, 1989.

Spence, Donald P. *Narrative Truth and Historical Truth: Meaning and Interpretation in Psychoanalysis.* New York: Norton, 1982.

Tavris, Carol, and Carole Offir. *The Longest War: Sex Differences in Perspective.* New York: Harcourt, 1977.

Thorne, Barrie. 'Political Activist as Participant Observer: Conflicts of Commitment in A Study of the Draft Resistance Movement of the 1960's.' *Symbolic Interaction* 2.1 (1971): 73–88.

Waite, Elizabeth. *Trauma and Survival: Post-Tramautic and Dissociative Disorders in Women.* New York: Norton, 1993.

Weinbaum, Batya. 'The American Feminist Concept of Motherhood: Test Practice in Israel as Evaluated through Oral History Research.' *Frontiers* 20.2 (1999): 87–101.

———. 'Challenges to Feminist Internationalism in Palestine/Israel.' *Journal of Progressive Judaism* 12 (1999): 29–55.

———. *D'ot shel nasheem b'Israel: Voices of Women in Dialogue on Politics, Reli-*

gion and Culture in Israel. 1990c. (Typescript available from University of Massachusetts at Amherst Library)

———. 'Impact of Children on Mothers' Activism and Vice Versa: Some Insights from an Examination of Oral Histories with Some Israeli Mothers, Summer 1999.' *Journal of Research on Mothering* 3.2 (2001): 113–22.

———. *Islands of Women and Amazons: Representations and Realities*. Austin: University of Texas Press, 1999.

———. 'The Radicalizing Impact of Children on Mothers' Activism: Insight from Oral Histories with Some Jewish Israeli Mothers, Summer 1999.' *Journal of Feminist Therapy*. 13.4 (2001): 23–40.

———. 'The Relationship between Gender Identity and Nationalism as Negotiated by an Oral History Subject: Between Zionism and the Experience of Rape by Muslims.' Paper presented at meeting of the Association of Jewish Studies, Chicago, December 20, 1999.

———. *Searching for Peace on Hostile Grounds*. Austin: University of Texas Press, forthcoming.

———. 'Searching for Peace on Hostile Land: Narrative from the Field, Palestine/Israel, 1989–1992.' In *Lost on the Map of the World: Jewish Women Writers' Quest for Home*, ed. Phillipa Kafka, 157–71. New York: Lang, 2001.

———. 'Shifting Gears in Life History Research: The Case of an Assimilated American Jewish Woman in Palestine/Israel, 1989–1991.' *Biography* 21.3 (1998): 301–17.

———. 'A Story Involving Participants in Life Research: Israel, 1999.' Paper presented at meeting of the National Women's Studies Association, Boston, June 2000.

———. 'Utopian and Dystopian Moments: Unintended Impacts of Women in Black Organization, Palestine/Israel.' In *Integrating Cross National Research*, ed. Russell Farnen, C. deLandtsheer, H. Suenker, H. Dekker, and D. German. University of Oldenurg, forthcoming.

Willis, Paul, and Mats Trondman. 'Manifesto for *Ethnography*.' *Ethnography* 1.1 (2000): 5–16.

Wyatt, Gail E., and Gloria J. Powell. *Lasting Effects of Child Sexual Abuse*. Beverly Hills, CA: Sage, 1988.

Chapter 4

Exploring Discursive Constructions of Lesbian Abuse: Looking Inside and Out

CINDY HOLMES AND JANICE L. RISTOCK

This paper critically examines the discursive constructions of lesbian abuse within (1) feminist, community-based, educational booklets that are used to help lesbians experiencing same-sex domestic violence, and (2) recent 'backlash' books that criticize feminist research on violence against women and focus attention on lesbian abuse to show how a feminist analysis is anti-male. In looking at texts and discourses (which we define as a set of assumptions, socially shared and often unconscious, reflected in language that frames knowledge), we explore the assumptions made about violence, subjectivity, gender, race, and sexuality in these writings and highlight some of their effects and implications. We think it is important to examine closely how lesbian abuse is being constructed both in lesbian feminist communities and in mainstream and anti-feminist contexts. In other words, we look inside our communities as two lesbians who are each researching, writing, and educating from a feminist perspective in this area, and we look out at the ways this issue gets constructed and represented by mainstream sources. Cindy examines three educational booklets on lesbian abuse produced in the 1990s. Her analysis explores the ways in which the texts present a seemingly unified, coherent, or universal narrative on lesbian abuse that masks complexities, obscuring certain knowledges and subjectivities. Janice examines constructions of abuse in three recently published books that focus on the topic of female perpetrators of violence and use lesbian abuse as an example to assert a discourse that shows women are just as 'bad' as men.

We frame our analyses through a feminist, anti-racist, postmodernist lens. Drawing on Foucault, we discuss the ways power circulates in the production of knowledge on lesbian abuse. We seek to make visible the way violence in same-sex relationships is being constructed by examining the material, social, and political context in which these discourses exist. We hope to encourage ongoing critical reflexivity among feminist educators and researchers producing knowledge about same-sex relationship abuse. We all need to think carefully about the socio-political implications of our work on this issue.

'Are Relationships Dangerous? – Myths and Facts': Insiders' Constructions of Lesbian Abuse

In this section Cindy examines three educational texts (two booklets and one pamphlet) on 'lesbian abuse' that were produced in Canada in the early to middle 1990s: *Abuse in Lesbian Relationships: A Handbook of Information and Resources* by Laurie Chesley, Donna MacAuley, and Janice Ristock (1992); *Assisting Abused Lesbians: A Guide for Health Professionals and Service Providers* by Cheryl Champagne, Ruth Lapp, and Laurie Lee (1994); and *Violence in Lesbian Relationships: Are Relationships Dangerous?* published by the University of British Columbia (no date). Here we focus on Canadian educational discourses; however, educational materials about same-sex partner abuse exist in other countries, such as the United States, Britain, Australia, and Argentina. We chose these examples to illustrate a dominant discourse on lesbian abuse that shows up in workshops, forums, feminist anti-violence programs, gay and lesbian centres, health and counselling centres, and universities. At the same time, it is important to note that these are not considered to be the central texts on the subject, nor are we suggesting they are representative of all education on woman-to-woman abuse.

Feminist educational discourses on lesbian abuse emerged – in the United States in the late 1970s to early 1980s (see Lobel) and in Canada in the mid-to-late 1980s – as both practical tool and political strategy. As practical tools, often published in booklet and pamphlet form, educational materials provide information and resources to communities in a relatively inexpensive and accessible manner. The purpose of educational pamphlets and booklets is necessarily to convey information simply. Their simplicity and ease of reading are their major strengths and the primary reason we as educators and front-line workers produce them. Nevertheless, certain stories are told and others not, and in the process these pamphlets and booklets influence what comes to be known as 'facts' or 'truths' about the topic.

While educational materials on lesbian abuse do exist and many communities have organized workshops, such resources are not found everywhere. Due to pervasive heterosexism, a reliance on a hetero-sexual model of gender-based oppression, and investments in the con-struct of 'lesbian utopia,' many anti-violence organizations refuse to discuss abuse in same-sex relationships or to provide services to women who have been abused by a woman partner (Ristock, 'Justice,' 418). As a result, many women fear they will not be believed when they disclose same-sex abuse. They may also fear that if they speak out about the abuse, others will reduce the experience to a 'relationship conflict' or assume the abuse is mutual. Additionally, many women have been reluctant to acknowledge the abuse for fear of perpetuating heterosexist or racist stereotypes about lesbians or people of colour and Aboriginal people as degenerate, abnormal, sick, violent, or pathological (Kanuha, 151, 152). The association of violence with masculinity, and heterosexist assumptions that lesbians are role-playing, are not 'real' women, and are really like men (Ristock, 'Kiss,' 147), may have further motivated some women in same-sex relationships to keep a lid on the issue of abuse in relationships.

In our work as community educators we have become increasingly concerned about truth claims made in the educational materials that have been produced. There is often an urgency amongst educators, researchers, and front-line workers (including ourselves) to make fixed claims about abuse in same-sex relationships so that we can move forward and respond to the violence. We speculate that the urgency may mask other motivations or investments (conscious and uncon-scious) for the claims made about these forms of violence – such as investments in theories of violence based in white, middle-class, West-ern feminism, or in certain notions about who can occupy the categories 'woman,' 'lesbian,' 'victim,' or 'perpetrator,' for example.

As well, in community workshops and coalitions frequent debates arise amongst women about many of the same issues that are presented as facts in educational materials (for example, debates about 'mutual abuse,' the participation of bisexuals and transgendered people within lesbian and women's spaces, definitions of abuse that include consen-sual S/M practices, how to understand and respond to violence in inter-racial relationships, and whether racism in queer or feminist communities falls within the definition of abuse, to name a few). However, these controversies and complexities do not usually show up in feminist educational texts, which present a unified and authoritative narrative.

Over the years, we have reflected on what was being said about 'lesbian abuse' and how these discourses may in fact produce and limit what can be seen, known, and done. As well, we began to wonder about the links between the knowledge that is disqualified or marginalized and the hierarchical power relations among women. For example, which voices have been excluded (such as bisexual, transgender, women of colour)? Following Foucault's work (Gordon 81), we are interested in interrogating the way 'regimes of truth' obscure or delegitimize certain knowledges, subjects, and experiences through the process of legitimizing and normalizing others.

We do not view these educational discourses on abuse in lesbian relationships as simply succeeding or failing. We view power moving through discourses, including the ones we study here, in productive and multiple ways. We see these materials both as disrupting the 'grand narrative' of violence against women and as reproducing binaries and problematic essentialist constructions and categories. Although these materials *have* helped and educated many women in abusive relationships and their friends, families, and service providers, at the same time the everyday, taken-for-granted assumptions about the category 'lesbian abuse' contained within them produce exclusions. Perhaps most importantly, we approach this with a reflective look at our own complicity in circulating and constructing these discourses – as white, middle-class, able-bodied lesbians, Cindy who is a survivor of abuse in a lesbian relationship and Janice who has not been in an abusive relationship.

The Texts

Abuse in Lesbian Relationships: A Handbook of Information and Resources (Chesley, MacAuley, and Ristock) was the first educational booklet on the subject produced in Canada. It was also the first information about abuse in lesbian relationships that Cindy discovered and read after leaving an abusive lesbian partner. It provided her with a discourse that she accessed to make sense of her experience. Janice is one of the authors of this booklet, which was first produced in 1991 by the Toronto Counselling Centre for Lesbians and Gays, at a time when little had been published on the topic in Canada. It was revised and reprinted in

1992 and 1994. In 2003 it was revised again and is published and distributed by the Canadian National Clearinghouse on Family Violence. While these different editions are used in feminist anti-violence organizations and queer communities across Canada, we analyse the 1992 version because it has been most frequently reproduced in other educational texts and used in community organizations. It addresses various audiences: women who might be in an abusive lesbian relationship (identifying as either abused or abusive), friends and relatives, lesbian communities, and professionals.

In 1993 the London (Ontario) Battered Women's Advocacy Centre produced the booklet *Confronting Lesbian Battering* and then, in 1994, *Assisting Abused Lesbians: A Guide for Health Care Professionals and Service Providers* (Champagne, Lapp, and Lee), as part of their anti-heterosexist and anti-racist initiatives 'to respond to all abused women in more diverse, complex and accessible ways' (Lee, n.p.). The 1994 booklet is directed at health care and service providers.

Violence in Lesbian Relationships: Are Relationships Dangerous? (UBC) is a pamphlet first produced by Student Services of Simon Fraser University and then reproduced by Student Services of the University of British Columbia. It seeks to educate university students by providing information about 'date rape' and 'relationship violence.' Although it was not produced by a feminist or queer organization, we include it here because it cites lesbian and feminist texts in its suggested resources list and relies on many of the same central assumptions from feminist and lesbian theories of violence. However, of the three texts examined here, it relies least on lesbian feminist analyses and there are more contradictions in this text, which is perhaps reflective of the context within which it was produced (university student services).

All three texts challenge heterosexist and utopian assumptions by discussing myths and facts about lesbians and abuse, forms of abuse, and similarities with and differences from heterosexual abuse. The first two include information for service providers on how to work with abused lesbians from an anti-heterosexist or lesbian-positive perspective. Champagne, Lapp, and Lee include anecdotes involving abused lesbians seeking health care services. All three include resources and phone numbers for women in abusive relationships. Excerpts from the first two have been reprinted in other educational booklets in Canada. The texts range in length from two pages (pamphlet) to thirty (booklet).

We look at these texts as examples of a dominant educational discourse on lesbian abuse. We identify common themes and explore the assumptions embedded in what is being said and the limitations left by what is not said, in the interest of disrupting harmful regimes of truth and exploring strategies for change.

'Abuse Has Been Hidden' Discourse

The educational discourse in the pamphlets begins with the foundational claim that 'abuse has been hidden in Western society until recently,' and specifically that abuse in lesbian relationships has been hidden or difficult to publicly acknowledge (Chesley, MacAuley, and Ristock 1; Champagne, Lapp, and Lee 2; UBC). It also states that violence in lesbian relationships is something that lesbians do not usually discuss or know about each other (UBC; Champagne, Lapp, and Lee 2) and that has been 'kept "behind closed doors" until fairly recently' (Chesley, MacAuley, and Ristock 1).

The texts list the following reasons contributing to invisibility and silence: homophobia and heterosexism; fear that discussion about abuse will fuel negative stereotypes about lesbians; denial that women can hurt other women; inappropriate batterer/victim identification (people assume it is mutual and deny the abuse); the assumption that abuse occurs only in heterosexual relationships; and reluctance on the part of 'the lesbian community' and 'the battered women's movement' to destroy the myths of a 'lesbian utopia' and that 'all violence is caused by men' (UBC; Champagne, Lapp, and Lee 3; Chesley, MacAuly, and Ristock 1).

The narrative highlights the difficulties lesbians face in naming our experiences of violence in the context of heterosexism. While certain forms of abuse have indeed been hidden until recently, this dominant story may also make it difficult to tell other stories. The discourse focuses primarily on hidden abuse in the domestic or private sphere. We are interested in unpacking the assumptions in this discourse, in part because debates have emerged in educational forums among white women, women of colour, and Aboriginal women that revolve around white women's failure to see how assumptions about private violence can re-centre a white, Eurocentric conceptualization of violence by ignoring the past and current effects of racism and the different experiences of private and public spaces (Almeida et al.; Bhattacharjee). Part of the work of disrupting a colonial conceptualization of violence involves exploring how women are positioned hierarchically in relation to one another (Razack) and the rigid lines we have drawn between public and private/domestic spaces.

Perhaps the 'hidden abuse' narrative may apply most clearly to those groups of women who have been able to claim the privileges of privacy. In other words, it may best describe the experiences of white, middle-class lesbians. One wonders whether the violence that working-class or racialized women experience has been similarly cloaked in secrecy *or* for the same reasons. For example, in some working-class lesbian communities, violence 'in the home' has not always been hidden, but talked about and known; in addition, much of the violence in intimate relationships took place in public, in the bars. In working-class lesbian communities in Buffalo, New York, in the 1950s and 1960s, lesbians have indicated that violence in intimate relationships was not usually kept secret, nor were lesbians who experienced violence isolated or ashamed of it (Kennedy and Davis 319). As well, working-class and racialized women (for example, First Nations and Black women) have been marked as being more violent (and thus more criminal) than white, middle-class women (see, for example, Allard; Faith; Razack; West). It is possible that, for these groups, violence in intimate relationships may have been more visible, although naturalized and not necessarily acknowledged as anything but the 'degeneracy' of racialized populations. As well, individual and community silence about abuse may be directly related to the fact that these groups of women *do not* have the privilege of privacy. In other words, violence being hidden can be a response to the public violence of racism, which constructs certain women of colour as inherently violent, as well as a response to systemic racism as a barrier to accessing help (Waldron; Taylor and Chandler).

So, while the 'abuse is hidden' discourse highlights the invisibility of some forms of violence in lesbians' lives, it may have a universalizing effect, obscuring the experiences of women who have not had the privilege of privacy as well as ignoring the effects of racism on silence.

Lesbian Identity Discourse

Providing descriptions of lesbian identity that challenge heterosexist and utopian constructions is seen as a necessary first step in educating heterosexual service providers about lesbian abuse. This remedial discourse is a central part of all three texts, which attempt to complicate the concept of a 'universal lesbian' with references to 'diversity' and to the problem of generalizing about lesbians as a group (Chesley, MacAuley, and Ristock 3–4). Even though they contain some disruptions to an unified identity, the texts still reinforce essentialist constructions of sexuality and gender and use a narrative of diversity that relies on an additive model. The central figure in the texts is a woman whose life is structured primarily by her sexuality and her private experiences of violence.

The texts do not explicitly state that gender and sexuality are products of biology, nor do they say that they are socially and historically constructed or fluid. However, statements such as '10 percent of the population is lesbian or gay' (Champagne, Lee, and Lapp 5; Chesley, MacAuley, and Ristock 3) present gay and lesbian identity as fixed and stable. In one text this statement is presented as a 'fact' in response to a 'myth' that 'same-sex relationships are not natural' (Champagne, Lee, and Lapp 5), and therefore implies that homosexuality is a *naturally* occurring part of human sexuality, thus promoting an essentialist approach to understanding sexuality. Using the '10 per cent' strategy to promote acceptance or tolerance of gays and lesbians (a common educational strategy in anti-homophobia education) relies on biological explanations of sexuality – we *just are* lesbians (or heterosexuals). And yet, contradictorily, these texts also highlight the social power relations that regulate sexualities by emphasizing that heterosexism is a form of oppression based on 'the assumption that heterosexuality is the norm, that it is (or should be) *the* universal sexual/intimate experience' (Champagne, Lee, and Lapp 2; Chesley, MacAuley, and Ristock 21).

The narrative of these texts focuses on dispelling stereotypes or myths such as the notion that there is an identifiable lesbian 'type' (i.e., 'masculine in appearance,' 'non-mother,' 'man-hater,' 'feminist'). Although one booklet makes the statement that 'lesbians are women who have primary intimate/sexual relationships with other women' (Chesley, MacAuley, and Ristock 3), implying that lesbians may have secondary relationships with men, there is no overt mention of bisexuality or of the possibility of complex and shifting sexual and gender identities (such as transgender identities) that might not be easily slotted into categories.

Two texts argue that 'most lesbians do not explicitly adopt butch/ femme "roles,"' that lesbians cannot be put into two gendered categories in appearance or relationship practices, and that lesbians are not necessarily masculine or butch in appearance but fit all physical descriptions (Champagne, Lee, and Lapp 5; Chesley, MacAuley, and Ristock 3). (One booklet presents this statement as a 'truth,' but in another place in the same text there is an acknowledgment that some lesbians do adopt such roles: 'lesbian battering does not only occur in relationships where women practice butch/femme roles' [Champagne, Lapp, and Lee 3].) The intent is to challenge stereotypes about lesbians mimicking male-female roles in heterosexual relationships and to emphasize the wide range of expressions of lesbian identity. As well, all three dispel the notion that violence occurs solely in butch/femme relationships or that abusive women are always butch. Given the pervasiveness of these stereotypes and their connection to a pathologizing sexology discourse, it is crucial to challenge them and emphasize the many expressions of lesbian identity. However, one of the effects of exposing 'butch/femme roles' as myths is that we may be constructing a 'normal' lesbian as a woman who does not identify or express herself as butch, femme, or in drag. As well, this narrative doesn't acknowledge the possibility that social identities are not tied to biology; that, for example, the social identities of biological females could be male, masculine, shifting, or variable.

When challenging stereotypes, it is important that we as educators ask ourselves if we are fostering disavowal of these stigmatized gender identities. Commenting on her anthology *The Persistent Desire: A Femme-Butch Reader*, femme activist Joan Nestle writes:

> I wanted to do this book because, as a lesbian, I never want to hear again in my lifetime the defensive disclaimers I grew up with: not all lesbians are truck drivers; not all lesbians dress like men; not all lesbians play at being husband and wife. I am tired of these disavowals. We, of all people, must be able to cherish the woman in the stereotype and the cunning in the transformation of gender restrictions into gender rebellion. (18)

In all three texts, multiple identities and oppressions are described in an additive fashion. By examining the relational quality of categories that are produced through this discourse, we can see how the category 'lesbian' comes to mean 'white lesbian.' In the following example, an additive approach secures whiteness as the invisible centre: 'Lesbians have to face not only the sexist culture, but also a homophobic one as well. Lesbians of colour must face sexism, heterosexism and racism' (UBC n.p.). Whiteness is concealed as neutral throughout two of the texts (Chesley, MacAuley, and Ristock; UBC), while white lesbians (and lesbians of colour and disabled lesbians) are explicitly named in the third text (Champagne, Lee, and Lapp 9–10).

In these texts, First Nations lesbians are subsumed within the category of 'lesbians of colour.' While lesbians of colour and Two-Spirited women share the experience of racist-heterosexism in the context of white supremacy, this discursive move of not naming First Nations women not only negates the historical specificities in experience of these groups in Canada, but also negates the existence of First Nations lesbians.

As these examples show, the texts are effective in disrupting certain essentialist constructs (such as 'lesbians are nonviolent' and 'lesbians all look the same'), but a reliance on essentialist and biological definitions of 'woman' and 'lesbian' shuts down the socio-historical construction of identity. As well, the texts reveal that lesbian identity is often structured around whiteness.

Causes of Abuse Discourse

All three texts draw on existing feminist theories about abuse in intimate heterosexual relationships to inform the analysis of violence in lesbian relationships, and all three rely on a 'comparison' model (i.e., similarities and differences with heterosexuals). Some ambiguity about the usefulness of this approach is expressed in one text with the statement 'some studies have attempted comparisons but the question remains whether these comparisons are useful or valid' (Chesley, MacAuley, and Ristock 7). A comparison model could also be identified as an additive discourse that places the dominant Western feminist discourse on male violence against women (gender-based analysis of power) at the centre and then adds 'differences.'

The causes of abuse are described in two texts as lying in a society that sanctions and maintains systems of domination and teaches and reinforces power-over as acceptable behaviours and values; and acquired unhealthy patterns from families and society, where some individuals learned to use violence to gain control and power in relationships (Champagne, Lee, and Lapp 3–5; Chesley, MacAuley, and Ristock 4–5). In addition, two emphasize that there is no simple cause-and-effect relationship between factors such as 'childhood violence, stress, substance abuse and provocation' and abuse in lesbian relationships, emphasizing that an 'abuser is responsible for her behaviour and can choose to control it' (Chesley, MacAuley, and Ristock 8; UBC n.p.).

Challenges to a psychological discourse that attributes abuse to pathology or family dysfunction show up in two texts. Here violence is explained with a feminist analysis of the social context of oppression (Champagne, Lee, and Lapp 3–5; Chesley, MacAuley, and Ristock 4–5).

The third text (UBC) is a slightly different case, in that it loosely draws on a feminist discourse but also reproduces the notion that lesbian relationships are inherently dangerous. The cover includes a photo of two young women smiling at one another. The question 'Are Relationships Dangerous?' appears in bold, large capitals above the photo. In smaller, light print, the line 'violence in lesbian relationships' is almost lost on the cover, while the word 'dangerous' stands out.

Although all three texts refer to multiple systems of oppression, the social context of violence in lesbian relationships is primarily described as patriarchy and heterosexism. The Toronto booklet discusses internalized patriarchy, heterosexism, and homophobia as part of the causes and effects of abuse (Chesley, MacAuley, and Ristock 5, 11). Two texts argue that heterosexism and homophobia affect everyone – heterosexual, gay, or lesbian (Champagne, Lee, and Lapp 4–5; Chesley, MacAuley, and Ristock 21) – yet all three texts describe racism and classism as issues for 'other people' (Champagne, Lee, and Lapp 4) or lesbians of colour and working-class lesbians only (Chesley, MacAuley, and Ristock 5; UBC n.p.). This claim can hinder an examination of who is oppressing whom and obscure the complicity of white and middle-class women in the oppression of women of colour, Aboriginal women, and working-class women. Both the Toronto and London booklets make attempts at integrating the effects of racism, classism, and ableism into the framework; however, a gender- and sexuality-based analysis of power remains at the centre of the model, and these 'additional oppressions' are not fully integrated into the entire framework.

To sum up, we can see from the pamphlets that the central figure in the text is a woman whose life is structured primarily by her sexuality. Explanations for the abuse mention multiple systems of domination and refer to feminist psychological explanations, but focus primarily on patriarchy and heterosexism. One text suggests that internalized patriarchy and heterosexism are part of the cause of abuse. The implication is that this de-raced and de-classed woman is abusive because she has internalized or learned power-over from her internalized sexism and heterosexism, rather than from internalized dominance. Relying on the narrative of internalized oppression as the cause of violence can construct women/lesbians primarily as victims in relation to men/heterosexuals. This misses an interlocking analysis of oppression that would examine how women are currently positioned hierarchically to one another and how certain women have historically abused power over other women (for example, through slavery and colonization).

The Nature of Abuse Discourse

The texts state that in an abusive lesbian relationship one woman most often or always exerts power and control over her partner. Consistent with feminist and criminological explanations, a perpetrator/victim dichotomy is used. All three challenge the notion that abusive lesbian relationships are mutually abusive and emphasize that defending oneself against abuse does not make one an equal contributor.

Each text includes detailed descriptions of types of abuse, which are categorized as physical abuse, sexual abuse, psychological abuse, threats, economic abuse, and property destruction. The Toronto and London booklets include heterosexist tactics as forms of abuse, and the Toronto text also includes racist, classist, and ableist forms of abuse and threats that affect child custody arrangements or legal or immigration status.

Two texts use the construct of 'vulnerability' or 'double jeopardy' to describe multiple forms of oppression. The London booklet includes two 'case illustrations' of abusive lesbian relationships, one in which Megan, a forty-five-year-old woman of colour with a disability, is being abused by Karen, her white, able-bodied, thirty-eight-year-old partner (Champagne, Lee, and Lapp 10). While the description of abuse hints at the presence of ableist, ageist, and racist abuse, it does not overtly state this and instead names race, age, and disability as reasons that 'women like Megan' are 'vulnerable to abuse.' The Toronto booklet also mentions that disabled lesbians are 'a particularly vulnerable population' (Chesley, MacAuley, and Ristock 26). The intent is to highlight the 'higher rates of assault and sexual exploitation' (26) that disabled women experience. Nevertheless, using a framework of vulnerability has the effect of implying that 'women from historically disadvantaged groups are more vulnerable because they are more vulnerable' (Razack 138). This can privatize the violence of ableism, racism, and ageism rather than examining how these social relations are produced to position women differently and unequally (139).

Although they do not speak in a unified voice, the pamphlets discussed above show us a dominant discourse in lesbian abuse education – the one granted the status of truth, the agreed-upon framework of language and meaning (Mareck). In part because of risks in naming the abuse and the context of material constraints and limitations, educators have relied on a simple conceptual framework as represented in the pamphlets. This framework makes complexities around gender, sexuality, race, disability, and class, as well as complexities around the violence itself, hard to introduce. While simplicity helps when educators are faced with the risks and limitations in a short pamphlet, the cost is the privileging of white, middle-class, able-bodied women's experiences.

By deconstructing these discourses in educational materials that have been produced to respond to lesbian abuse, we can see how our constructions may obscure and delegitimize certain knowledges and subjectivities. It is important for those of us using these discourses to ask not only what kind of subjectivity is produced through them, but also the related question of what kind of subject can access this discourse. Who is 'in' this 'insider' category, and what conditions make it possible for someone to inhabit this space? It is crucial for those of us in dominant positions to critically examine the links between the hierarchical relations among us as women and the knowledge that is produced. The questions raised through this process of deconstruction create further dilemmas for those of us who might position ourselves as 'insiders' (women who have participated in the circulation of these educational discourses): How can we write about and talk about violence? How do we recognize social, cultural, and historical specificity and broad categories and still write a simple booklet with a limited, narrow focus? What should be our goal in producing and circulating educational discourses? What is possible within an educational booklet? Who should produce such booklets and for what purposes? And on what should they focus when addressing violence in relationships: all violence, lesbians, queers, women in same-sex relationships, women in general? How can we provide information on a category while still recognizing the dangers of what we are producing? How can we show complexities and connections between oppressions within a short educational booklet?

In analysing these texts, we are not saying we should stop producing concise, short educational pamphlets, or that past and present educational materials are useless. But we want to suggest that many of the assumptions in the discourse are connected to the continued marginalization of the knowledge and experiences of women of colour, Aboriginal women, and working-class, bisexual, transgendered, and disabled women. In order to respond to and end violence in its various forms and locations, we must examine what these discourses produce and limit. Rather than focusing simply on whether they are 'right' or 'wrong,' we need to recognize and explore their multiple effects and be strategic about how we deploy them.

'When She Was Bad' – Outsiders' Constructions of Lesbian Abuse

The questions and struggles that we as insiders producing educational discourses need to be aware of are also relevant when examining the discourses being produced about lesbian abuse by outsiders – those writers who seek to discredit feminist research on violence against women. In recent scholarship on domestic violence, there is often a tension between those who continue to demand that a gender analysis be part of our theorizing and research and those who feel a gender analysis in feminist theorizing is too limiting and cannot explain examples of violence where women are perpetrators, such as the realities of lesbian domestic abuse. A recent collection from the United States on same-sex partner abuse has explicitly dismissed feminist theorizing (Renzetti and Miley) and suggested that we must instead adopt a psychological framework that emphasizes treatment of the batterer (Island and Letellier) or a social psychological model that emphasizes an analysis of social and individual power (Merrill). These moves trouble us for their similarity to backlash writers who have dismissed feminist theorizing and research on violence as wrong-headed and deceitful in denying the facts about women as perpetrators.

Research on violence has been attacked by many conservative writers who dispute the discourse and statistical claims of feminist approaches. Writers such as John Fekete, in his book *Moral Panic: Biopolitics Rising*, suggest that feminists are creating a moral panic and generating research that reflects their own agenda. Fekete argues that the statistics are implausible and reflect bad science. Further, he argues, feminist discourse cannot account for examples where women are violent towards men: 'women are victims of the system, and accountable for nothing. Anything they may do in response is either a manifestation of their vulnerability or an example of fighting back' (96). Similarly, Katie Roiphe, a self-defined feminist, disputes the claims of research on date rape. She accuses feminists of creating 'date rape hype' that reinforces the status of women as victims and emphasizes women's fragility. She sees a cult of victimhood: 'there is power to be drawn from declaring one's victimhood and oppression' (quoted in Faludi 37). Authors such as Camille Paglia, Christina Hoff Sommers, and others make similar claims about feminist research and discourse on violence against women; they suggest that women are presented only as victims yet can be perpetrators of violence. The main argument these texts have in common is that they point to a gender bias in feminist scholarship. They claim we cannot use gender as part of our analysis of the dynamics of battering relationships, and suggest that a feminist analysis ends up presenting a limited understanding where women are seen as good/ victims and men as bad/perpetrators.

Backlash texts are certainly not new in the history of feminism, but they do seem to be getting more specific in their attacks, focusing in on the topic of female perpetrators of violence as an Achilles' heel of feminism. What made two of the three recent texts we review below such alarming favourites of the media is that the authors are self-defined feminists, approximating, in public relations value to the patri-archy, the repented homosexual. Christina Hoff Sommers describes herself as 'a feminist who does not like what feminism has become' (18), while Donna Laframboise writes with the credentials of an under-graduate degree in women's studies from the University of Toronto. These writers are not raving anti-feminists out to destroy the move-ment. In this section Janice reviews Sommers's *Who Stole Feminism: How Women Have Betrayed Women*, Laframboise's *The Princess at the Window: A New Gender Morality*, and Patricia Pearson's *When She Was Bad: Violent Women and The Myth of Innocence* as a way of examining the construc-tions of same-sex violence they put forth. We wanted to ask: Do they pose useful questions for feminists? Are they providing an alternative analysis? Is there something to be gained from reading these texts rather than dismissing them out of hand as backlash? Are we, as back-lash writers charge, dismissing female violence as a rare, exceptional event? Are we, as they claim, denying, hiding, explaining away rather than explaining women's violence?

Who Stole Feminism is an attack against 'gender feminists,' whom Sommers defines as believing that 'women are virtually under siege because of an oppressive system of male-hegemony' (16). She feels that gender feminists have been dominating American feminism even though they hold a minority analysis. In the area of violence against women, Sommers accuses gender feminists of using erroneous statistics and being unwilling to scrutinize their beliefs in the face of facts that dispute their claims. She mentions lesbian abuse studies as one such example that could help shed light on the dynamics of battering relationships yet is ignored by gender feminists. She refers to the research of Claire Renzetti, which suggests that violence in lesbian relationships occurs with about the same frequency as violence in heterosexual relation-ships, concluding that 'once again, it appears battery may have very little to do with patriarchy or gender bias. Where noncriminals are involved, battery seems to be a pathology of intimacy, as frequent among gays as among straight people' (200).

Similar to the view of Sommers is the work of Donna Laframboise in *The Princess at the Window*, which is particularly critical of the report prepared by the Canadian Panel on Violence against Women. She feels this government-sanctioned panel constructed a report that claims men's violence is always an example of 'deliberately carrying out a political agenda of oppression whenever they mistreat female persons' (92). She believes women who are violent are held to a different standard and brings in the example of lesbian abuse, raising the question 'Why do lesbians who batter other lesbians get to blame it on the stress that a society hostile to lesbians places them under? What is so unique about this sort of pressure that nothing remotely approximates it?' (94). To support her claim of double standards for men and women, she quotes directly from the report, which says the following regarding lesbian abuse:

> Although research into the incidence and prevalence of lesbian battering is virtually non-existent in Canada, women who spoke to the panel contend that it is the result of institutionalized heterosexism which isolates lesbians and adds pressure to their relationships (96).

Laframboise acknowledges that this is one form of women's violence that the report does discuss, but is critical of the fact that it ignores research done in the United States that suggests lesbian abuse is just as prevalent as heterosexual abuse (referring to the same report by Renzetti [94–5] that Sommers cited). Laframboise concludes that lesbian battering is excused as an example of women being doubly oppressed by patriarchy and homophobia, and that lesbian batterers are not held accountable in the same way that men are. Laframboise also applies this discourse of 'double standards' to Aboriginal people who have used violence. In her mind, oppression is used as an excuse for violent behaviour. She cannot imagine an analysis of violence that would include both individual accountability and systemic oppression.

Patricia Pearson, unlike the previous authors, does not locate herself as a feminist, post-feminist, or anti-feminist. She writes as a journalist who is critical of second-wave feminism for ignoring examples of women's violence and insisting on women's stance as victims. She challenges feminism to try to understand examples where women are violent, and acknowledges the context of patriarchy, which in her view makes women's violence more complex and more often indirect, as the result of needing to be relational in a patriarchal context. She too raises the issue of lesbian abuse as an example of women's violence. She even shows concern for gay and lesbian communities in bringing forward this example of violence:

> Feminists who refuse to admit that heterosexual women can be violent leave the gay community by itself out on a limb, vulnerable to further slander by self-appointed keepers of public morals. There is a long tradition in our culture of depicting aggressive or criminal women as sexually perverse. That link can only be fortified if feminists refuse to concede straight women's violence, forcing lesbians to appear as the only ones who abuse. (131)

Her review of research on lesbian abuse is far more extensive than those of Sommers and Laframboise. She presents some of the findings that challenge a feminist analysis of violence. For example, she says relationship violence cannot be understood in terms of male social and economic power because in many abusive lesbian partnerships it is the woman with the higher earning power and self-esteem who gets assaulted (again based on Renzetti's [132] work). She interviewed Toronto counsellor and lesbian feminist Laurie Chesley (co-author with Janice and Donna MacAuley of one of the booklets that Cindy examines), who commented on the pattern of some abused lesbians becoming abusers in other relationships (138) (something Janice's research has also confirmed; see 'Community-Based Research' and No More Secrets). Pearson's review of the lesbian literature then raises some interesting questions about the nature of power and the meaning of the discrete categories 'perpetrator' and 'victim.' Yet she too, like Sommers and Laframboise, relies on Renzetti's work, which claims that violence in lesbian relationships occurs with the same frequency as violence in heterosexual relationships, and adds 'with the smaller, more conventionally feminine partner often being the one to strike' (117). It appears these authors all accept the results of the few incidence and prevalence studies on lesbian abuse without applying to them the same scrutiny they do to feminist research.

In our view, we simply do not yet know if violence in same-sex relationships occurs with the same frequency as heterosexual abuse. For example, some of this prevalence research does not differentiate between the different forms of abuse – so lesbians who indicate they have experienced abuse may have been subjected to emotional rather than physical. One author recently suggested that lesbians may in fact experience less physical abuse than heterosexuals and more verbal and emotional abuse in our relationships; this remains a question for the prevalence research. It has also been suggested that lesbians may be more likely to recognize and name abuse than heterosexual women because many lesbians have been politically active and aware of issues like violence against women. We need to examine the micropolitics of power, asking how abuse in lesbian relationships is both similar to and different from heterosexual domestic abuse. Pearson uses lesbian abuse to show the problems with a feminist analysis of heterosexual battering, but misses opportunities to ask more complex questions and does nothing to contribute to an understanding of the dynamics of abuse in lesbian relationships.

So what patterns emerge when we examine the discourse of these texts? What is their strategic purpose? In our view they seem to be intent on creating a seamless discourse that shows women as bad or just as bad as men rather than really asking new questions or offering an analysis that moves beyond a psychological view. In Foucauldian terms, a 'regime of truth' is enforced in these texts that produces gender as a neutral category.

It is important to acknowledge that many feminists working in the area of violence have also been critical of the emphasis on 'survivors' and 'victims' in violence research, which can deny women's agency. We are critical (as we stated above) of a tendency in feminist standpoint research and theorizing on violence to offer the all-explanatory theory or grand narrative that shows how violence is used as a form of social control over women in a patriarchal context. We acknowledge that this grand narrative can exclude specific examples of abuse, such as abuse in lesbian and gay relationships, where there is no male/female dynamic, and abuse within Aboriginal communities, where the violence of colonization and racism interlock with patriarchy (see Ristock; Ristock and Pennell; see also Razack).

Backlash writers are not in any way interested in widening the analysis from gender to include race, class, or sexuality. Yet their criticisms of feminist discourse allow for a reflexive moment for us to ask: Do our current discourses let us speak about women who abuse their children or their elderly relatives? Or lesbians who have experienced abuse within their relationships? Or gay men who have been sexually assaulted by straight men? Or the ways in which women use racist, classist, ableist violence against other women? How does a will to ignorance and the pursuit of respectability operate in our discourses on relationship violence?

There is now a substantial body of material addressing lesbian abuse, so we cannot say the issue has been ignored by feminists, as some backlash writers would have us believe. But neither has there been a groundswell of attention to this topic, which one might expect feminists interested in theorizing domestic abuse to want to understand. There are by now tens of thousands of feminist texts on male battering. Of the thirty-three journal articles in our working bibliography of the area of lesbian abuse, fewer than half are feminist. We have found seventeen book chapters, of which twelve are feminist. Unfortunately, this tends to support Pearson's observation that in a special issue of *Ms.* magazine on wife assault, 'lesbian violence was discreetly confined to one column with a feeble attempt to distinguish it from what men do' (131). It must also be acknowledged that most feminist work in the area focuses on victims, and thus avoids having to deal with the hard question of women's violence.

Femininst researcher Ellen Faulkner describes three positions within the work on lesbian battering: what she calls a 'liberal feminist and system theory position' but we will call liberal, in which violence emerges as a gender-neutral psychological problem; a radical feminist framework in which lesbian violence is explained within a theory of male domination; and a cultural feminist perspective that sees violence as a male biological trait and argues for the development of lesbian communities and ethics as a way to prevent violence, thus sidestepping the issue of lesbian abuse.

Faulkner's overview of the lesbian abuse literature is useful for examining what is being constructed both inside and out. The liberal position, which ignores gender and patriarchy as a way of understanding lesbian abuse, is the research that is being used by backlash writers to support the view that men and women's violent behaviours are equal and that we therefore do not require a gender analysis of the causes of violence. This position poses some strategic dangers in that, being most intelligible within the terms of mainstream discourses, it can get taken up without a transformative political analysis, inadvertently contributing to the still widespread pathologizing discourse on lesbians, and inadequately covering the context of lesbians' lives. For example, in Janice's university the Applied Counselling program of Continuing Education asked her to develop a course on lesbian abuse, yet this program does not have courses that examine racism, sexism, and heterosexism in counselling practices and service delivery; nor were they interested in developing such a course when she suggested it. The Applied Counselling program at the University of Manitoba is not in backlash mode and is not out to prove feminism wrong: they simply want to add lesbians to their existing curriculum on domestic abuse, focusing on helping the lesbian victim. The liberal analysis of lesbian abuse can easily be inserted into a curriculum that keeps heterosexuality at the centre of a crime-control discourse predicated on neat gender-based distinctions between perpetrators and victims and deeply embedded in the institutional practices of the social welfare and justice systems.

The other positions within the literature on lesbian abuse operate from an additive model of oppression, where lesbian abuse is plugged into existing theories that have been used to explain heterosexual abuse. The feminist research on lesbian abuse, with its emphasis on lesbians as victims rather than batterers, or essentialist assumptions that lesbians are different, can be read as supporting the seamless feminist construction of good girls/women as victims that backlash writers are critiquing. So, in an odd twist, much of the literature on lesbian abuse as currently constructed can support both of the claims of backlash writers: that women's violence is like men's, and that feminist writers focus on women's innocence.

We therefore need to see, not that backlash writers are right that women's violence is just like men's, but that some of their criticisms do reveal the limitations of an analysis based solely on gender and patriarchy. We can quite readily see how regimes of truth are being constructed in backlash research. We also need to be prepared to ask continuously, What are the regimes of truth – in Foucault's terms, the systems of exclusion and rewards – in feminist discourse on violence in lesbian relationships?

Final Thoughts on Inside/Out

As our analyses of texts both inside and outside lesbian feminist, anti-violence communities have shown, the discourse of lesbian violence is a political morass, with backlash writers often using the issue to fortify a claim that women are bad. Talk gets polarized yet again into pro- and anti-feminist camps, and neither side concedes a shred of insight or useful thought to the other. In our review of the backlash texts, we found no other explanatory effort apart from 'women are bad.' That being said, there is a certain regime of truth or perhaps gallantry at work in feminist discourse that we are at times uncomfortable with. The result sometimes is a commitment to a clearly inadequate theory of violence that does indeed see women as victims, even when they punch another woman in the face. What we would like to see is work that explores the complexity of violence between women, preserving gender analysis as an important but not sufficient explanation for lesbian abuse. It is not that we need to learn that patriarchy is not all-explanatory: for years feminists have been working at understanding the role of other axes of difference in women's lives. But on the subject of lesbian abuse, there sometimes seems to be a recourse to simplistic, essentialist thinking and a desire to steer the discussion away from what is happening between women, back towards the issue of male violence. And as we have demonstrated, many of the feminist educational materials on lesbian abuse have a tendency to re-centre a white, imperialist feminist discourse. In the process, we don't learn much about the complexity of violence in relationships, or the ways in which systems of oppression mutually construct and depend on one another.

We need to look at connections between subjectivity and our analytical frameworks and make the link between the hierarchical relations among women across race, class, sexuality, ability, etc., and the kinds of theorizing that circulate in feminist or queer circles. We must ask: How are 'we' continuing to conceptualize violence in a colonialist and/or heteronormative manner? What are the connections between violence in same-sex relationships among women and other forms of violence perpetrated by women? What happens when we expand our definitions of violence perpetrated by women to talk about the racist, colonialist, classist, or ableist violence enacted by white, middle-class, heterosexual, and able-bodied women against women of colour, First Nations women, working-class, lesbian/bisexual/transgendered, and disabled women?

Two events in recent years stand out as reflections of current popular constructions and understandings of interpersonal violence in North American culture. One was the killing of Reena Virk, a Victoria, British Columbia, teenager beaten to death by a gang of her peers. The media focused on the unusual fact that the perpetrators were primarily girls and on the question of whether girls were becoming more violent. Erased from the mainstream media coverage was any discussion of the ways in which racism and classism worked simultaneously with sexism (and other forms of oppression) to contribute to Reena's death. Her identity as a young South Asian woman was not mentioned in most of the reports, nor were the racial identities of the youths who attacked her. Sheila Battacharya's research into this case explores how the absence of research on racist violence committed by women in colonial sites contributes to the sensationalism of 'girl violence' by making it seem as if violence committed by women is a new phenomenon. Battacharya draws attention to the relations of power that contextualize acts of violence committed by women as a way of shifting the focus from the surprise that women are violent. Much of this surprise reaction to women's acts of violence is bound up with racialized (classed and also gendered) notions of femininity. People are not surprised by violence enacted by certain women; it is expected.

In contrast to this incident were the reports of the shooting deaths of four young girls and one female teacher at a school in Arkansas. In this case the perpetrators were two boys, eleven and thirteen (one of whom was said to want to get back at girls who had broken up with him). Here the media focused on the issue of gun control and kept referring to 'the students' or 'schoolchildren' involved without specifying the gender of the victims or the shooters. Media representations and editorial page discussions that followed were strikingly similar to the discourse surrounding the Montreal massacre in 1989, where the discourse focused on gun control and the 'madman' killer, rather than acknowledging the fact that it was fourteen women who were singled out and killed. We mention these examples as the 'outside' cultural backdrop to the work we are doing as researchers and educators in the area of same-sex partner abuse.

As 'insiders' we need to keep pushing the limits of our thinking on this issue (and on violence in general) and to theorize politically about the complexities that exist. At the same time, as Cindy heard in her focus group with women educators on this issue, women are anxious about bringing forward complexities for fear that disrupting current regimes of truth will allow a gender-neutral, liberal analysis to prevail that will be taken up and used against women (Holmes 81–2). This has happened in British Columbia, where gender-neutral language in legal policies (initiated with the intention of being inclusive of lesbians who had been abused in a relationship) has been co-opted and used against women who've fought back in self-defence against abusive men. Educators in Cindy's research talked about this dilemma, but also concluded that we cannot afford to rigidify our analysis out of fear; we need to be strategic and continually talk about our political analysis and goals to distinguish them from those with a liberal or conservative agenda.

It is important for those of us engaged in this work to explore the assumptions within the discourses we use and to ask what these constructions offer and to *whom*. Many women involved in research, service provision, advocacy, and education in this area *are* concerned about the very questions we raise in this paper and are often skeptical about the concepts used in our work. Many are calling for more complex frameworks for understanding violence in general and are pushing each other to struggle with difficult questions. What we would like to see is a feminist discourse on the topic that is both less timid and less self-regulated and more focused on understanding what is going on in lesbian abuse. Bat-Ami Bar On, writing more broadly, calls for a 'nuanced feminist rethinking of the relationship between women and violence: in a manner that necessarily problematizes the neat, clean distinctions that feminist paradigmatic understandings of violence assume' (4).

Note

Cindy would like to thank Janice Ristock, Sherene Razack, Anne Fleming, and Caroline White for providing useful comments on various versions of this paper. Janice acknowledges the support provided for her research through grants from the Social Sciences and Humanities Research Council of Canada and the Lesbian Health Fund of the Gay and Lesbian Medical Association. She would also like to thank Cindy Holmes and Catherine Taylor for their helpful comments.

Works Cited

Allard, Sharon. 'Rethinking Battered Woman Syndrome: A Black Feminist Perspective.' *UCLA Women's Law Journal* 1.1 (1991): 191–207.

Almeida, R., R. Woods, T. Messineo, R. Font, and C. Heer. 'Violence in the Lives of the Racially and Sexually Different: A public and Private Dilemma.' *Journal of Feminist Family Therapy* 5.3/4 (1994): 99–126.

Bar On, Bat-Ami. 'Introduction to *Hypatia*: Special Issue on Women and Violence.' *Hypatia* 11.4 (1996): 1–4.

Bhattacharjee, Annanya. 'The Public/Private Mirage: Mapping Homes and Undomesticating Violence Work in the South Asian Immigrant Community.' In *Feminist Genealogies, Colonial Legacies and Democratic Futures*, ed. Chandra Mohanty and Jacquie Alexander, 308–29. New York: Routledge, 1997.

Bhattacharya, Sheila. 'Racism, "Girl Violence" and the Murder of Reena Virk.' Master's thesis, Ontario Institute for Studies in Education, Toronto, 2000.

Canadian Panel on Violence against Women. *Changing the Landscape.* Ottawa: Minister of Supply and Services, 1993.

Champagne, Cheryl, Ruth Lapp, and J. Lee. *Assisting Abused Lesbians: A Guide for Health Professionals and Service Providers.* London: London Battered Women's Advocacy Centre, 1994.

Chesley, Laurie, Donna MacAuley, and Janice L. Ristock. *Abuse in Lesbian Relationships: A Handbook of Information and Resources.* Toronto: Toronto Counselling Centre for Lesbians and Gays, 1992.

Faith, Karlene. *Unruly Women.* Vancouver: Press Gang, 1993.

Faludi, Susan. *Backlash: The Undeclared War against American Women.* New York: Anchor, 1992.

Faulkner, Ellen. 'Woman-to-Woman Abuse: Analyzing Extant Accounts of Lesbian Battering.' In *Unsettling Truths: Battered Women, Policy, Politics, and Contemporary Research in Canada*, ed. K. Bonnycastle and G. Rigakos, 52–62. Vancouver: Collective Press, 1998.

Fekete, John. *Moral Panic: Biopolitics Rising.* Montreal: Robert Davis, 1994.

Gordon, Colin. 'Two Lectures.' In *Power/Knowledge: Selected Interviews and Other Writings 1972–1977 by Michel Foucault*, 78–108. New York: Pantheon Books, 1972.

Holmes, Cindy. 'The Politics of Naming the Violence: Examining Constructions of "Lesbian Abuse" in Community-Based Educational Discourses.' Master's thesis, Ontario Institute for Studies in Education, Toronto, 2000.

Island, D., and Patrick Letellier. *Men Who Beat the Men Who Love Them.* New York: Harrington Park Press, 1991.

Kanuha, Val. 'Compounding the Triple Jeopardy: Battering in Lesbian of Colour Relationships.' In *Confronting Lesbian Battering: A Manual for the Battered Women's Movement*, ed. Pam Elliot, 142–57. St Paul: Minnesota Coalition for Battered Women, 1990.

Kennedy, Elaine, and Madeleine Davis. *Boots of Leather, Slippers of Gold: The History of a Lesbian Community.* New York: Penguin, 1994.

Laframboise, Donna. *The Princess at the Window: A New Gender Morality.* Toronto: Penguin, 1996.

Lee, J. Letter attached to *Confronting Lesbian Battering: A Manual for the Battered Women's Movement* ed. Pam Elliot. London: London Bottered Women's Advocacy Centre, 1993.

Lobel, Kerry, ed. *Naming the Violence: Speaking Out about Lesbian Battering.* Seattle: Seal Press, 1986.

Mareck, J. 'Trauma Talk in Feminist Clinical Practice.' In *New Versions of Victims: Feminist Struggle with the Concept*, ed. S. Lamb, 158–82. New York: New York University Press, 1999.

Merrill, Gregory. 'Ruling the Exceptions: Same-Sex Battering and Domestic Violence Theory.' In *Violence in Gay and Lesbian Domestic Partnerships*, ed. Claire Renzetti and Charles Harvey Miley. New York: Harrington Park Press, 1996.

Nestle, Joan, ed. *The Persistent Desire: A Femme-Butch Reader.* Boston: Alyson, 1992.

Paglia, Camille. *Sex, Art and American Culture.* New York: Vintage Books, 1992.

Pearson, Patricia. *When She Was Bad: Violent Women and the Myth of Innocence.* Toronto: Random House, 1997.

Razack, Sherene. *Looking White People in the Eye: Gender, Race and Culture in Courtrooms and Classrooms.* Toronto: University of Toronto Press, 1998.

Renzetti, Claire. *Violent Betrayal: Partner Abuse in Lesbian Relationships.* Newbury Park, CA: Sage, 1992.

Renzetti, Clare, and Miley, C.H., eds. *Violence in Gay and Lesbian Domestic Partnerships.* New York: Harrington Park Press, 1996.

Ristock, Janice L. 'Community-Based Research: Lesbian Abuse and Other Telling Tales.' In *Inside the Academy and Out: Lesbian/Gay/Queer Studies and Social Action*, ed. Janice L. Ristock and Catherine G. Taylor, 137–54. Toronto: University of Toronto Press, 1998.

———. '"And Justice for All?" ... The Social Context of Legal Responses to Abuse in Lesbian Relationships.' *Canadian Journal of Women and the Law 7* (1994): 415–30.

———. 'Kiss and Kill: Some Impacts of Cultural Representations of Women's Sexualities.' In *Undisciplined Women: Tradition and Culture in Canada*, ed. Pauline Greenhill and D. Tye, 139–50. Montreal: McGill-Queen's University Press, 1997.

Ristock, Janice L. *No More Secrets: Violence in Lesbian Relationships.* New York: Routledge, 2002.

Ristock, Janice L., and Joan Pennell. *Community Research as Empowerment: Feminist Links, Postmodern Interruptions.* Toronto: Oxford University Press, 1996.

Roiphe, Katie. *The Morning After.* Boston: Back Bay Books, 1993.

Sommers, Christina Hoff. *Who Stole Feminism? How Women Have Betrayed Women.* New York: Simon and Shuster, 1995.

Taylor, J., and T. Chandler. *Lesbians Talk Violent Relationships.* London: Scarlet Press, 1995.

University of British Columbia Student Services. *Violence in Lesbian Relationships: Are Relationships Dangerous?* Vancouver: UBC, n.d.

Waldron, Charlene. 'Lesbians of Colour and the Domestic Violence Movement.' In *Violence in Gay and Lesbian Domestic Partnerships*, ed. Claire M. Renzetti & C.H. Miley, 43–51. New York: Harrington Park Press, 1996.

West, Angela. 'Prosecutorial Activism: Confronting Heterosexism in a Lesbian Battering Case.' *Harvard Women's Law Journal* 15 (1992): 249–71.

Chapter 5

Shattered Dreams:
A Material Rhetorical Reading of
Charlotte Fedders's Memoir of
Domestic Abuse

CATHY A. COLTON

> Unto the woman [God] said, I will greatly multiply thy sorrow and thy conception; in sorrow thou shalt bring forth children; and thy desire shall be to thy husband, and he shall rule over thee.
>
> *Genesis* 3:16

On 25 February 1985 the *Wall Street Journal* broke the story of the 'legal and personal problems' of John Fedders, the well-respected chief enforcement officer of the United States' Securities and Exchange Commission. Fedders was in the middle of what became a highly publicized divorce trial in which he admitted to having beaten his wife, Charlotte, on a number of occasions over the course of their seventeen-year marriage. After publication of the article, Fedders resigned his position to avoid further embarrassment to the Reagan administration, with its professed commitment to 'family values.' Two years later, Charlotte Fedders and journalist Laura Elliott published *Shattered Dreams*. The memoir is told in the third person (Elliott's writing) with extended narrative quotes from Fedders about her experiences. Fedders also conducted the bulk of the research about domestic abuse for the book. It begins with a recounting of her strict Roman Catholic upbringing in the 1940s and 1950s, explicitly attributing to Catholic teachings on marriage, family, and women's role Charlotte's willingness to work so long on an abusive marriage. As I read it, the complex entanglement between desire and domination, which comprises part of the curse or description[1] in the above passage from Genesis, accurately reflects the bind of Charlotte Fedders and of many battered women. They are brutally ruled over by their husbands, whom they also desire, love, and often need economically. As an author, Fedders places herself squarely within a Christian (specifically Roman Catholic) discursive realm to construct an interpretation of her married life, a critique of domestic abuse, and the Charlotte who is the heroine of *Shattered Dreams*.[2]

In the book, both Charlotte's religion and her culture prepare her to desire the role she was supposed to fill in life. She writes, 'All I ever wanted to be was a wife and mother. To marry a man who could give me children and a comfortable life, filled with love and little strife. That was my dream' (37). As if she is responding to God's curse of Eve (directed at all women, according to many interpreters), Charlotte's desire is for a husband, though she is not anticipating the accompanying punishment. She married John Fedders in 1966, fully expecting her dream to come true. In this essay, I work to develop a material rhetoric of domestic abuse, arguing that rhetoric is not only linguistic but also physical and sometimes violent. I first lay the theoretical groundwork for this revised understanding of rhetoric, and then offer my rhetorical analysis of Fedders's narrative of her abusive marriage.

Rhetoric Reconsidered

Rhetoric has traditionally been termed the art of persuasion. While I would concur that rhetoric is largely about persuasion, I veer from the traditional understanding in asserting that rhetoric is not always an art, as the classical rhetoricians understood that term. I understand persuasion to occur through the construction of meaning in such a way that it is difficult for the one being persuaded to see the issue any other way. Such persuasion works whether through a rhetor leading an audience step by step through a logical, persuasive argument, using enthymemes (what Aristotle termed 'the very body and substance of persuasion' [Cooper 1]); through an audience's engagement in a story, filmic, oral, written; through socialization; through example of action; through immersion in a worldview/ideology; or through the means of physical violence. It is important to expand our understanding of rhetoric to include the physical, even physical violence. The distinction between persuasion and physical coercion or violence is a blurry one. If we tend not to see violence as rhetorical, crucial aspects of domestic abuse go unnoticed, impeding efforts to combat such abuse. If we tend not to see violence as rhetorical, our understanding of the field of rhetoric is incomplete.

Sharon Marcus's theories of rape offer a way of understanding physical violence as rhetorical. In 'Fighting Bodies, Fighting Words: A Theory and Politics of Rape Prevention,' she suggests thinking about rape as language in order to effectively combat it, proposing that a

> way to refuse to recognize rape as the real fact of our lives is to treat it as a *linguistic* fact: to ask how the violence of rape is enabled by narratives, complexes and institutions which derive their strength not from outright, immutable, unbeatable force but rather from their power to structure our lives as imposing cultural scripts. (388–9)

This is not to see rape as *only* linguistic or immaterial, but to recognize the role that discourse plays in such violent actions. What she says about rape can be applied appropriately to domestic abuse, offering a theoretical construct for understanding such violence against women as a language. Such a construct allows us to see the narratives that enable the perpetuation of the traditional nuclear family and of domestic abuse in some of those families. Male power is in part constructed through language and through stories that we tell about family. The power of men to abuse is conceded through the structure of the patriarchal nuclear family and what we believe are the rights and responsibilities of the different members of those families. The languages of family, including those that many Christian churches present women like Charlotte Fedders, offer women a script in which we are invited to position ourselves as subordinate, powerless, victim, nurturer, caretaker, etc., while inviting men to position themselves as powerful, coercive, dominant, and protective. The structures within this script that position persons relative to others can be called the grammar of domestic abuse. Marcus writes that 'the rape script takes its form from what I will call a *gendered grammar of violence*, where grammar means the rules and structure which assign people to positions within a script' (392). Physical violence, then, has the form and structure of a language, able to fit within more traditional understandings of rhetoric.

When persuasion or the art of rhetoric is understood as only a mental or immaterial activity, rhetoric is situated on the mind side of the body/mind dualism. A related dualism then is that between traditional understandings of persuasion and physical coercion. I present a case for sexual seduction as the mediating term between the two of persuasion/physical coercion. Such seduction involves both physical and mental aspects and plays a strong role in domestic abuse.

There is both rhetorical theory and much feminist literature on violence against women that see persuasion and physical coercion as two completely different phenomena.[3] Feminism, in its desire to stand with female victims of violence, has often stressed the distinction between reasoned choice (persuasion) and coercion. This makes sense in a culture where blaming the female victims of violence is common. Many people see women who are battered not as coerced but as exercising completely free choice to stay in a violent relationship. Hence the commonly asked question 'Why doesn't she leave?' Yet this cultural situation only stresses the importance of addressing the complicated nature of the relationship between physical coercion and persuasion, the entanglement of desire and domination represented in Genesis 3:16, in which seduction plays a predominant role.

In her discussion of Marvell's poem 'To His Coy Mistress,' Alicia Ostriker defines seduction as follows:

> It differs on the one hand from the act of rape, where X subdues Y by force, and on the other from the proposal, where X promises Y an exchange of goods and services: come live with me and be my love and I'll give you this and that. In both rape and the proposal, X and Y remain distinct beings with separate sets of wishes. In the seduction this separation is less certain, less absolute. As Marvell suggests, seduction depends on X *convincing* Y that she already secretly desires the same amorous play that X desires, and that she has the potential to amalgamate with Y into a single being, a 'we' that will replace 'I' and 'you.' (154–5) (emphasis mine)

This definition puts seduction squarely in the camp of rhetoric. The seducer (Ostriker here assumes the seducer is male) takes on the task of convincing – persuading – another that her desires actually coincide with his. Yet this also implies a subtle kind of force. If the object of the seduction does not really desire the same thing the seducer does, then for the seduction to be successful, the seducer must rechannel the desires of the seduced until they coincide with his.

This blurring of the boundaries between persuasion and physical coercion and the recognition of the role of seduction in both is important in the development of a rhetoric of domestic abuse. It is a lack of understanding of this dynamic that allows for the question 'Why doesn't she leave?' Abused women often love and desire their husbands or boyfriends, with whom they can share good experiences when he is not violent, as well as hate the abuse to which the men subject them.

Perhaps the strongest classical rhetorical statement positing persuasion as coercive is that found in Gorgias' 'Encomium of Helen.' In this speech, Gorgias offers a defence of Helen, arguing that she should not be blamed for going to Troy with Paris. She should be seen as blameless, Gorgias argues, because she went either at the wishes of Chance or the gods, because forced, because persuaded, or because of love. In his discussion of persuasion, Gorgias describes speech as a 'powerful ruler' to move people (23). Though he asserts that persuasion is not the same as compulsion (25), he posits that one can be influenced by speech against one's will, just as if one were attacked with violence. Though he places force and persuasion in two separate categories, his description reveals that the line between them is blurred in his thought. Whether Helen was forced violently or persuaded through the power of speech, she was made to act against her will – hence coerced, as are present-day battered women.

In order to better understand and ultimately combat domestic abuse, we need to recognize the rhetorical structure of such violence. We must understand how violence serves a persuasive – as well as a coercive – function. If we deny its rhetorical function, the commonsense conditions for such violence will not be changed or even discussed.

While traditional rhetorical theory has not interpreted violence rhetorically, some contemporary reworkings of rhetorical theory create an opening for doing so. In *Rhetorical Dimensions of Popular Culture*, Barry Brummett defines rhetoric as 'the social function that influences and manages meaning' (xii). It is not a kind of act or object but rather a part of or function of acts and objects, that part that 'influences how social meanings are created, maintained, or opposed' (38). Such a definition of rhetoric allows for an understanding of rhetoric not just as a linguistic act but as a *process* that occurs when people engage in social meaning-making. Rhetoric thus occurs through the enactment of and contemplation of any type of action or artifact. While Brummett uses this construction of rhetoric to analyse rhetorical functions of popular culture artifacts like movies, and issues like race relations, utilizing his definitions and methodology in an examination of the rhetorical dimensions of domestic abuse can be very helpful.

The usefulness of Brummett's theory becomes most apparent in his discussion of the levels of rhetorical function: the exigent, the quotidian, and the implicative, particularly the last two. The exigent function involves what many rhetorical theorists are used to considering as rhetoric: 'it addresses exigencies of the moment, pressing problems, perceived quandaries, and frank questions ... Any time a pressing need arises that implicates the management of meaning, rhetoric then functions at the exigent level' (39).

The quotidian function of rhetoric is that level at which 'the public and personal meanings that affect everyday, even minute-to-minute decisions' are managed (41). This is where a social group's commonsense is managed. Rhetoric at this level operates through 'appropriational manifestations' (42), whereby individuals appropriate various 'bits' of information and experience they encounter in their lives and piece them together into messages or 'mosaics' that allow them to make sense of the world (64). In the instance of domestic abuse, a person could construct her understanding of what this issue means by appropriating 'bits' from news stories on the trial of O.J. Simpson, a movie about a battered wife on the Lifetime channel, discussions she overhears in the cafeteria at work, and a poster for a hotline glimpsed on the side of a bus as it drives by her.

Brummet's third function of rhetoric is implicative, which involves 'the conditions for common sense, the ways a society constructs its categories of thought and language, ... its fundamental values, its most unquestioned priorities.' Rhetoric at the implicative level is carried out through 'conditional manifestations' (44). This manifestation is 'rarely thought of at all, and when it is, it seems like a ghost haunting the houses of "real" texts, faintly seen assumptions and conditions hovering just beyond the clear and concrete signs and utterances of speeches and everyday life' (45). Conditional rhetoric functions below the conscious level and provides the grounding for the other forms of rhetoric. Genesis' Eden story constitutes an example of conditional manifestations of implicative rhetoric. It is a story pervasive in Western culture, influencing everything from literature to public policy decisions. Whether or not people hold it to be authoritative, its influence is so widespread as to affect our 'fundamental values.' In *Shattered Dreams*, other religious texts also function as conditional rhetoric in persuading Charlotte, as they do so many women, to work harder at her abusive marriage.

Analyses of the implicative and quotidian functions of the rhetoric of violence can lead to a more effective intervention at the exigent level. If we deny violence's rhetorical aspects, we deny the complex nature of violence within intimate relationships – the blurring of the line between persuasion and coercion, the role of seduction – an understanding of which is necessary to combat such violence.

Brummett writes that 'we are socialized by our cultures to see the world and to make the world in certain ways. If we could see how we are influenced to do so, if our repertoires for making reality were broadened, we might make the world into something different' (xxii). So, if we as a society were able to make changes in the values that ground and make possible domestic abuse (i.e., religious stories pervasive in our culture), we could conceivably make a world in which such violence is much less pervasive. Becoming aware of how our cultural and religious values function rhetorically – at an implicative level, below our consciousness – and identifying those parts of our repertoire for making reality that can be dangerous to women in families is a first step in changing the grounds of male/female relationships.

The Rhetoricality of Domestic Abuse in *Shattered Dreams*

Charlotte Fedders's account of her husband's abuse provides further evidence for my contention that the boundary between persuasion and physical coercion is a blurry one. I interpret her account as illustrating that one can be persuaded by physical violence, that rhetoric can be beaten into someone. This rhetoric of violence becomes embodied in the battered woman. Seduction also plays a role, this time revealing the importance of audience and the prerogatives of power to choose whether to become the audience of another or not.

It must be noted that a difficulty in working with a text such as *Shattered Dreams* is that it represents the interpretation a battered woman puts onto her experience from a distance of a significant amount of time. How she constructed her experience as the beatings were occurring is something unavailable to us, for it is then that the inexpressibility of suffering is at its highest. Women cannot record interpretations of their experiences of violence as they are occurring. The construction of written memoirs is necessarily one created with time and distance for reflection.

In her study of torture in *The Body in Pain*, Elaine Scarry posits that 'it is the intense pain that destroys a person's self and world ... Intense pain is also language-destroying: as the content of one's world disintegrates, so the content of one's language disintegrates' (35). Through the narrative of violent episodes in her marriage, Charlotte Fedders illustrates the breakdown of a woman's linguistic order – of her power to make meaning of her own – as a result of physical violence. Her husband's worldview then replaces hers. Persuasion is accomplished through means of violence. Scarry describes this dynamic with regard to the interrogation involved in torture: 'The question and answer also objectify the fact that while the prisoner has almost no voice – his confession is a halfway point in the disintegration of language, an audible objectification of the proximity of silence – the torturer and the regime have doubled their voice since the prisoner is now speaking their words' (36). While political torture and wife abuse are different and, in the Fedders case, they also vary widely in the degree of pain inflicted, there are similarities that this section will examine.

The following is Charlotte's account of the first time her husband hit her:

> I was sitting in a side chair next to the dining table. I think it was a Saturday morning. We had been talking for awhile. All I remember is that this conversation seemed to be going well. That we were really conversing, sharing ideas. We were not fighting, we were not being sarcastic or nasty. I swear we were just talking. But I think it was the first time I disagreed with him and was sticking to my guns. I was arguing my point calmly, but I was holding to it. I got his right hand to the left side of my face ... It was one good sock to the left side of my ear. Then I heard this ringing sound. I found out later that he had broken my eardrum. (77–8)

At this point, Charlotte describes herself as expressing and maintaining her own point. She is the creator of her own symbolic order different from John's. This appears to be what provokes his violence. As Ann Jones writes, it is 'vital to understand that women are battered *because they will not give in*' (94). Women who are battered do often resist their husbands' attempts to control their lives, actions, and thoughts, and it can be this resistance that leads men to increase the severity of attempts at control – attempts to persuade women to see things their way. This appears to work for John in the short run. The aftermath of this violent incident includes a breakdown or 'shutdown' of Charlotte's ability to create meaning: 'I kept wondering what I had done wrong, like a child who had been spanked ... I think he left and went to work. I sat and cried, a really sad cry at the table. Then I just shut down. I felt sick. I couldn't eat' (78).

Charlotte's thoughts get sidetracked from a construction of her own argument and ideas to the impossible task set her by her husband – trying to figure out what she had done wrong. The only worldview in which she's done something 'wrong' is that of her husband, which holds that a woman should not have any thoughts or ideas that are not her husband's. To solve this riddle, therefore, Charlotte would have to place her mind in the thought patterns of that worldview – one not her own. Her own symbolic order has to be placed in subjection to another. Since she has already been persuaded to a large degree to women's secondary status, she finds it difficult to hold on to her own symbolic structure at this point. Charlotte writes of going to a doctor to see to her broken eardrum: 'I was ashamed to be going to a doctor because my husband had hit me. I sat in that examining room in a dental-type chair for ten minutes going back and forth, "Should I tell him how it happened or not?" ... Of course, I didn't tell him. I fought hard not to show any emotion and I lied. Said that I had blown my nose and suddenly heard this ringing' (78). The replacement of falsehood – a story of which John would approve – for her truth represents another destruction of Charlotte's symbolic order and ability to make meaning for herself.

This process is a recursive one. Rather than a linear set of events, in which Charlotte's power to make meaning is completely destroyed and remains so until she is able to heal and reclaim her own worldview, Charlotte's experience (like that of many battered women) involved moving back and forth between attempts at self-assertion, giving up her meaning for that of the scripts her church and husband provided for her, and later experimenting with alternative scripts.

Another beating, this time while Charlotte was pregnant with their first child, occurred while she was again standing up for a position she felt strongly about: buying a house that was not on a busy street. She writes:

> So again, I was sticking to my guns. I was on the sofa ... He towered over me ... He was very angry. He loomed over me and hit me in the abdomen, three, maybe five times, hard. I bent over, trying to protect my tummy. They were powerful blows. It felt like taking a heavy fall. It's not like the pain you feel when you fall into a heavy object and bruise. It seemed like it went on forever, although the whole thing probably only lasted thirty seconds, maybe a minute ... I tried to push him away, which only seemed to make him madder. He yelled that he didn't care if he killed me or the baby. (82)

Like before, this beating apparently occurred to beat Charlotte's own opinions and ideas out of her, to take away her ability to shape her own worldview. Consciousness of her own world seems to have stopped for a time after this incident: 'I don't remember how it stopped ... The next thing I remember clearly is sitting in the doctor's office' the next day (82). This time she does tell the doctor what happened because she fears for the fetus she is carrying, but she clearly had John's viewpoint beaten into her:

> It was humiliating. I thought that I had 'openly defied' John, so that I deserved being hit. I was already making excuses for John. He had been tense and I was nagging him. We had found a perfect little house and I was being stubborn. I had been sick and unable to take care of the apartment the way I was supposed to and he was justifiably angry. (82–3)

Charlotte's recounting of this scene suggests that rhetoric is something that can be beaten into someone. After this beating Charlotte was persuaded, by means of violence, to construct the situations in their marriage as her husband did. His point of view became hers. He persuaded her not by force of a good argument, but by force, period. This has important consequences for a theory of rhetoric. It suggests that the boundary between persuasion and physical coercion is a blurry one. Rhetoric is not just an ideal form of communication or even a sophistic one. It involves the physical as well as the mental, the body as well as the mind.

Charlotte sought an authority outside of herself to define the situation for her, but the doctor did not say that what John had done was wrong. He did suggest she leave, but 'it wasn't what I wanted to hear. I was pregnant. I was convinced I couldn't take care of myself anyway. How could I take care of a baby too, on my own?' (83). She turned to her religion – the symbolic structure with which she was most familiar – for comfort and guidance. Upon getting home from the doctor, she prayed the rosary and looked for guidance in her meditation book, *Women before God*. In it she encountered prayers like the following:

> Lord, bless and preserve my cherished husband, whom you have given to me. Let his life be long and blessed, comfortable and holy; let me ever be a blessing and a comfort to him, a sharer in all his sorrows, a consolation in all the accidents and trials of life. Make me forever lovable in his eyes and forever dear to him ... Keep me from all ungentleness; make me humble, yet strong and helpful. (83–4)

Fedders and Elliott interpret Charlotte's reliance on these prayers as the force that kept her in her marriage to John despite his violence. This is an important factor. The prayers and what the church taught Charlotte dictated that she was to see him as a blessing and work to please him, no matter what. The symbolic structure offered by the Catholic Church in her prayers is imaginatively limited to a world in which husbands do behave in 'holy' ways and find their wives always 'lovable.' It forecloses the possibility that the husband might behave violently towards his wife. The 'good wife' is to pray for control over her actions – that she might be sharing, consoling, loving, gentle, humble, helpful, etc. But what happens when the husband – someone beyond the realm of her control – does not behave according to the paradigm of the 'blessed' marriage? The script, to use Sharon Marcus' term, of the 'good wife' provided by the church has no room for such possibilities, so someone who attempts to construct her experience according to that script has her options foreclosed. Her worldview is reoriented from one of someone with ideas and opinions to offer to one focused solely on serving her husband.

Yet this is too limited a view of Charlotte's rhetorical situation. In Charlotte's world, turning to the church was the moral thing to do in crisis. Suffering was a beautiful option and there was a mystical, soothing, peace-generating quality to the process of praying the rosary. Charlotte did construct a prayer of her own; it is fully within the boundaries of this Catholic paradigm, but she was using her agency to make sense out of her world within the framework available and most attractive to her. She recalls praying something like the following:

Hail Mary, full of grace, you are so wise. You are so loving. You were a good wife. Help me to be more like you. I don't seem to be able to understand my husband. Help me to understand him so that I can be a better person, a better woman, a better wife. (84)

Mary, the paradigmatic 'good wife,' is called upon to help her be more responsible for her marriage. Within this worldview, there is no possibility of John's being responsible for his actions. For Charlotte and for the Catholic paradigm, being a good person, if one is a woman, is equivalent to being a good wife. Being a good wife means being understanding, loving, consoling, etc., regardless of the husband's behaviour. Full responsibility for the marriage is placed upon the woman, someone who has very little self. Part of this responsibility means putting up with the material beatings her husband administers to keep her in line with the rhetoric of submission.

Such destruction of Charlotte's capability for language and symbolic structures is one consequence of these beatings. A willful withholding of language, however, can be a conscious action used to abuse another and further that other's symbolic and material destruction. John Fedders frequently chose such a tactic. His wife termed it 'psychological torture' (92). He would refuse to talk to her for days, sometimes weeks at a time. The silences appeared to her to be completely arbitrary – she could never tell what would set them off or what would end them. They were a feature of her life over which she had no control. This particular form of 'torture' did destroy much of Charlotte's capacity for constructing her own symbolic structures and creating her own language. So, she took on those of John, speaking and acting for him. This is best exemplified in the following scene, which I will quote at length:

> There was nothing I could do to make him come out of [the silence]. He came out of it when he was ready, not before. I would get more and more emotional, trying to get a response, and he would get more and more silent. Self-control was very important to him, it was important in the Catholic Church, and I think he viewed my getting upset, losing control, as being very wrong, a sin. He would look at me with disgust. Or if he answered, it was terse and icy. 'Look in the mirror,' he'd say. 'There's our problem' ... He was lying in bed ignoring me. I tried to seduce him. Making love had always seemed to settle arguments between us, to make things better. The culture at the time told us that sex was the way to make men happy, that that was the main thing they wanted. So I tried everything ... he rejected me. I was humiliated and hysterical. Finally I said, 'Maybe you're queer.' The way he turned and looked at me terrified me. I was sitting in the rocker ... and I slapped myself in the face, several times, hard. 'I'm so stupid,' I said, whack, 'I'm so ugly,' whack, 'I'm so fat,' whack. He watched me do it. By Pelham [a place they lived], I would do what he told me to. I'd look in the mirror, at the cause of all our problems, and say, 'I hate myself,' over and over again as I slapped. His response was, 'You see, you're crazy. That proves my point.' (93)

As she describes it, Charlotte's interests and her self are obliterated as she takes on John's role of insulting, belittling, and beating her. She has become victim and perpetrator of the verbal and physical violence in her marriage. She violently inscribes upon her body internalized messages, from both her husband and the culture at large. She not only has become persuaded by her husband and culture to believe these messages, but has herself become the persuader and the text upon which those messages are inscribed. The three classical elements of rhetoric (rhetor, audience, and text) are all embodied in Charlotte. This embodied rhetoric is problematic. When all of the rhetorical elements are located in one person, that person is isolated from others. Embodied messages need to be translated so they can be communicated verbally to another. In the case of the text inscribed on a battered woman (that she must submit to her husband), the message must be translated so that it can then be refuted. As a woman like Fedders begins to put her story into words and communicate it to others, she can begin to believe that her husband's treatment of her is unjust and must be fought. She can begin to create a new text of self-understanding and communicate it to an audience that includes herself, but reaches farther to include others. This does not mean that she no longer has bodily memories of the text written upon her, but that she can read them in new, more liberatory ways and share them with others.

Yet Charlotte also used her body rhetorically in attempts to communicate with her husband. Following a script of how the culture suggested a 'good wife' should behave, Charlotte used her body sexually to communicate her desire to get along better with her husband. This rhetorical use of the body is further illustrated in the following scene. At a point in time later than the last scene discussed, Charlotte was at what she describes as her lowest point. During another of John's long silent periods, she followed him around pleading with him, asking him to go with her to a marriage counsellor, but getting no response except the typical, 'Look in the mirror. There's our problem.' As he was leaving for a week's trip with a friend, Charlotte 'ran after him. I threw open my nightgown and started rubbing myself all over my body. I don't know what I was trying to do. Seduce him to stay, I guess. He looked at me and said with this icy tone of voice, "You have proved my point. You're crazy"' (184).

By the end of this scene, not only is Charlotte an embodied rhetoric of female submission, she is *only* body. In a culture that regularly denigrates the female body in favour of the 'male' mind, such a reduction is an ultimate degradation. Since it is through language use, our rational faculties, our ability to create symbolic structures, that we are typically seen to be fully human, this is ultimately a dehumanizing scene. Charlotte has again enacted the part of the female that John and the culture prepared for her. Women are then put down for fulfilling the role they are supposed to play. She does, though, use her body in an attempt, however ineffective, to communicate. Her rhetoric is embodied – is material – because she expresses it through her body.

These attempts at being rhetorical, of persuading John to stay with her, fail, however. In her own words, she tried to *seduce* John so that he would not leave angry. Interestingly, she tried to seduce John by touching herself, not him. Her body, not his, is still the text being written upon. And, given John's refusal to heed her, she is once again her own audience. Earlier, I posited seduction as the mediating factor between persuasion and physical coercion. Seduction is part of a rhetoric of abuse. For rhetors to be effective, though, they must have an audience. John refused to be Charlotte's audience, so her attempts at using seduction as a means of persuasion failed. Seduction could not work as part of her rhetoric because she did not have the power to claim an audience for herself. John had the effective power within the relationship and so was able to decide when and whether to use his violence as a means of persuasion and when and whether to serve as an audience to Charlotte. His long, angry silences can be interpreted as a refusal to play the role of audience. Despite Charlotte's attempts, she did not have control over the rhetorical situation. She did not have the power to command an audience, and hence felt crazy.

These feelings led Charlotte to see a female counsellor, the first person from whom she ever sought help who told her that the way John treated her was 'unacceptable behaviour.' The seemingly simple act of labelling a man's violent and abusive actions as 'unacceptable' opened up a new rhetorical arena of possibility for Charlotte, providing her with a new 'bit' of experience to weave into her 'mosaic' of meaning. For the first time, she 'really got the idea that there might be something wrong with John's behavior' (185).

Possibilities for a Material Rhetoric of Self-Affirmation

Up until this point, I have illustrated the destructive power of a material rhetoric of female submission for women. But women's agency is complicated, and battered women use theirs in ways to empower themselves too. Charlotte used literacy as a way to rebuild her own capacity for creating symbolic structures – her own use of language. She began this with John, finding that sometimes when she wrote him letters, rationally explaining her feelings and position, it could help to bring him out of a silence or to calm him down. These provided times when John was willing to be an audience, to allow Charlotte to be a rhetor, and she was creating her own texts in an effort to become a better wife. But the power still was definitely with him, and his willingness to allow Charlotte's rhetoric didn't last; he didn't seem to want a wife who had her own position and could articulate it.

Charlotte finally turned to other avenues. She joined a book group, rather late in their marriage, which provided her with a support group, something entirely new for her. Before that, John had always 'censured her friendships ... mostly limiting their social acquaintances to his business or sports friends, people Charlotte would never have felt comfortable confiding in' (157). She said about the book club that 'these nights were really good for me, because it got me dressed up and out of the house ... The discussions were so good for me. I would be absolutely floored that these educated women I thought so highly of would actually listen to me. It was so exciting' (157–8). As Denise Gogarty, another member of the club, said, 'reading prescribed books on a variety of topics allowed all of us to think about something beyond the scope of our homes and children. Also, I think it was a community ... it was inclusive, had a sense of commitment, was a safe place for people to be themselves' (158). This group met a need for Charlotte to have a community that operated on the basis of a different story or script than she was accustomed to.

At first she saw these acts of assertion as good for her marriage too. But the reading group also offered an alternative script with which Charlotte could experiment. Such a script calls for more collaborative behaviour, an egalitarian ethic of listening and knowledge creation, as opposed to the hierarchical model of the Catholic script of 'good wife' to which Charlotte was accustomed. With an expanded repertoire of scripts to draw upon to help her make sense of her world, Charlotte participated in a self-affirming and material rhetoric that relied upon the physical presence of other women; food and dressing up were also big parts of the evening, focused on fulfilling bodily as well as intellectual needs.

Fedders and Elliott interpret this book club as allowing Charlotte to widen the scope of her worldview, enabling her to see multiple possibilities for how to be a self in the world. The first book the group read and discussed together was Marilyn French's *The Women's Room*, the feminist novel about a woman gaining her self and life back after a marriage devoted solely to husband and children ended. Laura Elliott writes that the 'book club would nurture Charlotte and gradually wean her from total dependence on John for her self-esteem, helping to build the strength she would need to eventually stand on her own' (157). Her rhetorical possibilities were expanding; she was being exposed to new ideas that could persuade her to construct a different perspective that that of her husband and her church.

Conclusion

Fedders and Elliott's narrative of the Fedders' marriage offers a helpful opportunity to explore and develop a rhetoric of abuse. It exposes some of the conditional rhetoric of abuse in our culture. The book's limitation, in my estimation, lies in the fact that it does not question the 'shattered dreams' themselves. The myth of the 'good wife' and a woman's desire to be one are not critiqued; it is only suggested that one should not be punished for holding on to such a dream. Yet traditional marriages based on a rigid distinction between spheres for men and women always have within them the potential for danger to women. This danger comes from her unequal economic status, often making it impossible for her to leave a violent marriage, and from her denigrated positioning within the various binaries of body/mind, private/public, etc. Until women are constructed as the equals of men in our culture, women will always be subject to the abuses of men.

Shattered Dreams does, however, offer some critique of the traditional categories of male and female. Although at the end Charlotte still upholds the ideals of traditional marriage, while decrying the violence that can accompany them, she has rewritten her understanding of success into a more 'feminine' one. And she includes her sons in this definition. At the end of her memoir, she writes of her sons:

> I want happiness for them. And my definition of happiness is very different today than it would have been five years ago. Before, I would have identified the means of happiness as being good in sports, getting into college, becoming a doctor or lawyer, having a successful career. Now, I want them to have the self-confidence that comes from liking themselves, not being afraid to try anything. To be good to their families and to really enjoy everything a family can bring. I don't agree that success and being nice are mutually exclusive. I want them to be nice because I believe the greatest success in life is being a warm person, capable of tenderness. (292)

This new definition of success Charlotte puts forth ultimately challenges both the public/private split and the related male/female split. To her, what is success for males is more like what is typically seen to be success for females: it is based more on 'private' sphere activities of the family and home that on 'public' sphere activities of work for money. These qualities of tenderness and warmth would then be infused into the 'public' sphere of work, transforming it, rather than allowing the current aggressive qualities of the public sphere to transform the home into a place of despotism and abuse. The feminism offered here is reminiscent of that in the nineteenth-century, one in which men are men and women are women, but the superior 'feminine' qualities are given sway not only at home, but in the public realm as well.

The memoir serves as a rhetorical call to such change. Despite years of abuse that broke down her meaning-making capacities, Charlotte became able to create new capacities for her own symbolic structures, which eventually culminated in the telling of her story to Laura Elliott, the mediation of that story through her new lens of awareness of Catholic rhetoric, and the collaborative publication of a book. As readers, we receive the story of a battered woman's engagement with the material rhetoric of female submission through the literate artifact of the text of *Shattered Dreams*. Despite years of her husband attempting to destroy her subjectivity by denigrating her body, Charlotte's book brings her and her perspective back to a central position. You, as readers, have further had this story mediated through my interpretive lens, the lens of someone seeking to construct an understanding of how rhetoric works materially. My work aims to make Charlotte's body and its messages central, as worthy of an audience, something her husband denied her. Charlotte Fedders, Laura Elliott, and I have all sought to create, through our writing, rhetorical texts that can have an impact on the material lives of women. We have taken a step towards changing the possibilities of violence for women when we can analyze the often quotidian and implicative ways in which rhetoric functions materially. When women can be empowered to disrupt and revise the scripts that enable them to construct their experience in harmful ways, instead embodying new scripts that are self-affirming, further change can occur. Material rhetorics can function both to violently force women's compliance with traditional understandings of the biblical epigraph and with the traditional scripts of 'good wife,' *and* to free women from the curse of their desire for men who dominate them.

Notes

1 For centuries, theologians and biblical scholars have argued whether the subordination of woman to man referred to in Genesis 3:16 is a created, and hence inherent, part of the difference between the sexes or is a result of the 'Fall.' Feminist rereaders of Genesis seek to put the book in its contemporary social context, removing the universalizing aspect of a verse like 3:16. Scholarship I have read, however, that discusses the verse as a curse, focuses on the 'curse' of childbirth pain or of male domination. The double bind of not only domination, but desire for the dominator, goes unremarked. See, for example, Pagels, Meyers, Bledstein.
2 I signify the distinction between author of and character in *Shattered Dreams* by use of 'Fedders' when referring to the author and 'Charlotte' when referring to the book's character.
3 While a number of studies examine the relationship between violence and the rhetoric or discourse about it or accompanying it, I have found none that explore the rhetorical nature of violent acts themselves. See, for example, Browne, Leeman.

Works Cited

Bledstein, Adrien Janis.'Are Women Cursed in Genesis 3:16?' In *A Feminist Companion to Genesis*, ed. Athalya Brenner, 142–5. Sheffield, U.K.: Sheffield Academic Press, 1993.

Browne, Stephen H. 'Encountering Angelina Grimke: Violence, Identity, and the Creation of Radical Community.' *Quarterly Journal of Speech* 82 (1996): 55–73.

Brummett, Barry. *Rhetorical Dimensions of Popular Culture*. Tuscaloosa: University of Alabama Press, 1991.

Cooper, Lane. *The Rhetoric of Aristotle*. Englewood Cliffs, NJ: Prentice-Hall, 1932.

Fedders, Charlotte, and Laura Elliott. *Shattered Dreams: The Story of Charlotte Fedders*. New York: Harper and Row, 1987.

Gorgias. 'Encomium of Helen.' Trans. D.M. MacDowell. Bristol, U.K.: Bristol Classical Press, 1982.

Leeman, Richard. *The Rhetoric of Terrorism and Counterterrorism*. New York: Greenwood, 1991.

Marcus, Sharon. 'Fighting Bodies, Fighting Words: A Theory and Politics of

Rape Prevention.' In *Feminists Theorize the Political*, ed. Judith Butler and Joan W. Scott, 385–403. New York: Routledge, 1992.

Meyers, Carol L. 'Gender Roles and Genesis 3:16 Revisited.' In *A Feminist Companion to Genesis*, ed. Athalya Brenner, 118–41. Sheffield, U.K.: Sheffield Academic Press, 1993.

Ostriker, Alicia. 'Anne Sexton and the Seduction of the Audience.' In *Seduction and Theory: Readings of Gender, Representation, and Rhetoric*, ed. Dianne Hunter, 154–69. Urbana: University of Illinois Press, 1989.

Pagels, Elaine. *Adam, Eve, and the Serpent*. New York: Random House, 1988.

Scarry, Elaine. *The Body in Pain: The Making and Unmaking of the World*. Oxford: Oxford University Press, 1985.

Chapter 6

When the Daughter Tells Her Story: The Rhetorical Challenges of Disclosing Father-Daughter Incest

BRENDA DALY

> Having survived, am I supposed to say something, do something, be something?
>
> Dorothy Allison

Writing autobiographical narratives can be therapeutic, according to many trauma experts, writers, therapists, and literary critics.[1] Having written a scholarly book, *Authoring a Life*, in which I disclosed the experience of father-daughter incest, I understand this claim and, to some extent, agree with it. Yet critics sometimes forget that writing, like speaking, is a social act: without listeners or readers, there is no story.[2] The audience's response is especially important for trauma survivors because, if the act of narration is to be therapeutic, the audience must be willing to *affirm* the teller's story despite memory gaps (Herman, *Trauma and Recovery*). Yet women's incest narratives, particularly those that claim to be based on actual experience, such as memoir and autobiography, have been challenged with increasing frequency during the 1990s. For example, some critics charge that the gaps in the traumatized daughter's memory are filled with fiction implanted by therapists rather than with actual experiences (Loftus and Ketcham). Despite the escalating intensity of such attacks, women are being encouraged to continue telling their stories of trauma, for reasons both therapeutic and political. The feminist hope is that if a woman translates her trauma into narrative, she may become an agent in her own recovery, and that if she exposes her father, whether in a court of law or in a memoir, she may become an agent of social change. Unfortunately, regardless of where she tells her story, the daughter's rhetorical situation has become complex as a result of the current backlash.

It is important to remember, as Louise Armstrong reminds us, that in the early years of the second wave of the women's movement, it was a political act – not a therapeutic task – for a woman to disclose her incest experience. As Armstrong states, 'It bears remembering here that consciousness-raising was conceptually *antithetical* to therapy' (11).[3] Because the more powerful father had imposed secrecy on the incested daughter, forcing her to bear the burden of his violation, feminists encouraged traumatized daughters to break their silences in the public sphere. An early example of such a collective feminist effort is the anthology *Voices in the Night: Women Speaking about Incest*, edited by Toni A.H. McNaron and Yarrow Morgan (1982), which includes only one story by a well-known writer, Audre Lorde's 'Chain.' Most of the women in *Voices in the Night* were not famous, not writers, and did not aspire to be. Telling their stories, especially telling them together, was a political act. In addition, feminist literary scholars began to recover the incest narratives by 'lost' women writers and to champion contemporary narratives such as Maya Angelou's autobiography *I Know Why the Caged Bird Sings* (1969). In short, despite the risk of public disclosure, as daughters began to tell their stories, a canon of incest narratives emerged, some of which continue to be taught in college literature classes.[4]

Prior to the women's movement, as Christine Froula observes, the situation of literary daughters mirrored the relationship of daughters in the incestuous family, as described in Judith Lewis Herman's *Father-Daughter Incest* (1981). Because the daughter is 'prohibited by her father from speaking about the abuse,' Froula explains, '[she] is unable to sort out her contradictory feelings of love for her father and terror of him, of desire to end the abuse and fear that if she speaks she will destroy the family structure that is her only security' (112). Feminists worked collectively to challenge a canon that mirrored this 'family structure,' a challenge that helped to fuel the canon debate beginning in the 1970s and 1980s. In addition, in the early 1970s feminists challenged the Freudian theory that hysteric patients had only fantasized paternal sexual abuse. In 1971, at a conference on rape sponsored by the New York Radical Feminists, Florence Rush presented one of the first theoretical papers to argue that incested children, usually girls, were not to blame and that sexual abuse, most often committed by fathers, should be understood as part of a 'pervasive pattern with antecedents of social acceptance that reach far back into history' (Brownmiller, Introduction to Rush ix). In the 1980s, numerous studies (Rush; Herman; Miller) criticized Freud's theories and confirmed the pervasive pattern of father-daughter incest. According to Herman, the estimates of women who survive some form of sexual abuse in childhood and/or adolescence range from one in three to one in five (*Father-Daughter Incest*, 12).

During the 1990s, the importance of political protest was often lost: despite the backlash against the daughter's incest story, critics began to place increasing emphasis upon individual recovery in the privacy of a therapist's office or in the privacy of journal writing.[5] This backlash has taken a variety of forms: members of the False Memory Foundation, founded by parents accused of sexual abuse, attack therapists for implanting false memories in their patients; reviewers attack memoirs and novels for lacking artistry or for being too artistic to be credible; some reviewers state that they have grown tired of 'pathographies' while others argue that the public is suffering from compassion fatigue. Ironically, the growing canon of the daughter's incest stories has helped to turn the public against them. One reason for such resistance is that, as Louise Armstrong phrases it, these stories are 'rocking the cradle of sexual politics.' Another reason is that such stories are deeply disturbing and, according to Judith Lewis Herman, none of us is immune to the attractions of denial. That is why, she argues, the history of psychological investigations of trauma illustrates such patterns of forgetfulness, with periods of 'active investigation' followed by periods of 'oblivion' (*Trauma and Recovery*, 7). Neither changes in fashion nor loss of interest can account for such a pattern, Herman argues; rather, because traumatic events force bystanders to take sides, they can exhaust us.

As a result of such resistance, the incested daughter faces a complex rhetorical situation: she needs to break her silence, and she needs affirmation, but whether she tells her story in a therapist's office, in a court of a law, or in the form of a memoir, she may encounter responses ranging from neutrality or indifference to exploitation or hostility. To illustrate these rhetorical problems, I examine two father-daughter memoirs published in 1997: Linda Katherine Cutting's *Memory Slips* and Kathryn Harrison's *The Kiss*. In addition to publishing their incest memoirs during the same year, both women were sexually violated by minister-fathers. Both had also published novels before turning to memoir, and prior to publishing their memoirs both were recognized professionals – Cutting as a concert pianist and Harrison as a novelist. A major difference, however, is that Cutting's abuse began when she was only three years old; by contrast, Harrison's incestuous relationship with her estranged father began when she was twenty. As a result of these differences, each woman must use rhetorical strategies that make her vulnerable to attack: Cutting employs modernist techniques to represent gaps in her memory, whereas Harrison borrows scenes from previously published novels to write an anti-romance.

As I shall illustrate, the reception of these stories raises the question: How much public authority, how much credibility, does a daughter have in the 1990s? As Susan Lanser argues, 'Discursive authority ... the intellectual credibility, ideological validity, and aesthetic value claimed by or conferred upon a work, author, narrator, character, or textual practice – is produced interactively; it must therefore be characterized with respect to specific receiving communities' (6). Despite variations in specific receiving communities – Cutting describes encounters with two therapists and a church authority who fail to affirm her story, whereas Harrison was attacked after publishing *The Kiss* – I shall demonstrate that the reception of the daughter's incest narrative always has an ideological component: each listener (or reader) must decide whether to affirm or attack, to support or exploit, to bear witness to the trauma survivor's suffering or to challenge her credibility. While keeping in mind that some women may, in fact, be lying when they claim to have been sexually abused, I intend to focus on two memoirs that are, in my view, not only well written but also credible. I begin my analysis with *Memory Slips*, in which Cutting addresses the problem of memory gaps, as well as the reception she encountered when she attempted to tell her story to different adults in positions of authority.

Rhetorical Strategies and Receiving Communities: Cutting's *Memory Slips*

While studying to become a concert pianist, Cutting managed to contain her trauma; however, as an adult, she found the delayed symptoms of post-traumatic stress[6] becoming so severe that she frequently contemplated suicide. Aware of the backlash against stories of childhood sexual abuse, Cutting says in her Prelude, 'So much has been done to discredit the memories, and silence the voices of those who have struggled against great odds to be heard'; then she adds, quoting Judith Lewis Herman, 'But healing requires the reconstruction of memory; the unspeakable must be spoken and heard' (2). Cutting's reconstruction of traumatic memory in her memoir is offered, then, both as an effort to speak the unspeakable but also out of a need – as part of her healing – to be heard and believed. Although Cutting had already published a novel, she chose to write a memoir in order to make certain truth claims that she could not make in a work of fiction. In my view, because the author of a memoir is vulnerable to charges of lying in ways that a novelist is not, Cutting was taking a greater risk, and she was doing so for political rather than artistic reasons.

Although it has become fashionable to blur the boundaries between fiction and memoir – and, for the writer, the shift from autobiographical fiction to memoir is often made – receiving communities differentiate between these genres. As Marie-Laure Ryan explains, 'The "language game" of nonfiction ... bind[s] sender and receiver in a communicative contract ... The text of nonfiction is to be evaluated in terms of truth, [but] the text itself is unable to establish its own validity. The reader evaluates the truth-value of the text by comparing its assertions to another source of knowledge relating to the same reference world ... The need for external validation means that the nonfictional text stands in a polemical relation with other representations' (166). In short, Cutting's authority as the writer of a memoir – the reliability of her perception of reality – can be validated only by comparing her 'truth' to other sources of knowledge, knowledge often controlled by male-dominated institutions, such as the ministry.[7] But even prior to going public – whether through the courts or through publication of a memoir – victims of sexual violation face a formidable narrative task, the task of integrating unspeakable acts into narratives that meet conventional expectations of socio-linguistic coherence.

While sexual abuse is a physical trauma, a violation of the body's integrity, it also shatters the victim's coherence, her sense of self, particularly her trust in others. This shattering of identity creates a complex problem of identity and narration.[8] For example, after her own survival of a near-fatal sexual assault, feminist philosopher Susan J. Brison explains that the mind/body problem had been so complicated by 'the bodily nature of traumatic memory' (17) that 'rejecting the body and returning to the life of the mind was no longer an option, since body and mind had become nearly indistinguishable' (17). Like many victims, Brison suffered from 'hypervigilance, heightened startle response, insomnia, and other PTSD symptoms' (17), as well as anxiety and depression, all of which resist categorization as either mental or physical. As a result of these experiences, Brison concluded, 'If memories are lodged in the body, the Lockean distinction between the memory criterion and that of bodily identity no longer applies' (18). Brison's experience of sexual violation differs from Cutting's: Brison, a highly verbal adult, felt that she had 'outlived' her previous identity after a single assault by a stranger.

By contrast, Cutting was a child, not yet three years old and still in the stage of language acquisition, when she was repeatedly sexually violated by her minister-father. Thus, the task of narrative is even more formidable for survivors like Cutting, who, at the time of her violation, had no vocabulary for her betrayal trauma. Cutting's adult struggle to find words for what she was too young even to name was further complicated by the fact that her father had forced her to make a terrible bargain: aware that she loved to play the piano, he promised that if she would keep silent about the abuse, he would buy her a piano. To recover her memories and speak about them, she would have to break this unstated emotional contract with her father. Even as an adult, Cutting would face harsh consequences for breaking her silence: she would lose the love of her father and, possibly, her mother's love as well. Elizabeth Loftus, a board member of the False Memory Syndrome Foundation, has used her research to argue that such silenced, or repressed, memories are a myth, that memories such as those recovered by Cutting are implanted by therapists. By contrast, Cutting argues that fathers often implant 'forgetting' with bribes and threats. She writes, 'Survivors don't only forget because of the trauma, though that in itself would be enough. They forget because they were told to forget. Whether by threats ("if you tell, I'll kill you") or by edict ("this did not happen"), reality gets reshaped' (2).

Memory is a complex problem for survivors and therapists. For example, because Cutting's memories were lodged wordlessly in her muscles, she needed a therapist who understood, as Herman explains in *Trauma and Recovery*, that traumatic memories may be stored in a part of the brain not immediately accessible to language. As Jennifer Freyd explains, memory is not 'monolithic' (89). For example, repression and dissociation are not the same, although some kind of blockage occurs in both, despite the public's confusion of these terms; dissociation is a defense that occurs during the event while 'repression is an after-the-fact defense in which memory for the event is in some way impaired' (107). Because the human brain is multifaceted, Freyd explains, there are many kinds of memory, just as there are many kinds of learning. She identifies the following kinds of memory, while cautioning that the terms are undergoing change resulting from ongoing study: declarative (knowing what) and procedural knowledge (knowing how); explicit (recall and recognition involving conscious remembering) and implicit memory (no conscious effort), which may be dissociated from each other; episodic (time-dated) and semantic (not time-dated); generic event memory (familiar event, such as driving to work), episodic memory (information about time and place), and autobiographical memory (part of one's life story); and sensory memories, which may be visual, auditory, or tactile.

Freyd says, 'Although information may be blocked from entering conscious awareness and/or declarative memory stores, sensory traces, or procedural memories, may well be laid for traumatic events' (115). Psychotherapist Babette Rothschild agrees, as her title asserts, that 'the body remembers.' Yet somatic memory, Rothschild says, is 'neither more nor less reliable than any other form of memory' (xv). Sometimes these memories can be recovered 'with relative accuracy,' while at other times 'false memories can be inadvertently created or encouraged – by the therapist as well as the client' (xiv). Nevertheless, Loftus claims that 'no evidence exists to support the claim that muscles and tissues respond in a way that can be interpreted reliably as a concrete episodic memory' (161). Many survivors disagree with Loftus, insisting that there is a difference between 'sense' memory and 'thinking' memory, a distinction formulated by Holocaust survivor Charlotte Delbo and cited by Roberta Culbertson. A survivor of childhood sexual abuse who currently is director of the Institute on Violence at the Virginia Center for the Humanities, Culbertson says, 'We lose sight of the body's own recall of its response to threat and pain ... because this wordless language is unintelligible to one whose body is not similarly affected' (170). Culbertson adds that bits of memory often 'appear in nonnarrative forms that seem to meet no standard test for truth or comprehensibility' (169).

Fortunately, because Cutting is a professional pianist, she is aware of the differences between what Culbertson calls thinking memories and sense memories. Cutting's name for sense memories is 'muscle memories,' and she employs a musical analogy to explain how it works. 'The muscles retain everything,' she says; just as her 'fingertips hold the minutest memories' of complex musical passages, she knows 'from sleepless nights' that 'muscles remember too' (7). For years, without knowing why, Cutting slept with a baseball bat – not with a bat and a mitt, only a bat. Therapy helped her to understand why:

As a child I spent my nights in vigilance, watching the bedroom door for the crack of light or listening for the sound of footsteps. Though I know in my mind he's not coming into my bedroom tonight, that it's been decades since he last came, my muscles don't know it. Not yet. I am hoping to teach them, the same way I taught them to aim for the faraway note and strike it dead center. (7)

At the same time, Cutting cautions, 'Muscle memory, by itself, is not reliable' (8); that is because muscles cannot distinguish between 'a loving gesture in the present' and 'an assault from the past' (8). Further-more, says Cutting, 'If the memory of the original gesture has been eclipsed, there is no way to understand the muscles' reactions' (8). Muscle memories may, however, serve as an avenue for recovering repressed memories – thinking memories – of sexual violation.

To illustrate the differences between thinking memory and sensory memory, Cutting borrows, once again, from her experience as a musi-cian. When teaching music, she tells her students that 'there are three kinds of memory slips': one that doesn't prevent you from 'losing a beat,' another where you don't recover 'until the downbeat,' and a third that requires you to stop and 'restart the music' (6). There is also, she writes, a fourth memory slip that she does not explain to students: a slip of much longer duration, the ten years it took to 'recover the life I forgot I had lived. The life that began before music or words' (6). The process that enables Cutting to recall the life before music or words does not, however, begin with words, but rather with images externalized through painting and sculpting. Through these artistic processes Cutting trans-lated muscle memories into images that eventually became words.[9] Loftus cautions therapists against such a use of art therapy. 'While drawing pictures might access blocked feelings, is it wise to use those feelings to explore "the deeper nuances of suspicion and fear"?' she asks; 'If memories are triggered by a client's drawings or visual repre-sentations, the therapist has no reliable way of determining whether these memories are accurate or inaccurate' (167). Here again is an example of how Loftus, who is consistently more concerned with the rights of accused fathers,[10] challenges therapeutic techniques designed to facilitate the translation of painful memories into words.

Words, as Linda Cutting explains, are essential to the recovery pro-cess. 'I need music. But I know I also need words,' she writes; 'Giving a voice to what was once unutterable has saved my life' (237). Why is this 'giving voice' so important? The answer is that without telling her own story, Cutting cannot assert her own reality, nor can her reality be affirmed, thereby restoring her shattered trust. But Loftus challenges even the therapeutic use of narrative because, she argues, 'In the process of creating our own stories, we run the very serious risk of mistaking imagined events for memories of actual experiences. We end up believing in the stories we tell' (158). Yet Cutting's memoir illustrates a survivor's need not only to tell her story, but at least initially to tell it in a safe place. Cutting sought therapy in order to be heard by an ethical and affirming listener; unfortunately, she initially found skepticism and even exploitation. One therapist asked, after Cutting had described her father's continuing habit of French-kissing her, 'Was that memory or fantasy?' (146). Cutting, suicidal at the time, never returned to this therapist.

Another therapist, a man old enough to be her father, sexually exploited her. In her vulnerable state, Cutting says, she gave this man almost everything – except her voice, which he had asked to audiotape. 'It was the only thing I could not give him,' she says; 'I gave him tapes of my playing, I gave him access to my body and soul, but I would not give him my voice. If I had given him that, he would have had all of me. I kept one part of myself that would enable me to go on without him' (117). Needless to say, when a therapist enacts his own incestuous desires with the victim, she is neither heard nor healed; instead, she is traumatized again. The father's desire is the blind spot in Freudian theory and practice, according to feminist psychologist Ellyn Kaschak. This blindness is well illustrated in the behaviour of Cutting's psychiatrist, a father-surrogate who tells his patient that he is in love with her. While engaged in an affair with this therapist, Cutting learned, to her dismay, that he had a daughter about the same age to whom he had sent the very same romantic poetry. The failure of Cutting's therapist to analyze his own incestuous desires made it impossible for him to provide the kind of affirmative listening that Cutting requires. Understandably, Cutting did not want incestuous fatherly love from her therapist; instead, she had hoped, based on her experience with at least one of her two brothers, for a form of 'brotherly' love. 'I wanted him to love me in the same way my brother had,' says Cutting, 'but not leave' (as her brother did, when he committed suicide) (110).

Anticipating judgmental readers – those who will argue that she was free, as an adult, to say no – she speculates about how much responsibility she shares for engaging in the affair: 'I've often wondered,' she writes, 'what I did to bring that on' (111). Cutting herself does not answer this question, but the answer seems obvious: once Cutting had disclosed to her therapist that, even as an adult, she felt helpless when her father continued to French-kiss her, the therapist knew how vulnerable she was to a father-figure's advances. He is, therefore, culpable. By contrast, because she has been taught that her body belongs to the father, she does not know how to resist her therapist when he violates the ethics of therapeutic practice. She has been taught, as most women have been taught, to accept 'father rule.' I shall return to this issue – the problem of the daughter's complicity – in my analysis of Kathryn Harrison's memoir *The Kiss*, which recounts the incestuous affair her father initiated when she was twenty. At this point, I want to emphasize that when Cutting sought therapy she was a vulnerable adult: she needed a mature and ethical therapist, someone who would affirm her suffering rather than exploit her need for nurture. As Shoshana Felman and Dori Laub assert in *Testimony*, all trauma victims need respondents who are willing 'to bear witness'; if this willingness is absent, the possibility for healing is seriously diminished. In fact, its absence may actually endanger the victim's life. Cutting's response to her exploitive therapist makes this point: after this therapist's repetition of her childhood trauma, she attempted suicide. Fortunately, she survived

Some time later, when her suicidal impulses were intensified by the suicide of a second brother, she found a therapist capable of bearing witness. Cutting dramatizes the moment that she began to trust her therapist: when that therapist took an affirmative stance.[11] When first asked, 'You were remembering your mother's response to catching you in her bed with your father. Is that what made you want to hurt yourself?' (98), Cutting remains silent. Her trust begins after her doctor asks, 'Don't you think it's nuts to watch your husband beat and molest a child? Then tell her she has demons and that's why she feels so bad?' (99). For years Cutting had kept disturbing thoughts out of her piano playing by writing in a private journal; however, this strategy did not, finally, prevent her from attempting suicide. Nevertheless, when her therapist asks permission to write something in her journal, Cutting almost refuses because it has been her only means of defending herself against her 'mother's voice inside which says, "This didn't happen. You just imagined it"' (100). After Cutting grants permission, the doctor opens the journal to its last blank page:

[She] draws a line down the center of the page, then another across the middle. In the top left-hand box she writes, 'Fantasy – nothing happened,' and in the box underneath, 'Bad Pain – price you pay.' In the top right-hand box she writes, 'Reality – yes it did,' and in the box underneath, 'Good Pain – feelings about any real thing that happened. 'We're going to be filling in these boxes,' she says. 'Suicidal feelings go on the left under "It didn't happen." Crying goes on the right under "Yes, it did."' (100–1)

Because Cutting decides to trust her therapist, she gives up the journal that had kept her alive – her defense against her mother's denial of the abuse – but that now threatens her with isolation and, ultimately, sui-cide. This trust, earned by a therapist willing to believe and affirm her, begins the healing process.[12]

Tragically, however, therapists are now being criticized, even sued, for just such a therapeutic technique. Why? According to Loftus, 'The techniques of journal writing strike many cognitive psychologists as potentially "risky," particularly when therapists suggest that their pa-tients strive for a noncritical, stream-of-consciousness flow, writing down whatever comes to mind without stopping to evaluate the con-tent. The possibility that this technique will lead nonabused people to create false memories and beliefs is compounded when journal writing is accompanied by other therapeutic techniques and/or the therapist's expressed beliefs about memory recovery' (161). Loftus has no clinical experience – she is a research psychologist at the University of Wash-ington, not a clinician – yet she attacks the work of experienced therapists. In my view, this is an irresponsible use of her research. Yet based upon Loftus's argument, feminist literary critic Elaine Showalter takes the position in *Hystories* that therapeutically recovered memo-ries cannot be trusted. Despite the fact that Loftus's conclusions have been challenged by research psychologists such as Jennifer Freyd and psychiatrists such as Herman, Showalter states, 'I have come to doubt the validity of therapeutically recovered memories of sexual abuse' (147). While Showalter's scepticism may be understandable, one might ask why she shows no scepticism towards Loftus's research findings, but is sceptical of stories told by a female survivor of childhood sexual abuse.[13]

Despite such a lack of affirmation of the daughter's incest story, sympathetic readers might conclude that Cutting's recovery is com-plete. Indeed, the book jacket of *Memory Slips* informs readers that the author currently teaches at the Longy School of Music in Cambridge and has recently returned to the concert stage. This impression is also conveyed by Cutting's subtitle, 'a memoir of music and healing.' But it must be remembered that, according to Herman, recovery is not fully complete until a survivor decides what action to take against the injustice she has suffered. It is for this reason, to take action against injustice, that Cutting's memoir exposes the actions of ineffective or unethical therapists, as well as the church's failure to take action against her father. According to Cutting, upon hearing her story, Michael Robertson, director of pastoral relations at the National Association of Congregational Churches, says, 'I can appreciate the turmoil ... But at this point, what you are saying is nothing but hearsay' (151). When Cutting explains that her father, who once had five children, has lost two to suicide; that he has sexually abused two of the surviving children, daughters of different marriages; and that she can prove her father lied about how her brothers died and that she herself is now in a hospital 'trying to find a safe way to live with what I know happened' (151), Robertson replies, 'If information that's germane to a minister's ability to function is left off a dossier we would certainly pass that along, but we need proper documentation' (152). Based on past experience, Robertson explains that even if a victim does produce 'verifiable' evidence, 'the church will be reluctant to believe your story' (152).

In other words, church fathers – some of whom abuse their children – discredit the stories of sexually abused daughters.[14] Thus, what Cutting learns, as many incested daughters have learned, is that because the father has far greater authority, his story is likely to be believed while hers will be challenged – even in the face of legally valid evidence.[15] During the past decade, it has also become increasingly difficult to persuade juries of a perpetrator's guilt, even when there is material evidence, often because child abusers have found psychologists such as Elizabeth Loftus who, as expert witnesses in court, are willing to attack the credibility of survivors who claim to have recovered (repressed) memories of their trauma during therapy. According to Loftus and other members of the False Memory Syndrome Foundation, repressed memory is a myth. In *The Myth of Repressed Memory* Loftus and her co-author Katherine Ketcham[16] criticize a range of therapeutic techniques because they may lead to the creation of what she calls 'fictional' memory. Although distinctions must be made between legal and therapeutic 'truth,' legal criteria have permeated the therapist's office as well as public reception of memoirs such as *Memory Slips*. As Leigh Gilmore observes, in the 1990s readers are more likely to take a 'juridical' stance towards such memoirs. Perhaps because the task of seeking legal redress is daunting – it is an expensive, exhausting, time-consuming process likely to lead to defeat – Cutting chose to stir public sympathy more directly: through her memoir.

To some degree Cutting succeeded; most reviews of *Memory Slips* were sympathetic.[17] Nevertheless, her memoir was certainly not a bestseller; furthermore, regardless of how much sympathy Cutting produced in readers, they are not likely to have much influence on professionals, such as research psychologists and judges, who have become increasingly skeptical of stories of child sexual abuse. In addition, there is growing evidence that reviewers are tiring of trauma narratives in general and incest narratives in particular. In 'Making the Incest Scene,' Katie Roiphie is openly hostile and disparaging towards such narratives, accusing women writers of using clichés to cash in on the public's fascination with incest, and in the *New York Times Book Review* W.S. Di Piero complains: 'I'm surely not alone in wishing there were fewer memoirists aching for our witness to their traumatic illnesses (depression, AIDS), addictions (sex, booze) or pathologies (incest, abuse) or what Freud called the family romance. A sour whiff of suffering as privilege rises from their pages, and I feel as though I'm expected to envy or even covet such privilege' (4). He describes these narratives as 'aching for our witness to ... traumatic illnesses,' but counters by asserting that such memoirs are usually aesthetically inferior. 'I want a style,' he says, 'that plays out the actual engagement of a mind encountering the contents of its experience and that does so without panting for our attention' (4).

This artistic requirement makes a heavy demand on the memoirist because it is difficult to achieve such 'modernistic' artistry while, at the same time, persuading readers of a memoir's 'realism' or validity. Once again the survivor who wishes to write a publishable narrative faces a complex linguistic challenge. Even though realism may be more credible to most readers, as Janet Walker explains, a modernistic style – the engagement of a mind encountering the contents of its experience – is actually more effective for survivor stories because realism is a mode that cannot successfully convey 'qualities of memory including repression, silence, ellipsis, elaboration and fantasy' (814). Because common responses to trauma include both fantasy and exaggeration – fantasy may provide a screen memory of the actual violation, while exaggeration may convey the emotional impact of violation – Walker argues that the techniques of modernism are more effective because they 'figure the traumatic past as meaningful yet as fragmentary, virtually unspeakable, and striated with fantasy constructions' (809). Modernism more accurately represents trauma, Walker asserts, because it allows for the creation of a 'fragmented structure that acknowledges the gaps of and resistances to history and memory' (817). Although Cutting's memoir is an artistic success – it reconstructs incidents of sexual violation in the fragmentary and elliptical manner of modernism – this style might also have led to charges of dishonesty.

Rhetorical Strategies and Reception: Kathryn Harrison's *The Kiss*

When the woman writer is a better known writer, as I shall illustrate, she may be accused of dishonesty simply *because* her memoir is, presumably, too artistic to be credible. For example, in his review of *The Kiss*, Christopher Lehmann-Haupt asked 'whether a memoir can ring too artistic for truth' and concluded that 'the mystery of her survival is a flaw in the memoir' (C18). James Wolcott's attack on Harrison's credibility is even more blatant: he points out that some scenes in *The Kiss* were taken from Harrison's previously published novels; therefore, by implication, her memoir is a 'fiction.' Nevertheless, the *New Republic* was so confident that readers would welcome Wolcott's mean-spirited review that in the July 1997 issue they tried to attract new readers with the question: 'Who else would have ... Dr. James Wolcott demolish Kathryn Harrison?'[18] The strength of the backlash against women's incest narratives is also evident in reviewers who state their desire for silence on the topic. For example, Cynthia Crossen offers 'two wise but widely ignored words of advice for Ms. Harrison *and her brethren*: Hush up' (16; emphasis added). By using the phrase, 'Ms. Harrison and her brethren,' Crossen makes Harrison representative of women who write incest narratives, an attack that made the latter a lightning rod for debates about the 'age of memoir.'

Part of Harrison's problem is that she is better known than Cutting – and thus a more visible target – but an even greater problem is that her incestuous relationship with her father began when she was an adult. While Cutting writes more from the position of a victim, Harrison writes as an agent: although younger and less powerful than her father, she is nevertheless an accomplice in their incestuous affair. Like her father, Harrison engages in the affair out of a desire for revenge against her mother. The father sought revenge against a woman who had divorced him six months after their daughter's birth, persuaded by her parents that he could not make enough money to support her. Harrison's desire for revenge was prompted by feelings of abandonment when her mother moved out, leaving her six-year-old daughter in the care of grandparents. For years a fear of abandonment fuelled Harrison's attempts to win her mother's love by at least appearing to submit to her demands. As Harrison plays obedient daughter – in contrast to her mother, getting good grades and avoiding boys – the unstated hostilities between mother and daughter escalate. One of the most disturbing examples of this conflict occurs when Harrison's mother takes her to a gynecologist before she goes away to college. Out of a desire to prevent her daughter from making the mistakes she had, she orders the doctor to provide her with a diaphragm. The doctor explains that, in order to do so, he must break the girl's hymen, but her mother insists. Using 'a series of graduated green plastic penises' (42), writes Harrison, 'The doctor deflowers me in front of my mother' (43).

Harrison does not, however, use this traumatic event to cast herself as a victim. Instead, she identifies her family romance – the mother-daughter-father triangle – as a variation on well-known fairy tales and myths. As Gilmore argues, 'The memoir's refusal of a conventional rhetoric of blame, judgment, and expiation blinded many readers to its allusive representation of incest and its evocation of mythic precursors, especially figures of Oedipus and Antigone and the doomed familial relations in which damage, debt, and agency develop' (711). The father's kiss does not awaken the daughter; instead, she becomes a 'sleeping beauty': following his French kiss, Harrison consents to a four-year incestuous 'romance' that her father calls 'God's will.' 'God gave you to me' (108), says Harrison's minister-father. 'Her father's kiss bewitches Harrison,' as Gilmore emphasizes, 'and the spell is finally broken only when she embraces her mother's dead body at the end of the memoir and saves herself by kissing the beloved's cold lips' (711). In contrast to Cutting's mother, who denies her husband's incestuous acts, Harrison's mother understands that her ex-husband is trying to injure her: '"You know," she says, pointing, "this isn't about *you*. It's about *me*"' (98).

Years later, Harrison acknowledges that she and her father were united in their effort to spite the elusive woman who failed to love them. This motivation explains why, according to Harrison, the affair ends abruptly after her mother dies. Harrison finds proof that her mother's analysis was right when she discovers, while reading her father's love letters to her mother, that 'I'll have read letters just like them: letters addressed to me' (100). Although Cutting remains blind to her own motives for entering into an affair with her therapist, a father-surrogate, Harrison – with the belated insight of an Oedipus – finally 'sees' and assumes responsibility for her actions. Of course, because Cutting was sexually abused from an early age, she did not understand that she had a right to bodily integrity; by contrast, Harrison states explicitly that she did not engage in sex – and was not 'deflowered' by a gynecologist – until she became an adult. In short, the bodies of both daughters are violated and their trust is betrayed; however, Cutting's abuse was more severe because it began so early and lasted so long. For these reasons, readers are likely to perceive the daughter in *The Kiss*, in contrast to *Memory Slips*, as more of an agent than a victim. Harrison is also more agent than victim because, as a daughter-writer, she confronts The Father on his linguistic turf, challenging his sacred (biblical) and secular (romance) scriptures. She directly challenges her father's claim that 'God gave you to me' (108), and she writes an anti-romance in which Beauty is not awakened by a kiss, but put to sleep with a kiss.

Harrison tells her story with audacity, evoking 'mythic precursors,' such as the Greek tragedy of Oedipus, who blinds himself when he recognizes his incestuous marriage with his mother, with scenes emphasizing sight and insight. For example, in a sparely written but evocative scene, the eleven-year-old Harrison opens the sealed eyes of five newborn kittens because, she explains, 'I couldn't bear to see their always sleeping faces' (90). She plays the part of the abuser when, taking up the first kitten, she 'carefully pulled its eyes open, separating one delicate membrane of flesh from the other. My heart was pounding and I was sweating with fear, but I accomplished the violation gently' (90). She pulls open the eyes of all five kittens but later denies that she had done anything. This scene complicates issues of guilt and innocence. Harrison is a child, but she is not 'innocent': she wants to see and know. However, readers are likely to recall that, earlier in the memoir, Harrison had described the anxiety she experienced as a child while watching her sleeping mother. She wants her mother to open her eyes in order to truly see her and love her, but, as evident in the scene in the gynecologist's office, Harrison's narcissistic mother rarely sees her daughter's needs or feelings. By contrast, once Harrison becomes an adult, her father's eyes devour her while, narcissistically, he denies her a father's generous and protective love. Thus, Harrison's self-portrait is complex: yes, she is victimized by selfish, self-serving parents; on the other hand, even as a child she is capable of injuring newly born kittens.

I shall return to the question of innocence or guilt, but first it is necessary to point out that critics who attack Harrison's use of fictional devices, such as allusions to myths and fairy tales, either fail to recognize her reversal of the conventional romance or, for ideological reasons, try to undercut her credibility by accusing her of writing fiction. For example, Laura Frost remarks that although 'none of these accusations that Harrison is lying about the affair has been convincing' (52), she holds Harrison herself responsible for the harsh attacks on her memoir, arguing that 'in moving from fiction to memoir, Harrison was also moving into a revelatory, confessional mode: a mode that ultimately exhausted her audience's sympathy' (55). In short, the value of Harrison's memoir is limited[19] because she fails to write as a penitent, according to the conventions of a confessional genre. According to Frost, 'The history of *The Kiss* ... shows how readily pleasure is contingent upon an assurance of proper genre conventions' (52), and the lack of reader pleasure is, thus, the result of Harrison's impropriety. Wolcott goes even farther, attacking Harrison's use of fictional devices to destroy her credibility. He writes, 'As Michael Shanyerson damagingly documented, some of the big set pieces in *The Kiss* (an incident involving kittens, the gynecological deflowering) are reprised from Harrison's first novel, *Thicker Than Water*' (35). Harrison also 'lifts' scenes from her second novel, *Exposure*, not in order to reveal the facts behind the fiction, argues Wolcott, but to 'cash in on her catharsis' (35).

Details from Harrison's autobiographical novels do, in fact, surface in her memoir; however, while Wolcott would allow a man this option (he names Philip Roth), he condemns Harrison for the same practice. In short, the misogyny in this review is blatant. Wolcott seeks to damage Harrison's reputation not only as a writer, but as a woman and a mother. He describes *The Kiss* as 'incest with a twist, trash with a capital "T"' (32), suggests that Harrison is selling her flesh by posing in 'fishnet stockings and a tacky dress slit thigh-high' (32), and mocks her writing, which, he says, goes 'from melodrama about hypnotic burning eyes to women's-magazine pap about "society's normative messages," from overblown omens ... to cardboard dialogue' (34). As Wolcott acknowledges, Harrison's agent 'advised Harrison to put aside the family saga novel that she was writing and tackle this obstruction as nonfiction' (35), but Wolcott asserts – despite growing evidence that disclosure can be therapeutic – that some secrets are better kept. It is, in his view, vulgar to write about such private things, and even more vulgar to make money, especially when the writer 'risk[s] injuring those most intimately involved' (35). Whether Wolcott is referring to Harrison's father or her children, one thing is clear: he wants Harrison and her ilk to keep quiet about incest. 'What was once quite possible to accomplish [women writing incest] has become impossible to stop' (32), he remarks.

As Lisa Alther points out in the *Women's Review of Books*, Harrison's story obviously created greater discomfort for most male critics than for most female critics. The struggle over Harrison's supposedly 'scandalous' memoir is clearly gendered; nevertheless, according to Gilmore, 'Gender is frequently an absent or submerged element in theories of memory and trauma' (701). Male critics faulted Harrison for a wide range of reasons: for selling her memoir and making money, for taking revenge on her parents, for injuring her children, and even for being beautiful. For example, after explaining that reviewers described *The Kiss* as 'calculating and mercenary,' a way of 'merchandis[ing] her pain,' and 'a calculated act of revenge' (151–152), John Paul Eakin asks: 'What exactly ... were the Harrisons and their burden of incest doing in the glossy world of fashion and luxury presided over by *Vogue*'s editor?' (153). Eakin implies that by making a private matter public, Harrison has failed to consider the consequences of her memoir on her children's lives. Therapists argue that keeping such secrets is damaging to families; however, Eakin implies that Harrison should sacrifice her own mental health, protecting her children by keeping her secret rather than writing about it. Another male reviewer, faulting Harrison for being too beautiful, quotes a remark by Paul Bogaards, direction of promotion at Knopf: 'If an unattractive woman were to write a book about sleeping with her father, it would not command the same media real estate as an attractive woman sleeping with her father' (Pogrebin 2).

What is not acknowledged by these reviewers is their own discomfort with the incestuous relationship Harrison describes in *The Kiss*. It is a father-daughter 'romance' similar to 'secret' but later highly publicized liaisons between such couples as Senator Ted Kennedy and Mary Jo Kopechne (Chappaquiddick),[20] President Bill Clinton and Monica Lewinsky, or, more recently, Chandra Levy and congressman Gary Condit.[21] These Washington affairs effectively illustrate Phyllis Chesler's observation that 'women are encouraged to commit incest as a way of life ... As opposed to marrying our fathers, we marry men like our fathers ... men who are older than us, have more money than us, more power than us, are taller than us' (quoted in Herman, *Father-Daughter Incest*, 57–58). As Chesler argues, father-daughter incest functions as a paradigm for this imbalance of power in heterosexual relationships; indeed, such May–December romances are not only commonplace but widely accepted. Relationships between older women and young men, especially men young enough to be their sons, are far less common and also far less acceptable. Given such imbalances of power, it is not surprising, as Herman remarks, and as is evident in both *Memory Slips* and *The Kiss*, that 'if the father chooses to eroticize the relationship with his daughter, he will encounter little or no resistance' (57). This is the open secret that Harrison exposes in *The Kiss*.

A similar gender imbalance exists in terms of society's expectations of innocence. Demands for the female victim's purity have escalated despite the fact that the law is far from 'pure' and public opinion often far from just, as Gilmore points out: 'Those who seek to represent trauma often say they feel compromised by or implicated in the degradation of the experience; few feel confident that anything like purity or innocence will emerge through trauma's representation and reception' (698). Even Cutting, victimized at age three, does not claim complete innocence, as evident in her disclosure of an adult affair with a therapist. While Cutting's motivations and experiences differ from Harrison's, as daughters they shared one powerful need: the need to be loved by a supportive and nurturing father, a father who would not leave them. Both women also needed fathers mature and healthy enough not to sexualize their feelings for their daughters or, at least, healthy enough not act on such feelings. Reviewers who portray Harrison as a 'sluttish' woman who wears fishnet stockings to sell her book, a woman who betrays her children to create a publishing sensation, are insecure: they are shoring up male authority by attacking a woman's character, credibility, and writing ability. In the 1990s it is, apparently, once again acceptable to blame the daughter in order to protect the Father.

As Herman says, 'It is very tempting to take the side of the perpetrator [because] all the perpetrator asks is that the bystander do nothing ... The victim, on the contrary, asks the bystander to share the burden of pain. The victim demands action, engagement, and remembering' (7). If such remembering, engagement, and action do not occur, can it be claimed that autobiographical writing has the power to heal? While the act of writing may have some healing effects, as DeSalvo, Henke, and others claim, it was the support of the feminist community that enabled me to tell my story and begin the healing process. The feminist community supported my writing and healing both by affirming the credibility of women's stories of childhood sexual abuse, and by providing me with the collective authority to write about it. Women such as Linda Katherine Cutting and Kathryn Harrison, along with unknown women such as those who published their stories in *Voices in the Night*, engage in writing not only to heal themselves, but to speak out against the continuing injustices against women and children. It is remarkable, in my view, that some of these stories are so beautifully written, but neither the aesthetic nor the therapeutic value of such narratives should be allowed to suppress their political value. As Louise Armstrong points out, the current emphasis on therapy and healing may actually divert attention from what is at stake, politically, when children tell stories – or when, as adults, they write and publish stories – that reveal what incestuous fathers prefer to conceal.

As Janet Walker reminds us, 'To the extent that they are remembered and believed, women's and men's claims of childhood incest and abuse have the ability to threaten male dominance and the subordination of women and children' (822). In short, those who attack the credibility of women's incest narratives, or those who attack their aesthetic value, may be disguising their own unacknowledged resistance to a loss of male dominance. Roland Summit explains:

> It is all of society, not just those immediately affected, that protects the secret of child sexual abuse. We have overlooked or outrageously trivialized this subject, not because it is peripheral to major social interests, but because it is so central that we have not yet dared to conceptualize its scope. (quoted in Freyd 32)

Freud discovered a century ago just how central child sexual abuse is to major social interests when he encountered resistance from his scientific colleagues. As a result of this resistance, Freud repudiated his theory that the sexual abuse of children leads to hysteria, asserting instead that 'hysterics lie.' The women's movement has challenged this Freudian view, insisting on the authority of women to tell their stories of sexual violation and on their right to be considered credible.

It may seem naive to affirm the authority and credibility of women's memoirs of father-daughter incest, especially in an era of intense debate over the reliability of memory as well as concern over how to effectively represent and respond to memory gaps in trauma memoirs; however, it should not be automatically assumed that all 'hysterics lie,' nor should it be assumed that all recovered memories are false. It is important to keep in mind, when reviewers and critics attack women who write trauma narratives, especially those disclosing father-daughter incest, that reviews or critical essays are sites of ideological struggle about control of, and representation of, women's bodies. As Gilmore argues, 'Gender animates scandal, in part, because critical and popular notions of truth telling are gendered' (701). During the continuing backlash against women's incest narratives, it is also important for readers to keep in mind the importance of social context for trauma survivors:

> To hold traumatic reality in consciousness requires a social context that affirms and protects the victim and that joins victim and witness in a common alliance. For the individual victim, this social context is created by relationships with friends, lovers, and family. For the larger society, the social context is created by political movements that give voice to the disempowered. (9)

In conclusion, I want to reiterate the argument that autobiographical writing can lead to partial healing at best, and then only when a survivor is supported, as I was, by the collective power of women who affirm the survivor's reality as well as her right to resist the tyranny of father rule. Because women such as Linda Katherine Cutting and Kathryn Harrison, along with many others, have been betrayed not only by their biological fathers but also by institutional fathers – religious, academic, psychiatric, and legal – complete recovery is not possible without the kind of social change advocated by feminists. That is what Rosaria Champagne means when she says, 'There is no such thing as healing the self in a sick society' (210).

Notes

1 In *Writing as a Way of Healing*, Louise DeSalvo lists many writers, including the following, who have claimed that writing is therapeutic: Alice Walker, James Baldwin, Virginia Woolf, Elizabeth Bishop, Anais Nin, Alice James, Charlotte Perkins Gilman, Henry Miller, D.H. Lawrence, Djuna Barnes, Toni Morrison, Isabel Allende, Dorothy Allison, Kenzaburo Oe, and Henry Miller. In *Shattered Subjects*, Suzette Henke argues that writing was therapeutic for Colette, H.D., Anais Nin, Janet Frame, Audre Lorde, and Sylvia Fraser. I would add Joyce Carol Oates to this list; see her 'Art: Therapy and Magic.' Writing can also be healing for students, according to DeSalvo.

2 As Karl Kroeber emphasizes, a written text, like an oral performance, is

'*by* someone, *to* someone, and *about* something' (41–2). Narrative is a social act, as psychologist Jerome Bruner also emphasizes; hence, without a listener or reader there is no story.

3 I agree with Armstrong's critique of therapy, however, even *Voices in the Night* (McNaron and Yarrow Morgan) includes a tribute to supportive therapists; moreover, since the 1960s, feminists have lobbied for changes in the therapeutic profession. Armstrong implies that reliance on therapists infantilizes women. In my view, some therapists may be guilty of this, but feminist therapists, like the one described by Linda Katherine Cutting, support a woman's effort to become healthy and self-reliant.

4 Those who wish to teach father-daughter incest narratives now have a great range of options, including Joyce Carol Oates's *them* (1969), Toni Morrison's *The Bluest Eye* (1970), Alice Walker's *The Color Purple* (1982), Jane Smiley's *A Thousand Acres* (1991), Dorothy Allison's *Bastard Out of Carolina* (1992), Margaret Atwood's *The Robber Bride* (1993), Marilyn French's *Our Father* (1994), Sapphire's *Push* (1996), and Sally Patterson Tubach's *Memoirs of a Terrorist* (1996). A collection edited by Karen Jacobsen Mclennan, *Nature's Ban: Women's Incest Literature* (Northeastern University Press), appeared in 1996.

5 Suzette Henke opens *Shattered Subjects: Trauma and Testimony in Women's Life Writing* with the assumption that the act of authorship mimics the therapeutic process. She asks, 'If one accepts the basic premise of Freud's talking cure – a psychoanalytic working-through of repressed memories brought to the surface and abreacted through the use of language and free association – then an intriguing question arises concerning the role of the analyst. Is he or she truly necessary?' (xi). She answers by claiming that writing alone can heal. Miranda Sherwin questions Henke's argument with emphasis on the role of the reader: 'If scriptotherapy is a mimetic enactment of the therapy process, then the audience/readers stands in for the therapist' (141). For this reason, unpublished diaries may not be as therapeutic since a reader other than oneself may never bear witness to the victim's suffering. In contrast to Henke, Louise DeSalvo warns in *Writing as a Way of Healing* that the act of writing cannot always take the place of therapy. Although DeSalvo agrees with James W. Pennebaker's claim that writing sometimes produces as much therapeutic benefit as sessions with a psychotherapist, she adds, 'I personally believe it is essential for people wanting to write about extreme situations to have skilled professional support while writing or to attend a reputable support group' (40).

6 In her introduction to *Trauma: Explorations in Memory*, Caruth explains that 'the precise definition of post-traumatic stress disorder is contested, but

most descriptions generally agree that there is a response, sometimes delayed, to an overwhelming event or events, which takes the form of repeated, intrusive hallucinations, dreams, thoughts or behaviors stemming from the event[s], along with numbing that may have begun during or after the experience[s], and possibly also increased arousal to (and avoidance of) stimuli recalling the event[s]' (4). Trauma is not defined by the event(s), which may or may not have been 'catastrophic,' because what traumatizes one person may not traumatize another; nor can trauma be defined as a 'distortion' because the event 'is not assimilated or experienced fully at the time, but only belatedly, in its repeated *possession* of the one who experiences it' (4; italics in original).

7 Probably because Kathryn Harrison was a better-known novelist, one reporter sought out her father to find out if his story would verify or discredit the story told in *The Kiss*. According to Warren St. John, the results were inconclusive, since Harrison's father neither confirmed nor denied his daughter's story.

8 For a fuller discussion of a range of theoretical approaches to this problem of identity of the 'self' or 'subject,' see Suzette Henke's introduction to *Shattered Subjects*. In *Shattered Selves*, James Glass, a political philosopher, argues – as a result of his study of women suffering from multiple personality disorder, all of whom are victims of paternal sexual abuse – that it is irresponsible for poststructuralists to base their arguments of fragmented identity on textual examples only. I agree with Glass but disagree that a return to the concept of a 'core' self is the only alternative. Since the concept of a 'core' self retains its associations with a normative 'masculine' subject, I prefer Julia Kristeva's notion of a 'subject in process.'

9 Bessel A. Van Der Kolk argues that, as Piaget points out, 'When memories cannot be integrated on a semantic/linguistic level, they tend to be organized more primitively as visual images or somatic sensations' (255).

10 For example, in *The Myth of Repressed Memory*, which is sold as a scientific book, Loftus and co-author Katherine Ketcham do not take a neutral stance; rather, they defend presumably 'innocent' fathers from their presumably 'lying' daughters throughout the book, but most explicitly in chapters 8 through 12.

11 While Herman emphasizes the need for an affirmative stance, psychologists Robert I. Simon and Thomas G. Gutheil call for therapist neutrality. See chapter 12 in Applebaum, Uyehara, and Elin, pp. 477–95.

12 What Suzette Henke fails to understand is that not only has the victim's bodily and psychological integrity been shattered, but also her trust in others. To restore such trust, an affirmative audience is necessary. Yet in a

court of law, this therapist's affirmation of her patient would lead Loftus and her cohort to the charge that the therapist had 'implanted memories' in her patient rather than assisting her in recovering them. Such 'expert' testimony by members of the False Memory Syndrome Foundation certainly undermines victims' efforts towards social justice.

13 Additional criticism of Showalter's position can be found in Haaken and Horvitz.

14 I am well aware that boys are also abused – as is evident in the current scandal over the sexual abuse of children by Catholic priests, which was for many years kept secret by church authorities – but my focus here is upon daughters.

15 According to Rosaria Champagne, quoting Irene Wielawski, 'Even "evidence" does not validate the survivor: "Physical evidence does not prove truth, merely that the memory has elements of reality"' (221 n. 10). Physical evidence is similarly devalued and dismissed in U.S. courts, according to Louise Armstrong.

16 I refer only to Loftus, rather than to Loftus and Ketcham, because Loftus alone gives campus lectures and television interviews. For example, Loftus was unaccompanied by her co-author when she gave a lecture called 'Crimes of Memory' at Iowa State University in Ames (15 October 1996), and Loftus appeared alone on the television show *48 Hours* (27 July 1998) to defend the views expressed in *The Myth of Repressed Memory*.

17 Brief but mostly sympathetic reviews of *Memory Slips* appeared in the *Kirkus Review* 64 (5 November 1996), 1648; *Booklist* 93 (5 December 1996), 703; *Library Journal* 122 (January 1997), 125; *New York Times Book Review* (9 February 1997), 18; and *New Yorker* 72 (6 January 1997), 73.

18 Since in 1982 Wolcott had published an equally mean-spirited, misogynist review of a feminist novel by Joyce Carol Oates, editors of the *New Republic* were well aware that they had chosen a man who would 'demolish' Kathryn Harrison. See, for example, Wolcott's 'Stop Me Before I Write Again,' a review of *A Bloodsmoor Romance*, *Harper's*, September 1982, 67–79.

19 Other survivors of father-daughter incest, such as Sylvia Fraser and Linda Katherine Cutting, have first told their stories under the disguise of fiction before writing memoirs, but they have not for this reason been accused of lying. The fact that Fraser and Cutting are not as well known as Harrison, and not as powerful, is surely a factor in how reviewers responded to *The Kiss*, as is the fact that Harrison was twenty when her father initiated the incestuous relationship.

20 In Joyce Carol Oates's novella *Blackwater* (New York: E.P. Dutton, 1992), based on events at Chappaquiddick, the erotic attraction between Kelly

Kelleher (Mary Jo Kopechne) and the Senator (Ted Kennedy) is portrayed as a variation on father-daughter incest.

21 Chandra Levy was reported missing in April 2001 and later reported dead. On its cover of 23 July, *Newsweek* reported 'The Frenzy over Chandra Levy' and featured a pin-up photo of Levy. Two smaller-print subheads promised more: an 'Exclusive' on 'Gary Condit: His Secret Life' and 'The Parents vs. the Congressman: Inside the Investigation.'

Works Cited

Allison, Dorothy. 'Deciding to Live.' Preface to *Trash*. Ithaca, NY: Firebrand Books, 1988.

Alther, Lisa. 'Blaming the Victim' (Review of Kathryn Harrison's *The Kiss*). *Women's Review of Books* 14.10/11 (July 1997): 33–4.

Applebaum, Paul S., Lisa A. Uyehara, and Mark R. Elin., eds. *Trauma and Memory: Clinical and Legal Controversies*. New York: Oxford University Press, 1997.

Armstrong, Louise. *Rocking the Cradle of Sexual Politics: What Happened when Women Said Incest*. Reading, MA: Addison-Wesley, 1994.

Brison, Susan J. 'Outliving Oneself: Trauma, Memory, and Personal Identity.' In *Feminists Rethink the Self*, ed. Diana Tietjens Meyers, 12–39. Boulder, CO: Westview, 1997.

Bruner, Jerome. *Acts of Meaning*. Cambridge: Harvard University Press, 1990.

Caruth, Cathy. 'Introduction.' In *Trauma: Explorations in Memory*, ed. Cathy Caruth, 3–12. Baltimore: Johns Hopkins University Press, 1995.

Champagne, Rosaria. *The Politics of Survivorship: Incest, Women's Literature, and Feminist Theory*. New York: New York University Press, 1996.

Chesler, Phyllis. 'Rape and Psychotherapy.' In *Rape: The First Sourcebook for Women*, ed. Noreen Connell and Cassandra Wilson. New York: NAL, 1974.

Crossen, Cynthia. 'Know Thy Father.' *Wall Street Journal*, March 4, 1997, p. 16.

Culbertson, Roberta. 'Embodied Memory, Transcendence, and Telling: Recounting Trauma, Re-establishing the Self.' *New Literary History* 26 (1995): 169–95.

Cutting, Linda Katherine. *Memory Slips: A Memoir of Music and Healing*. New York: HarperCollins, 1997.

Daly, Brenda. *Authoring a Life: A Woman's Survival in and through Literary Studies*. Albany, NY: State University of New York Press, 1998.

DeSalvo, Louise. *Writing as a Way of Healing: How Telling Our Stories Transforms Our Lives*. Boston: Beacon, 1999.

Di Piero, W.S. 'In the Flea Market of the Mind' (Review of *The Factory of Facts* by Luc Sante). *New York Times Book Review*, 28 March 1998), p. 4.

Eakin, Paul John. *How Our Lives Become Stories: Making Selves*. Ithaca, NY: Cornell University Press, 1999.

Felman, Shoshana, and Dori Laub, M.D. *Testimony: Crises of Witnessing in Literature, Psychoanalysis, and History*. New York: Routledge, 1992.

Fraser, Sylvia. *My Father's House: A Memoir of Incest and Healing*. New York: Ticknor & Fields, 1988.

Freyd, Jennifer J. *Betrayal Trauma: The Logic of Forgetting Childhood Abuse*. Cambridge: Harvard University Press, 1996.

Froula, Christine. 'The Daughter's Seduction: Sexual Violence and Literary History.' In *Daughters and Fathers*, ed. Lynda E. Boose and Betty S. Flowers, 111–35. Baltimore, MD: Johns Hopkins University Press, 1989.

Frost, Laura. 'After Lot's Daughters: Kathryn Harrison and the Making of Memory.' *a/b: Auto/Biography Studies* 14.1 (1999): 51–70.

Gilmore, Leigh. 'Jurisdictions: *I, Rogoberta Menchu, The Kiss*, and Scandalous Self-Representation in the Age of Memoir and Trauma.' *Signs* 28.2 (2003): 695–718.

Glass, James M. *Shattered Selves: Multiple Personality in a Postmodern World*. Ithaca, NY: Cornell University Press, 1993.

Haaken, Janice. *Pillar of Salt: Gender, Memory, and the Perils of Looking Back*. New Brunswick, NJ: Rutgers University Press, 1998.

Harrison, Kathryn. *The Kiss*. New York: Random House, 1997.

Henke, Suzette A. *Shattered Subjects: Trauma and Testimony in Women's Life Writing*. New York: St Martin's Press, 1998.

Herman, Judith Lewis, with Lisa Hirschman. *Father-Daughter Incest*. Cambridge: Harvard UP, 1981.

––––––. *Trauma and Recovery*. New York: Basic Books, 1992.

Horvitz, Deborah M. *Literary Trauma: Sadism, Memory, and Sexual Violence in American Women's Fiction*. Albany, NY: State University of New York Press, 2000.

Kaschak, Ellyn. *Engendered Lives: A New Psychology of Women's Experience*. New York: Basic Books, 1992.

Kristeva, Julia. *Desire in Language: A Semiotic Approach to Literature and Art*, ed. Leon S. Roudiez, trans. Thomas Gora, Alice Jardine, and Leon S. Roudiez. New York: Columbia University Press, 1980.

Kroeber, Karl. *Retelling/Rereading: The Fate of Storytelling in Modern Times*. New Brunswick, NJ: Rutgers University Press, 1992.

Lanser, Susan Sniader. *Fictions of Authority: Women Writers and Narrative Voice*. Ithaca, NY: Cornell University Press, 1992.

Lehmann-Haupt, Christopher. 'Life with Father: Incestuous and Soul-Deadening.' *New York Times*, 27 February 1997, p. C18.

Loftus, Elizabeth, and Katherine Ketcham. *The Myth of Repressed Memory: False Memories and Allegations of Sexual Abuse*. New York: St Martin's Press, 1994.

McNaron, Toni A.H., and Yarrow Morgan, eds. *Voices in the Night: Women Speaking about Incest*: Pittsburgh: Cleis Press, 1982.

Miller, Alice. *Thou Shalt Not Be Aware: Society's Betrayal of the Child*. New York: Farrar, Straus and Giraux, 1984.

Oates, Joyce Carol. 'Art: Therapy and Magic.' *Americal Journal* (July 3, 1973): 17–21.

Pennebaker, James W. *Opening Up: The Healing Power of Confiding in Others*. New York: Morrow, 1990.

Pogrebin, Robin. 'The Naked Literary Come-On.' *New York Times*, 17 August, 1997, p. 2

Roiphe, Katie. 'Making the Incest Scene.' *Harper's Magazine*, November 1995, 65, 68–71.

Rothschild, Babette. *The Body Remembers: The Psychophysiology of Trauma and Trauma Treatment*. New York: W.W. Norton, 2000.

Rush, Florence. *The Best Kept Secret: Sexual Abuse of Children*. New York: McGraw-Hill, 1980.

Ryan, Marie-Laure. 'Postmodernism and the Doctrine of Panfictionality.' *Narrative* 5.2 (1997): 165–87.

Sherwin, Miranda. Review of *Shattered Subjects: Trauma and Testimony in Women's Life-Writing* by Suzette Henke. *a/b: Auto/Biography Studies* 14.1 (1999): 137–41.

Showalter, Elaine. *Hystories: Hysterical Epidemics and Modern Media*. New York: Columbia University Press, 1997.

Simon, Robert I., and Thomas G. Gutheil. 'Ethical and Clinical Risk Management Principles in Recovered Memory Cases: Maintaining Therapist Neutrality.' In *Trauma and Memory: Clinical and Legal Controversies*, ed. Paul S. Appelbaum, Lisa A. Uyehara, and Mark R. Elin, 477–95. New York: Oxford University Press, 1997.

St. John, Warren. 'Kathryn Harrison's Dad Responds to Her Memoir.' *New York Observer*, 21 April 1997, 1.

Van Der Kolk, Bessel A. 'Traumatic Memories.' In *Trauma and Memory: Clinical and Legal Controversies*, ed. Paul S. Appelbaum, Lisa A. Uyehara, and Mark R. Elin, 243–60. New York: Oxford University Press, 1997.

Walker, Janet. 'The Traumatic Paradox: Documentary Films, Historical Fictions, and Cataclysmic Past Events.' *Signs* 22.4 (1997): 803–25.

Wielawski, Irene. 'Unlocking the Secrets of Memory.' *Los Angeles Times*, October 3, 1991, 3.

Wolcott, James. 'Dating Your Dad.' *New Republic*, 31 March 1997, 32–6.

Chapter 7

The Epistemology of Police Science and the Silencing of Battered Women

CHRISTINE SHEARER-CREMEAN

In 1995, in a large city in Ohio, police officers wrote the following narratives about domestic abuse:

> Complainant stated above suspect broke the front wooden door in half after a brief argument. Complainant indicated that the suspect presently resides with her and proceeded to punch her numerous times in the face. Complainant did not suffer any visible injury. Complainant did not wish to press charges and was very uncooperative at the time of this report being taken. Suspect had fled the scene before police arrival.

> Myself and Crew 112 was dispatched to ——— on an assault complaint. On arrival, we found the suspect holding the complainant on the trunk of a car in the rear parking lot of ———. Suspect stated that the complainant accidentally got sprayed with mace, when it accidentally went off in the apartment. Complainant's face was red, apparently from mace. Suspect's friends and relatives were in the parking lot. They told me that she went into an asthma attack, after suspect had jumped on her and choked her. All the witnesses were in fear of retaliation from the suspect and would not sign witness statements. Complainant herself refused to tell us, at first, that suspect did anything. She later told us that the suspect did choke her.

> Dispatched to the location on a report of an assault. On arrival, I spoke with the complainant, who stated that she and the suspect along with her baby approximately four months old was shopping at the ——— Plaza, when the suspect became angry because the complainant wanted to con-

tinue to shop, including picking up milk for their child. The suspect told the complainant to get in the car and while driving on Hillcrest enroute to the complainant's apartment the suspect started punching her in the face with his fist, telling her 'that she was going to have to start listening to him.' The complainant stated that when they arrived at her apartment, the suspect told her to 'Get out of the car.' As she was exiting the vehicle, the contents of her purse spilled on the ground and as she was bent over, picking up the contents of her purse, the suspect began striking her with what she called a nigger stick across her back and arms, leaving bruises and welts, including a swollen upper lip from being punched in the face. The complainant described the stick as being long and like tree bark. The neighbors were outside the apartment building and witnessed the assault. The suspect fled prior to police arrival. Neighbors stated that the suspect was yelling and screaming and was extremely violent. The complainant denied treatment for her injuries and was ordered into the Prosecutor's Office.

As the narratives above demonstrate, victims, perpetrators, and witnesses, when situated within the discursive framework of the police report, are not *of the law* but *subjects to the law.* The police officer/ author's rhetorical stance as the objective observer, in addition to the uniform, badge, bearing, and distanced, official manner, mark the space between 'citizen' and 'the law.' It is through the security of binary parameters at the site of officer-citizen interaction that the legal process is launched, establishing the troublesome paradigm whereby the citizen is the subject/object of examination and assessment and the officer is the powerful observer and recorder. The citizen's ability to assert agency in this context is extraordinarily difficult; even when one has nothing to fear, even when one is actively seeking police intervention to obtain safety and care, one can still feel exposed, objectified, and intimidated. For survivors of woman abuse, the ability to obtain safety is based upon the credibility she can acquire through her body, through her demonstration of trauma. Regardless of her consent or belligerence, the rhetorical situation necessitates she be examined as the potentially abused object. In each of the narratives above, the complainant's narrative credibility is substantiated (or not) through her physical condition.

The officers who wrote the narratives above conducted their investigations and examinations according to a generic protocol mandated by the State of Ohio after the initiation of the 1994 Violence against Women

Act. Further, all three narratives were written by officers who attended the same police academy and received the same report-writing training. Consequently, the three paragraphs share the same pattern of development, voice, and rhetorical stance. Each text demonstrates how the police officer functions as the agent of institutional power, the transcendent witness, and the objective purveyor of the Truth. The officers' identities are blurry and absent, and the complainants', perpetrators', and witnesses' voices and identities are paraphrased, distilled into essentialized characterizations of 'complainant,' 'perpetrator,' and 'witness.' Perhaps most importantly, readers take the narrative as *fact*, as The Story of What Happened.

One wonders how one of these narratives might read if it was composed *by* and *for* the person who provided the information rather than by an intermediary who imposes an institutionally based vision. How might a transcript of the complainant's story look? What nuances or digressions might it exhibit? The problem with this suggestion, unfortunately, is that such a narrative, such a potentially 'messy' text, would not meet the requirements of the legal arena and those operating within it – the supervising officers, the prosecutors and defense attorneys, the judges and the social workers. The text is definitely not written for those directly involved in the incident, as they are not the audience.

This is the sort of issue feminist theorists can raise, particularly those engaged in discussions about the development of a feminist jurisprudence. On a large scale, we can ask: Who are police reports written for? What are the epistemological assumptions inherent in this type of written text? How do these police reports indicate the professional assumptions inherent in criminal justice? Pursuing more focused questions pertaining to 'domestic violence' police reports, we should consider questions like: Is the abused woman's story fully represented? Is the officer's representation of her the closest to the Truth? How is the woman's body read, in order to substantiate her claims? Admittedly, all these questions are problematic, and certainly I will not attempt to answer them all here, but these issues seem to require an analysis of the epistemological nature of police writing and the representation of abused women's bodies.

The debate over feminist jurisprudence has been lively, particularly in terms of what kind of feminist jurisprudence should and can be developed. Carol Smart's critique of the theoretical debates, particularly in terms of the conflict between essentialist or non-essentialist feminist legal theories, is clearly articulated in her book *Feminism and the Power of the Law*. Smart discusses just how problematic it is to develop any one model of feminist jurisprudence, in part because theorists debate how positive social change for women can best be obtained. For example, she writes that 'feminist work which challenges the epistemological neutrality of the legal system (especially if it does not have a blueprint for a feminist alternative) is necessarily less attractive to those who equate politics with institutional forms of change' (84). However, feminists working within the legal system are plagued by essentialist, positivist epistemological assumptions and depictions of women that do not always meet their needs.

In spite of what seems to be an irresolvable dilemma, there have been positive strides in the fields of law and criminal justice, albeit strides that work within the system rather than outside it. Although postmodern critiques of the law have existed for some time, such as in those offered by Catherine MacKinnon in *Toward A Feminist Theory of the State*, for example, criminal justice has maintained a distinctly empirical foundation despite the fact that it is epistemologically wedded to the discourse of law and should, by extension, benefit from any current theoretical discussions present there. Even though rhetorical and critical theory has challenged the belief that Truth can be represented through language, a discussion that seems rather dated today, and scholars like Catherine MacKinnon have applied such a perspective to the legal arena, the activity of writing a police report is still an objective, fact-driven enterprise hinging on the belief that human events can be accurately and comprehensively represented through one text.

At crime scenes, police officers are trained to regard themselves as neutral investigators and examiners for the criminal justice system, instructed to erase their identities, locate the 'facts,' and synthesize those facts into a coherent, linear narrative useful to police supervisors and lawyers. In other words, officers must wade through a complex discursive field of contradictions, linguistic eruptions, nonverbal modes of communication, textual body-markings, and environmental clues, and compose a succinct, comprehensive, chronological gloss that establishes Truth. Lawyers read these texts from a subjective, postmodernist epistemological perspective, but the officers *writing* the texts operate from a positivist, empirically based one. While attorneys are trained to disrupt and question a discursive representations of events, officers' composing endeavours are guided by a strict interview and reporting protocol manifesting a particular vision of Truth. Despite important strides in community responses to domestic violence and woman abuse, the epistemological issues remain largely unchanged.

In the context of woman abuse, the police quest to identify the legal Truth narrows and confines the voice and humanity of abused women because only certain criteria – that which establishes *probable cause* – are considered relevant to the legal system. However, the battle of women's advocates to make domestic violence a crime, to establish shelters, and to raise awareness that battering is a widespread and serious social problem make it even more urgent that representations of woman abuse be appropriate to a wider range of discursive frameworks. Far too often, the abused woman's story of abuse is glossed and massaged to meet only the conventions and requirements of police discourse, even though police reports are often read by medical personnel, shelter supervisors, and caseworkers. This reality is inherently problematic for battered women seeking relief and healing, the first 'stage' of which is to obtain safety.

The examination protocols utilized by officers can be likened to a ritual or ceremony, the metaphor manifested in much of Michel Foucault's work. A Foucauldian analysis exposes the epistemological fissure that erupts when human beings are objectivified/subjectified in order to be situated within a specific institutional framework, primarily because of his exploration of the inherent power dynamics. In 'The Means of Correct Training,' he writes that in the process of examination 'are combined the ceremony of power and the form of the experiment, the deployment of force and the establishment of truth. At the heart of the procedures of discipline, it manifests the subjection of those who are perceived as objects and the objectification of those who are subjected' (quoted in Robinow 197). Police arriving at a domestic call are trained to enact an investigative 'ceremony' under the auspices of uncovering Truth, to examine incidents through an institutional lens and slough off details and observations failing to fit within a prescribed textual parameter. The interview patterns officers are required to enact fit Foucault's vision of examination as ceremony, because unfortunately the texts emanating from this ritualistic event are often to the detriment of abused women. Women (as well as all the subjects present in the report) are essentialized, their identities collapsed into a few select characteristics. While it is true that police reports make abuse and assault visible to the legal eye, this visibility occurs through the cataract of police power. Rhetorical techniques manifested in the epistemology of criminal justice are designed to hide the authorship of the reporting officer, who possesses the omniscient narrator role; it is through this process that police power is maintained and entrenched. Again, Foucault writes, 'Disciplinary power ... is exercised by its invisibility; at the same time it imposes on those whom it subjects a principle of a compulsory visibility. In discipline, it is the subjects who have to be seen' (199). Officers, cloaked in the costume of institutional power (as indicated by such artifacts as the uniform, the gun, the police car), literally *erase themselves*, rendering themselves invisible while the subjects experience heightened, albeit skewed, visibility.

Perhaps this reality discourages some women from seeking police intervention when they are abused, because from this point on their identities have been glossed and appropriated on an institutional level by a system infused with patriarchal assumptions about the nature of womanhood and violence. The reports reflect these cues; for example, most I read concluded with the statement 'The complainant was ordered into the Prosecutors' Office,' followed by instructions to arrive at a specific time. While officers may regard the Law as doing the 'ordering,' and, truthfully, all complainants regardless of crime are so ordered, abused women are uniquely sensitive to this firm direction, usually given by a male officer. Either way, the battered woman lacks personal agency – an inability to choose the timing and sequence of criminal procedures, to arrange childcare or work hours, to attend therapy. My bias is, perhaps, is that domestic violence is a crime should be handled differently, where factors like a woman's immediate situation should be considered. Given the complex power dynamics and relationships inherent in woman abuse, a physically and emotionally traumatized woman may actually feel *less* empowered once police intervention is introduced into the dynamic, or at the very least just as manipulated. But the police reports betray themselves, as the language used *does* tend to be directive in tone. Some abused women have said that police intervention increases their sense of powerlessness. Aboriginal women have sometimes reported that the police did not respond helpfully to their calls, saying, 'There was a lot of times I did not call them because I thought it was no use to call them' and 'they always seemed like they were getting disgusted with you, because it is repeated over and over again, being abused and then charge him, and then it would happen again' (McGillivray and Comaskey 96). Some women even stopped calling the police altogether, saying, 'You know, I really felt like, what's the use? They never did anything' (96). Others indicated that they feared their children would be removed from the home. This sense of disempowerment is the opposite of how abused women should feel when they call the police.

Further disempowering the abused woman is her awareness that her language and behaviour are under censure, as she is expected to maintain the role of the 'good woman' who dutifully respects the officers' commands and permits herself to be rendered an object. Women intuitively know this. When battered women assert agency that conflicts with an officer's preconceived notions of appropriate female behaviour, like appearing ungrateful, angry, dismissive, or aggressive, the women are represented negatively in the written discourse, labelled 'unco-operative' or 'belligerent,' the sorts of officer comments that have severe repercussions for battered women if the case goes to court. Her refusal to accept 'object' status is not without consequences, enduring punishment for her failure to defer to police power.

Therefore, the nature of police-citizen language – particularly within the context of domestic violence and woman abuse – can be understood clearly through the relationship between power and language in addition to a feminist lens. In *Human Nature*, Foucault writes, 'It seems to me that the real political task in a society such as ours is to criticize the working of institutions which appear to be both neutral and independent; to criticize them in such a manner that the political violence which has always exercised itself obscurely through them will be unmasked, so that one can fight them' (quoted in Rabinow 6). To this end, Foucault historically traces the methods by which 'human beings are made into subjects' (7); according to him, 'the subject is objectified through a process of division either within himself or from others' (8). Foucault, who maintains that knowledge and power are inseparable, develops a schema manifesting three distinct modes by which individuals are transformed into 'things' occupying a position of subjectivity. Rabinow summarizes Foucault:

> In the first mode of objectification (the dividing practices), the constituted subject can be seen as a victim caught in the processes of objectification and constraint – most obviously the case for prisoners and mental patients. Although there are parallel developments associated with the second mode of objectification (scientific classification), the relation to domination is more oblique. For example, in *The Birth of the Clinic* Foucault demonstrates how the body was increasingly treated as a thing during the nineteenth century, and how this objectification was paralleled

and complemented by the dividing practices instituted in the clinic's spatial, temporal, and social compartmentalizations. But the two dimensions – dividing practices and scientific classification – are not the same thing; nor are they orchestrated together by some unseen actor. (10)

My contention is that the police narratives presented above exemplify the discursive process of transforming an individual into a subject or thing, basically Foucault's first and second modes of subjectivity. The abused woman is seen as either a victim or a perpetrator, objectified. This status is made visible in documents describing police protocol and interview strategies. The police officer assesses her body, characterizes it, and represents it in institutional discourse; her personhood is compartmentalized through a process of pseudo-scientific classification. Wounds are classified as 'small' or 'quarter-sized,' for example. The narrative paragraph and the chronology drawn within it function as a field that creates parameters constraining and controlling the abused woman's voice, discourse, and identity. In addition, the legalese of police language transforms and diminishes traumatic incidences of abuse and the humanity of the individuals into neutral 'scenes' that are further worked on by the more rhetorically skilled, arguably sophistic attorneys. Passive voice, detached language, and the objectification and construction of the woman's body as an examined 'thing' testifies to how the author as well as the reader is thrust into the perspective of the dispassionate observer. The courtroom is pregnant with such discourse and textuality; many abused women following through with legal proceedings remark that they feel as if they are nonexistent and invisible in the courtroom. When trauma is transformed into institutional discourse, the humanity and individuality of the subject are lost.

Examinations of woman abuse that focus on the legal response, analysing the patriarchal nature of law and the social inequalities that propel the continued oppression of all women, are certainly one valid method of critique, although, as Smart points out, they maintain problematic essentialist tendencies. Even the consciousness-raising strategies employed by feminists reduce abused women to a set of shared characteristics. Smart articulates Segal's argument that '[consciousness-raising] works well where it involves a small group of homogeneous women; it does allow for apparently personal and individual misfortunes to be recognized as structural disadvantages [...] But it works badly where women are heterogeneous, where experiences are not alike, and their priorities are different. Under such circumstances some women can be silenced' (79). In contrast, Foucault's belief that knowledge and power are intertwined and his analysis of the process of subjectification offer a particularly useful schema to understand this problem of how, despite years of social activism, women have been unable to significantly impact police investigative practice and written narrative.

An abused woman – as a body/text – shifts through a number of discursive sites. The place of violence where her abuser verbally and physically assaults the abused woman is one; when the police are called, the official 'crime site' becomes the second discursive arena. In neither of these sites is the abused woman a fully liberated subject. (Later, when she is able to exercise more agency, she may express herself in discursive sites that are more empowering.) The police report is not, ironically, where she can expect to be represented in a manner of her own choosing. When her personhood is distilled into several key characteristics noted in a police report, she is still rendered less powerful and voiceless. She will likely encounter difficulty if she wants to see what has been written about her. In fact, the little rhetorical analysis conducted on police reports is partly due to the inaccessibility of these documents, a result of their controlled institutionalization. This essentialization is carried out on two different levels that can be best understood by invoking Foucault's principles; first, the abused woman's body is rendered a textual artifact subject to the gaze of the more powerful police officer/observer, and second, *her story* of her abuse is transformed into a glossed, patriarchal, legal narrative that may adequately function within the legal system, and more often than not fails to meet not only her need for personal safety but her emotional need for justice and healing. The epistemological nature of police work necessitates this process of subjectification; the objective, neutral foundational assumptions inherent in the field dictate that everyone is subject before the law.

To further complicate the rhetorical situation, although police officers and other law enforcement officials are encouraged to regard their composing process as the essence of objectivity and neutrality, and derive their power through the assurance that they are dealing with 'facts' only, police reports can also be understood as arguments, the enthymene being 'I carried out this course of action (as in, arresting the abuser, arresting the complainant, doing nothing, driving her to the battered women's shelter, etc.) because the following evidence was collected ...' This enthymeme mercilessly functions despite the good intentions of the many caring officers, social workers, prosecutors, and the like, because it is the *nature* of police discourse that compromises our response to abused women. It is the legal system's dependence on patriarchal language and objective epistemological assumptions that prevent us from responding to domestic violence and woman abuse in a manner that privileges and values the woman's voice, narrative, and personhood. As the author/composer of the offense report, the police officer, who has internalized the conventions and assumptions of the organization he or she represents, is the institution's discursive agent. The abused woman is made over into a legally accessible but silent object through her docile, material body, the *docile body*. The human experience of abuse is dubiously transformed into a linguistic, pseudo-neutral artifact measured only within a pseudo-scientific classification system.

The context of patriarchal criminal justice discourse is not the only place the survivor of woman abuse is discursively limited. Over thirty years ago, the feminist mantra 'The personal is the political' targeted the epidemic of violence against women, and woman abuse activists embraced opportunities to work with legal and criminal justice professionals. However, the process of transforming personal issues into political ones is fraught with language and textuality issues, primarily because our culture's 'ways of knowing' and understanding linguistic phenomena are generally derivatives of scientific, Cartesian reasoning. As a result, strategies utilized by feminists against domestic violence invoked essentialist representations of woman abuse because they relied on visual representations that would resonate within the existing discourse frames. Gayatri Spivak remarks in 'In a Word: *Interview*' that 'within mainstream U.S. feminism the good insistence that "the personal is the political" often transformed itself into something like "*only* the personal is the political." The strategic use of essentialism can turn into an alibi for proselytizing academic feminisms' (4). In the context of the movement to stop woman abuse, this 'essentialist strategy' took the form of individual, personal, and visual representations of battered women offered up for examination and assessment, satisfying the empirically minded. For example, raising consciousness about woman abuse has involved exposing *private* discourse (and I am considering the abused woman's *body* and the marking of physical violence it manifests as a form of discourse, as well as the verbal language uttered by the abuser) articulated within the hidden sphere of the home, and laying it bare, making it public; language must be transformed into that which can be used within public discourse frames. (Police reports also exposed this private abuse, for the purpose of transforming it for an institutional discourse frame.) So, early strategies to encourage public awareness of domestic violence included the introduction in public domains of posters depicting battered women's faces: on billboards, television, and the like. These images were the previously hidden textual markings of violence, but regrettably were raised to the status of being The Markings of Violence. Several years ago there was a public service commercial that ran regularly on television showing a man and a woman in bed, listening to the verbal abuse and vicious beating levied at a woman in the apartment above. The distressed woman rolls over and turns out the light; the sobbing of the abused woman can be heard through the darkness. The purpose of such forms of media is to transform the private shame of the abused woman and the callousness of others who could help into public outrage, challenging and disturbing long-standing assumptions about women's social role. However, the commercial inadvertently reinstates problematic assumptions; for example, in the commercial the non-abused woman defers to her, presumably non-abusive, husband. If he had made a move to intervene on the abused woman's behalf, would she have followed his lead? Further, do we, as viewers, direct most of our anger at *her*, for ignoring the cries of another woman or for not insisting that her husband intervene? Or are she and her husband regarded as victims too, since their sleep will undoubtedly be interrupted by the violence occurring upstairs and, as witnesses, they are also subjected to the verbal and physical abuse that the abuser sees as his right to inflict? These images of violence against women were designed to perpetuate community activism, through the woman's body rendered as an argumentative text.

However, this strategy for achieving safety for battered women invokes Foucault's concept of 'bio-power,' one 'pole' of which is the manner in which 'the human body [is] approached not directly in its biological dimension, but as an object to be manipulated and controlled' (quoted in Rabinow 17). Although the commercial's intention was the exact opposite, to free the woman's body from manipulation and control, the battered woman in the commercial is clearly under the control of her abusive spouse and anyone who hears the abuse but fails to act on her behalf. Furthermore, the other woman in the commercial is also a docile body, as she looks to her husband for the impetus to act. According to Foucault, in *Discipline and Punish*, 'a docile body that may be subjected, used, transformed and improved' is valued by systems of power (198), but of course on the terms that the system of power sets. The feminist project of female empowerment has, unwittingly perhaps, not only further objectified the battered woman but emphasized that her relief from abuse is dependent upon others' intervention – male intervention.

A woman's battered body demarcates the private/public line, exposing not only the manner in which she occupies the discursive space of being the private text written on by the batterer, but the manner in which she becomes the textual, classified, and empirically *known* subject of the *body* of the law. According to Alan Hyde, 'The body ... often mimetically represents a *private* world of domesticity, autonomy, and freedom, as well as a *public* world of politics, the social order. It thus often symbolically polices the line between public and private' (135–6). This dual conceptualization of the body appears to apply more for men's bodies than for women's. In terms of violence against women, the woman's abused body, made visible for the public gaze, speaks to men's understanding of their power in the context of 'domesticity, autonomy, and freedom,' *as well as* his control of the social order, evidenced within the legal system. Domestic violence, and more specifically the police report taken at the crime site, which fixes and transforms the battering into a legally palatable, empirically verifiable scene, ruptures the conception of the private domain as being one where the body is free. The private domain is clearly not 'free' for abused women and, some might argue, not for *any* woman. In other words, abused women are denied free, safe, public or private discourse frames. The poster of the abused woman's face plastered to the battered woman's shelter, or even the depiction of the married woman rolling over and turning off the light, thereby 'betraying' her gender, can remind women of what they *lack* and what needs to be overcome. The poster also testifies to the extent to which the woman's physical and emotional personhood can be manipulated and controlled.

These sorts of textual representation of woman abuse directly, and perhaps negatively, impact the operations of law enforcement, the practices of which are simply more pragmatic manifestations of the legal system. Dramatic visual or auditory representations of a 'battered woman' – black eyes, vivid red blood on the swollen mouth, dishevelled hair, tears – are the depictions designed to arouse sympathy, the images that say, '*This* is a battered woman.' Women's bodies manifesting less obvious signs of abuse, though, may arouse less concern and therefore minimal intervention. My examination of hundreds of police reports written over a two-year period indicates that often officers' narrative descriptions denote less 'severe' episodes of abuse. Officers are frequentley careful to note that bruises or scratches, if they are visible, are generally 'small.' Pictures taken at the crime scene often do not clarify the extent or severity of the abuse, since bruising has not yet appeared. It is also unclear whether the ethnicity of a battered woman affects the description of her physical injuries. In addition, medical research indicates that many women are abused in *private* 'bathing suit' areas, areas that few women willingly show police officers, particularly male ones, and certainly not in *public*. The abuser, who understands full well how to function ably within a patriarchal frame of power, generally strategically places these wounds. *Her* private areas and shame are within his domain. (Women who agree to go to the hospital may show their injuries to the nurse or physician, but so many women deny medical treatment for a number of reasons, including ones derived from husbands' financial control and threats of increased violence.) These problems are outcomes of a method of inquiry that scientifically measures human beings, isolating body parts, negating and narrating over the voices of abused women, with the officer's narrow gaze believed to transcend and capture a multi-perspectival occurrence, empirically fixing a Truth.

Police reports cannot, nor are they designed to, capture the emotional and physical trauma and pain of an incident, and perhaps, as Elaine Scarry's *The Body in Pain* argues, intense pain shatters the voice. Perhaps trauma is only verifiable via the materialism of the body, or perhaps verifiability is an illusion. Perhaps we want to believe trauma can be verifiable through the materialism of the body, because to acknowledge the illusion is psychologically painful. Clearly, though, in order to reduce the occurrences of woman abuse, we must turn our attention to the discursive practices that maintain the dynamics of power within legal institutions, challenging their epistemological foundations. Working within the context of patriarchal discourse, as current solutions (like the 1994 Violence against Women Act) have sought to do, has not adequately focused on the role of language and discourse in facilitating gendered conceptualizations of the dynamics of woman abuse. When an abused woman's trauma story is articulated within a discourse frame of male domination, the narrative undergoes discursive shifts and permutations to meet the requirements of the patriarchal discursive contours; a woman may either consciously alter her narrative in order to secure safety or unconsciously linguistically adapt.

However, one must question how successful any programs designed to reduce domestic violence can be as long as we deny the reality of how women's language functions in male-dominated discourse frames.

Epistemological Assumptions Inherent in Police Science

Postmodernism seemingly has had no effect on the field of criminal justice, particularly in terms of textual examination. Feminist and Marxist theoretical critiques have been applied to law, albeit rather grudgingly, but most examinations of the criminal justice system have focused on the more pragmatic elements of officer/citizen interaction. Criminal justice has endured review and censure in terms of its response to woman abuse, as in Eve and Carl Buzawa's *Domestic Violence: The Changing Criminal Justice Response* (1980) and Nancy Loving's *Responding to Spouse Abuse and Wife Beating: A Guide for Police* (1980). Linguistic research (e.g., McElhinny) demonstrates that female police officers will abandon 'feminine' discourse styles as they undergo 'professionalization' in the criminal justice field, and are required to adhere to the fact-driven conventions of their jobs. Unfortunately, these critiques are generally not epistemological in nature, and do not overtly infuse references to postmodern theory, not only theoretically dating them but challenging their effectiveness. The tenets of postmodernism, however, can challenge the epistemological architecture of criminal justice discourse.

Because of their mutual dependence, a critique of criminal justice and police report writing cannot begin without first engaging in an epistemological analysis of the discourse of law. Over a decade ago Gerald Wetlaufer, often regarded as one of the first 'post-modernist' thinkers, claimed that 'we are the sons and daughters of Gorgias,' but noted that law was slow to accept postmodernism rhetoricity, at least in the context of written documents (1554–5). This reluctance still exists today, which has serious implications not only for the courtroom but for the documents that lawyers analyse and write. Lawyers, and the entire legal profession, adhere to a 'linked set of rhetorical commitments ... These include commitments to a certain kind of toughmindedness and rigor, to relevance and orderliness in discourse, to objectivity, to clarity and logic, to binary judgment, and to the closure of controversies. They also include commitments to hierarchy and authority, to the impersonal voice' (1551–2). Despite the understanding that many lawyers have of the rhetorical nature of law, particularly in a verbal sense, they are nevertheless reluctant to realize the logical extension of that reality, which Wetlaufer sees as the 'law's deeply ironic resistance to rhetoric and the perspective it entails' (1554).

From a feminist perspective, the epistemological critiques of this irony have been powerful. Catherine MacKinnon has unmasked the problematics of legal epistemology, where male dominance masquerades as neutrality, at one site of woman abuse: pornography. In 1989 she argued that an examination of pornography and obscenity law exposes the patriarchal epistemological foundations of law. She writes that 'uncovering gender in this area of the law reveals women to be most invisible when most exposed and most silent when used in defense of speech. In both pornography and the law of obscenity, women are seen only as sex and heard only when mouthing a sexual script' ('Pornography,' 196). The phenomenon she identifies can also be understood in the context of domestic violence; as in pornography, woman's battered bodies are *seen* when they are marked upon, exposed, by the dominant man, seen as concrete evidence, a thing, from a male point of view. Further, women's words are more likely to be 'heard' when they 'mouth' an 'appropriate' abuse narrative that fits the contours of the police protocol, as I will demonstrate later. In addition, MacKinnon argues that in the context of obscenity law, 'although the posture this law adopts toward the problem it envisions has shifted over time, its fundamental norms remain consistent: public is opposed to private, ethics is opposed to morality, and factual is opposed to valued determinations. These distinctions are supposed gender neutral but are implicitly, socially, gender based: female is private, moral, valued, subjective; male is public, ethical, factual, objective' (200). The woman and her body are the material to be dissected and the male is the scientist who possesses the acumen to carry out the dissection. In the context of domestic violence, it is through the process of police report writing that the female's trauma narrative is transformed into the more legally palatable male-based form of discourse. Her body functions as a factual, concrete piece of evidence, registering according to male-dominated gaze.

MacKinnon points out in 'Toward Feminist Jurisprudence' that

in male supremacist societies, the male standpoint dominates civil society in the form of the objective standard – the standpoint which, because it dominates in the world, does not appear to function as a standpoint at all. Under its aegis, men dominate women and children, three quarters of the world. Family and kinship rules and sexual mores guarantee reproduc-

tive ownership and sexual access and control to men as a group. Hierar-
chies among men are ordered on the basis of race and class, stratifying
women as well. The state incorporates these facts of social power in and as
law. Two things happen: law becomes legitimate, and social dominance
invisible. Liberal legalism is thus a medium for making male dominance
both invisible and legitimate by adopting the male point of view in law at
the same time as it enforces that view on society. (237)

Feminists working to improve society's response to battered women
have experienced the bind of which she speaks. For example, the 1994
Violence against Women Act, signed by former president Bill Clinton,
provided states that reviewed and strengthened their domestic violence
laws with federal funds. Several years ago, I interviewed the head of
the domestic violence division of the police department in the large
Ohio city where I conducted most of my research. When I asked her if
she perceived that Ohio House Bill 335 (the then-new state legislation
ushered in to improve the police response to battered women) would
allow attorneys to more effectively prosecute abusers, she sighed, 'They
change the laws, but not the rules of evidence' (Harrison). What her
remark reflects is an epistemological disconnect; the entire notion of
evidence and the establishment of probable cause are constructs invoking all the subjective, interpretative qualities of the gendered discourse
system. As MacKinnon argues, 'in the liberal state, the rule of law –
neutral, abstract, elevated, pervasive – both institutionalizes the power
of men over women and institutionalizes power in its male form'
(Toward Feminist Jurisprudence, 238). And so, Congress can alter the
law, but it is unable to alter this fixed ordering of reality.

    This ordering of reality is based upon the phenomenon of examina-
tion, the primary epistemological task of the police officer. Theoretically, and problematically, the officer is the camera, the legal eyeball.
Because officers are regarded as the observers of reality rather than
constructors of it, the training officers receive is basically to familiarize
them with *ritual*. Police work entails enacting patterns of behaviour
over and over again to the point where the patterns become a part of the
officer, a ritual of which he or she ceases to be consciously aware. These
patterns are designed to minimize risk, maintain the integrity of an
investigation, reduce mistakes, and secure evidence that will aid in the
prosecution or defense of suspects. But this discursive ritual also serves
to maintain the architecture of power. Foucault writes, in 'The Means of
Correct Training,' that 'the examination is the technique by which power,

instead of emitting the signs of its potency, instead of imposing its mark on its subjects, holds them in a mechanism of objectification. In this space of domination, disciplinary power manifests its potency, essentially, by arranging objects. The examination is, as it were, the ceremony of this objectification' (quoted in Rabinow 199). The police arrange their subjects to more capably control the frame of discourse. This is one of a number of elements that shut down the language of abused women.

This phenomenon occurs in a very concrete sense at the site of a police investigation of a domestic violence call. In the spring of 1995, police officers across Ohio were given a new police protocol for dealing with domestic violence, spouse immunity, and domestic disputes. In the large city where I conducted my research, the protocol was labelled the '——— Police Department General Order' (the city will remain anonymous to protect the identities of those involved in the research). This document, which does not describe a protocol remarkably different from the one previously existing, except that police officers were now bound to a mandatory arrest policy, instructs officers as to the process through which they intervene at domestic violence disputes, collect evidence, and write their reports. Under the category of 'Responding to the Scene/Police Responsibilities,' officers are required to first describe the positionality of the various subjects, including the location of the suspect, complainant, and witnesses. All participants are then 'arranged' so that they can be interviewed separately; a direct quote from Ohio House Bill 335 is included in the protocol in order to emphasize the necessity of this dynamic: 'separate the victim and the alleged offender, and conduct separate interviews ... in separate locations.' This practice is common, and believed to protect the integrity of the interview, although it arguably isolates the battered woman from others who may be present to support her.

The PDGO requests that officers interview the suspect first, drawing a portrait of the abuser that might establish probable cause. The suspect/subject is Mirandized, if he is being detained or arrested, and then police are to 'question him/her about the incident.' The protocol instructs officers to 'describe in your report the suspect's physical condition (e.g., under the influence of alcohol or drugs, torn clothing, out of breath, or any other characteristics indicative of having just been involved in an assault). Describe suspect's injuries in detail and ensure the suspect's offensive injuries are photographed (e.g., bruised knuckles).' I rarely read a police report where such details were noted, sometimes, I presume, because the abuser had fled the scene. However, such details were frequently absent from the report even when the abuser was available for assessment.

The process of interviewing the victim is encapsulated under the heading 'Evidence Collection' in the protocol, which to my mind asserts the abused woman's textual, subjective nature, a classification that the suspect/subject does not inhabit; interviewing the latter is listed under a separate heading, 'Interviewing the Perpetrator.' Within the context of evidence collection, the abused woman ceases to be a person but functions primarily as documentation for the legal process. In terms of the investigative strategy laid out in the handbook, she is afforded no more than the same discursive status as the room where the abuse took place. Foucault addresses how one's personhood becomes subsumed into a discourse frame and thereby fixed into a object/subject space: 'The examination that places individuals in a field of surveillance also situates them in a network of writing; it engages them in a whole mass of documents that capture and fix them. The procedures of examination [are] accompanied at the same time by a system of intense registration and of documentary accumulation' (quoted in Rabinow 21). The police offense report *is* registration and documentation of the abuse, and officers might argue that even they are held in the grip of the criminal justice system. For example, officers are reminded that 'the police officer must conduct his/her Domestic Violence or Protection Order investigation in a manner allowing for successful prosecution without the availability or cooperation of the victim,' one of the legislative changes often referred to as a mandatory arrest policy. Epistemologically, the search for Truth – manifested in the concept of *probable cause* – thus transcends all human needs and wishes. What the abused woman wants is irrelevant. Mandatory arrest policies have split feminists, as some women's advocates argue that abused women need to feel in control of their situation, which mandatory arrest policies deny, even if being in control costs them the ability to obtain immediate safety. In addition, there is evidence suggesting that officers are not arresting at higher rates as a result. However, there is also research indicating that such policies are helping.

The PDGO, which establishes an architecture of knowledge that categorizes and classifies the abused woman according to overt and discernable characteristics, was regarded as perhaps not a breakthrough for abused women in the metropolitan area I studied, but at least as movement in a positive direction. The problem, in my view, is that the empowerment goals women's advocates sought cannot be realized within the current patriarchal discursive framework, which functions to maintain gender-based stereotypes of battered women. Foucault notes that, in terms of the structure of the examination:

> Thanks to the whole apparatus of writing that accompanied it, the examination opened up two correlative possibilities: first, the constitution of an individual as a describable, analyzable object, not in order to reduce him to 'specific' features ... but in order to maintain him in his individual features, in his particular evolution, in his own aptitudes and abilities, under the gaze of a permanent corpus of knowledge; and, second, the constitution of a comparative system that made possible the measurement of overall phenomena, the description of groups, the characterization of collective facts, the calculation of the gaps between individuals, their distribution in a given 'population.' (quoted in Rabinow 202)

Even the most cursory examination of the PDGO illustrates this development. Although suspects do not suffer this object-classification to the same extent, the victim still maintains the space of 'Evidence' and is examined in terms of her location, mental and physical state, and manner, for the purpose of identifying a pattern that can be understood and appropriately responded to. In this sense, the motivation is at least altruistic. Unfortunately, it appears that battered women cannot be *made sense of* unless it is in the context of 'a permanent corpus of knowledge.' For example, the PDGO's instructions to officers state that:

> When interviewing the victim, the police officer should note in his/her report the following:
> a. The location of the victim when the police officers arrived.
> b. The victim's emotional and physical state (crying, bruised, swelling, redness, complaint of pain, hysterical behavior, intoxication, fearful, et cetera.)

Furthermore, officers are reminded, 'at trial a prosecutor may be able to introduce any "excited utterances" made to a police officer by the victim (or any other witness), which implicate the defendant even though the victim refuses to testify or retracts his/her statement.' A definition of what is meant by 'excited utterances' is provided, and then the PDGO reads, 'A police officer should fully document in his/her report all such statements, specifically noting when the statement was made in relation to the assault and the emotional state of the victim at the time the statement was made (e.g., shaking, anxious, excited, upset, nervous, hysterical, crying, sobbing, dazed, et cetera).' These references describe how the personhood of the battered women is ordered according to a particular schema, using a spatial discursive approach. She is classified not only according to a series of 'typical' characteristics 'seen' in battered women, but also according to those characteristics considered *appropriate* to battered women, including the sorts of injuries one might expect to see on an 'authentically' battered woman. Women who exhibit other, perhaps more 'male' characteristics are simply not 'understood' within the architecture of knowledge and are characterized as belligerent, a trend I noticed when I examined reports of this nature. For example, in one report, a severely beaten woman refused the police entry into her home, saying she had children inside. She refused to answer the officers' questions, and was characterized as 'belligerent' in the police report. Her refusal to admit entry to the police was in direct contrast to a more appropriate female response, which would be to defer to authority and allow the officers into the sanctity of her home.

Again, it is important to emphasize that this phenomenon is not gendered solely in terms of man/woman, but in addition to a patriarchal dynamic existing between the institution and the individual, indicative not only in the incident report script but in officer-citizen training processes. Bonnie McElhinny examines how female police officers feel they must, in order to be accepted into the criminal justice profession, transform their linguistic and behavioural approaches when on the job. She asserts that 'police officers learn to act like "tough cops" who limit their conversation to the formalities of the investigation because increased interaction offers further opportunities for excuses, arguments, complaints, or worse ... If they cannot minimize the amount of interaction or contact, they can engage as little as possible – with terse comments, body positioned half-turned away, or lack of eye contact' (316). Although McElhinny references research suggesting that 'reducing the amount of interaction affords others some personal space in what is often an intrusively intimate, if necessary, interaction with a stranger' (316), another way to regard this lack of human recognition and contact is that it maintains the institutional barriers between examiner and subject/object. Female police officers learn to adopt a 'professional' manner that maintains the power dynamic, considered by many in the field as necessary to the officer's personal and emotional protection. This discursive shift, as McElhinny's case studies show, requires that police officers – both male and female – deny not only the humanity of the subject but their own. McElhinny maintains that 'masculinity is not referentially (or directly) marked by behaviors and attitudes, but is indexically linked to them.' As a result, 'female police officers can interpret behaviors that are normatively or frequently understood as masculine (like noninvolvement or emotional distance) as simply "the way we need to act to do our job" in a professional way' (322). Where McElhinny and I part company, however, is that she sees this occurrence in a far more positive and hopeful light, believing that 'female officers are also redefining masculinity and femininity' (322) and 'in the end, such redefinitions could free women and men from the tyranny of the everlasting binary associations we find in our culture between masculine/objective/rational/strong/cultural and feminine/subjective/emotional/weak/natural' (323). On the contrary, the binaries she speaks of are further entrenched and even more malicious in their invisibility. The linguistic techniques utilized in the interview process are quite literally *fixed* in a system of documentation positing male discourse as normative. MacKinnon clearly identifies the problematic nature of *that*.

Perhaps the reason postmodernist and feminist critiques have left criminal justice discourse relatively untouched grows out of an uncomfortable tension between that discourse and the law. Ultimately, the police report's function, according to Fisher, is 'to justify the arrest and clear the case,' which he argues is accomplished 'by confining reports to what is necessary to satisfy the probable cause standard' (8). This understanding is critical to my analysis, but Fisher's claim is not without controversy. An attorney who worked both as a prosecutor and for the defence, Fisher argues that police reports were 'created primarily to serve various internal needs of the police department' (5), and although they are obviously used in the legal process, they tend to function more as an '"internal memorandum" serving the perceived needs of the police department' (7). Fisher's project entails examining why police officers often omit exculpatory evidence in their police reports, particularly when details of this nature typically aid the defence. He maintains that police officers, who must compose written texts under intense time constraints, are pressured to leave out details that could 'cast doubt on the arrestee's guilt, thus exposing the police to potential embarrassment or even civil liability for the false arrest' (8–9). Furthermore, 'aware of how attorneys might discover their reports and put them to hostile use, police have a negative incentive to report exculpatory facts' (9). These concerns seem an occupational hazard of working within such a structured, measured, and tenuous environment, but it is also clear that officers and others within the institution perceive the 'other,' in this case, the court system and particularly defence attorneys, to be a hostile threat. Police reports are part of the arsenal of protection against what the officers often regard as devious attorneys. The conflict is epistemological; criminal justice demands empiricism and verifiability and, from an officer's perspective, that he or she has established the facts. Yet the courtroom is often viewed as the place where criminals are released due to rhetoric and legal loopholes. The power struggle emerges as prosecution and defence theoretically seek to establish the Truth. As a consequence, officers often perceive that justice has been compromised and their hard work was all for nothing.

In fact, police reports are not really composed to establish facts to initiate the legal machine, but are arguments designed to justify police behaviour. Fisher notes that law enforcement studies demonstrate that police are not sufficiently trained to conduct investigations, and are shackled to their investigative protocols (20). McElhinny makes this observation, noting that during an interview with a woman allegedly punched by her son-in-law, the officer 'said very little aside from getting the woman's address, date of birth, and other information necessary for the incident report'; as a result, the officer 'doesn't react with horror or sympathy, as other interactants might (and do)' (317–18). Later, after the officer has shut away her notebook, clearly indicating that her comments are off the record and outside of her official capacity, she offers a few words of advice (318). Fisher's assessment, if correct, could explain observations such as McElhinney's; perhaps officers are uncomfortable deviating from the police protocol script because they have not obtained the investigative and rhetorical training to do otherwise. However, police officers can and do direct their ire at the court of law, seen as undermining the criminal justice system, with all the lawyers' theories, rhetoric, and linguistic gymnastics. This antipathy actually gives rise to apathy, compromising all aspects of the investigation. Fisher argues that in fact 'the relative indifference of the police to post-arrest proceedings results in inadequate police investigation and the loss of crucial inculpatory evidence' (21).

A further complication of an already difficult situation is that police are less motivated to attend domestic violence scenes than other crime scenes. Fisher's research focuses primarily on those calls that are identified as 'authentic,' such as robberies, assaults, and drug busts. Officers become frustrated because they perceive their work on the street as being undermined in the legal system. However, domestic violence has long been seen as unexciting social work. Gender stereotypes about battered women are also commonplace. Over ten years ago Kathleen J. Ferraro identified this problem, asserting that many police view battered women as aggressive, uncommitted to leaving their batterers, or easy liars (68, 70). Escorting women to shelters is regarded as social work officers should not be asked to do, a task that diverts resources from 'real' police work. Frequently, then, even with mandatory arrest policies in place, officers neglected to make arrests or enact the procedures legislation mandated. Although mandatory arrest policies establish new criteria for determining probable cause, the officer is still the agent verifying that the criteria have been met, a rhetorical act.

As I have tried to demonstrate, this dereliction is epistemologically permissible because of the minimization of the role of language. It is dangerous to assume that reports possess a lens-like quality: that officers have done what they say they have done, that they have seen what they say they have seen. Perhaps a police report, then, can best be understood as a translation of an event, a subjective understanding of circumstances. If we regard such a document as a translation, perhaps we can effect strategies that will give voice to abused women.

Strategies

One of the primary epistemological fissures between police officers and abused women is that the latter are in the midst of trauma – often characterized by linguistic disconnection and fragmentation – and yet police intervention necessitates that the abused woman verbally engage coherently and rationally, while comporting herself in a gender-driven, 'appropriate' manner. Research indicates that abused women call the police after at least several episodes of abuse, so it is relatively safe to assume that the majority of these women are suffering from traumatic stress; is it fair to expect such responses from abused women? In Judith Herman's *Trauma and Recovery* she explains, 'The traumatized person may experience intense emotion without clear memory of the event, or may remember everything in detail but without emotion. She may find herself in a constant state of vigilance and irritability without knowing why. Traumatic symptoms have a tendency to become disconnected from their source and to take on a life of their own' (34). Trauma, Herman maintains, is characterized by fragmentation, whereby the traumatized person has difficulty making sense of her emotions, responses, memories, thoughts, and feelings. An abused woman frequently also experiences extreme isolation and disconnection with others as a result of the restrictions enacted by her abuser. Furthermore, Herman points out that 'traumatic events, once again, shatter the sense of connection between individual and community, creating a crisis of faith' (55). An abused woman may fail to seek, or may be prevented from seeking, connections with social work agencies, friends, family, or the police; she may have little faith these sources will help her. The prolonged trauma she has endured may make it impossible, or at least intensely difficult, for her to articulate her experiences at all. This insight into traumatic stress has been a part of psychological approaches to treatment for a good while, but as I have tried to show, the nature of the legal system blocks an abused woman's ability to see police intervention as a step towards healing.

The abused woman who calls the police herself, or asks someone else to call the police for her, asserts an agency that could be the critical act in initiating the process of healing. Herman maintains, 'Because traumatic life events invariably cause damage to relationships, people in the survivor's social world have the power to influence the eventual outcome of the trauma. A supportive response from other people may mitigate the impact of the event, while a hostile or negative response may compound the damage and aggravate the traumatic syndrome. In the aftermath of traumatic life events, survivors are highly vulnerable. Their sense of self has been shattered. That sense can be rebuilt only as it was built initially, in connection with others' (61). Abused women who initiate police intervention are taking a tremendous emotional – and physical – risk by seeking police help. For poor and black women, this risk is especially great. Abused women who do not call the police – in cases where the police are called in by neighbours or witnesses – have the opportunity to connect with another human being who can help them. But the police are the primary network of social contact for poor women, as they have fewer accessible resources. The officer, like it or not, may very well be the abused woman's only connection in her attempts to seek safety. In many cases, she is seeking validation, the sense that her feelings are legitimate as well as her decision to open up to officers and speak of her abuse. Research like McElhinny's shows that women do not generally obtain that sort of response from the police. Yet Herman demonstrates that establishing safety lays the foundation for healing. Therefore, officer intervention can have a tremendous impact on a woman's decision to embark on the healing process, increasing her physical risk if she leaves her abuser.

Often, this is the context in which abused women are fixed when police officers attend crime sites. But because police intervention depends upon those linguistic qualities diametrically opposed to the conditions inherent in trauma (i.e., order, coherence, 'rationality,' and empiricism), when abused women are not able to or do not demonstrate those qualities, officers often characterize them as 'hysterical,' 'unco-operative,' or 'belligerent' rather than seeing those responses as exemplifying prolonged abuse. This is especially true if the abused woman behaves in a stereotypical 'unfeminine' manner, as in the midst of anger. The fragmentary or 'inappropriate' response to police intervention should be regarded as *evidence* of violence, rather than evidence that the woman is somehow responsible for the abuse. Unfortunately, such characterizations are more frequently considered as challenges to officer authority and a rejection of the subject/object status designated for battered women. Furthermore, as a battered woman negotiates the legal system, which she can be forced to do if she lives in an area with a mandatory arrest policy, she will find that her subject/object status is continually enacted in the courts. Her body functions as a purely textual signifier. If justice is obtained, it may seem accidental. But it is, perhaps, human nature to resist compartmentalization, classification, and essentialism, and it is based on this phenomenon that a strategy for giving voice to abused women can be conceived.

The language of abused women – the manner in which they give voice to their suffering in this early stage of recovery – simply cannot be validated within the criminal justice discourse frame in its current epistemological condition. Of course, I am assuming that the court system should have something to do with healing and emotional validation, and how those conditions can be reached through the humane, *human* administration of justice. I am also suggesting that we need to move from a *police state* model of criminal justice, with an emphasis on control and power, to a *peace officer* approach, which in my view would focus on establishing connection, validation, safety, and calm.

Additionally, I contend that the writing of police reports can be understood as a political, rhetorically engorged act of 'translation,' whereby the police officer filters the traumatized words of the battered woman and rewrites them into a new linguistic code meeting the language requirements of an institutional culture, necessary for the discursive entrenchment and distribution of power. Thus, a useful strategy would be to encourage and embrace alternative discourses that challenge the reliance on one institutionally derived text. Perhaps the most useful approach to understanding how the language must change is suggested by Gayatri Spivak:

> If you want to make a text accessible, try doing it for the person who wrote it. The problem becomes clear then, for she is not within the same history of style. What is it that you are making accessible? The accessible level is the level of abstraction where the individual is already formed, where one can speak individual rights. When you hang out and with a language away from your own (*Mitwegsein*) so that you want to use that language by preference, sometimes, when you discuss something complicated, then you are on the way to making a dimension of the text accessible to reader, with a light and easy touch, to which she does not accede in her everyday. If you are making anything else accessible, through a language quickly learned with an idea that you transfer content, then you are betraying the text and showing rather dubious politics. ('The Politics of Translation,' 191)

Domestic violence police reports are not written for abused women; the reports are administrative documents written for police supervisors, although other readers might have access to them. Abused women offer up their texts when they speak to police, but their words are regarded as unsuitable for administrative purposes, and so are dismissed, 'written over,' or disregarded. The field of criminal justice must move from a model of writing for the institution to writing for justice. This requisite is rarely if ever met for abused women, who may sign witness statements or offense reports but are not encouraged to review them in a critical manner, and who may not always understand how they are being linguistically represented. For a number of reasons, ranging from the intense traumatic stress they are in the midst of to the underdevelopment of literacy skills due to poverty, many women are not able or prepared to challenge police officers on that literal level. Further, they are simply not empowered to do so. Although, ironically, the police are supposed to protect them, to include them as subjects of composition in the process of composing would betray the subject/object power dynamic intrinsic to the police examination.

However, as I noted of the three reports profiled at the opening of this paper, one can discern women's attempts to assert a self that resists categorization as well as direct orders. The officer's notations of these linguistic eruptions testify to her effectiveness at being heard at some level. For example, in the sentence 'Complainant did not wish to press charges and was very uncooperative at the time of this report being taken,' even the passive voice cannot obscure the fact that the abused woman refused to be made docile and malleable. In the second report, the complainant at first refuses to tell the officers what her abuser did but eventually admits 'the suspect did choke her.' Disclosure was no doubt more difficult for her than it was for the other witnesses, who were not directly involved and stood as a group but nevertheless were 'in fear of retaliation from the suspect and would not sign witness statements.' The officer's orchestrated arrangement of the parties did not effect the disclosure of truth they were trained to expect, and the brevity of the narrative suggests that the reporting officers dispensed with much of the detail prompted by the DPGO. In the third report, the complainant 'denied treatment for her injuries' despite what appears to have been quite a vicious assault. The officer's use of the word 'denied' is perhaps a device attributing more agency to the abused woman than she may have felt. It is possible that asking to be escorted to the hospital emergency room would have been a more assertive action than refusing to go.

A concern I have about my analysis is that I have been positioning officers and abused women in purely dichotomous terms, regarding them as adversaries. Theoretically (and otherwise), it is counterproductive to do so. Spivak, in *In Other Worlds: Essays in Cultural Politics*, writes that 'the greatest gift of deconstruction [is] to question the authority of the investigating subject without paralyzing him, persistently transforming conditions of impossibility into possibility' (201). If we regard a police officer as also a subject of the criminal justice system who is required to write the abused battered woman into subject/object status, who is not free to do otherwise and might appreciate the ability to break off epistemological chains, we can perhaps see a way that the two can work together, cultivating a more comprehensive albeit still fragmentary conception of a truth. To an extent, the woman's body would experience coding, but it would be impossible for this *not* to occur; this is a concession that Spivak makes when she remarks, 'As a text, the inside of the body (imbricated with the outside) is mysterious and unreadable except by way of thinking of the systematicity of the body, value coding of the body. It is through the *significance* of my body and others' bodies that cultures become gendered, economicopolitic, selved, substantive' (20). A pastiche of collated text acknowledging its rhetoricity, however, could very well be more healing and ultimately advantageous than the method currently being advocated. To be sure, we are not as a culture effectively keeping battered women safe; we are not ending the epidemic of woman abuse; we are still living in and endorsing a culture ultimately hostile to women. Seen in this light, taking the risk of an alternative to the way *things have always been done* seems minimal indeed.

For example, when considering the inception of mandatory arrest policies, women's advocates can – and do – consider whether this legislative change has proved effective. What has emerged with clarity, however, is that no matter how one cuts it, mandatory arrest policies do not give abused women choices. Transforming domestic violence from a private family matter into a crime worthy of police intervention has seemingly necessitated the entrenchment of one-size-fits-all responses to battered women. True, before the inception of the new domestic violence policies, many women had even fewer choices; police generally did nothing at all. However, the adoption of a mandatory arrest policy does not mean that women will be treated more individually or uniquely; the discourse frames have merely been adjusted to accommodate new rules, the epistemological foundations altered little.

How can such a complex web of discourse be navigated? I will make the leap of arguing that abused U.S. women as a group must be regarded as manifesting tremendous complexity, and that even women's advocates and academic feminists can make the mistake of marginalizing them, making them 'other,' just as police officers are required to do, when institutional discourse is the frame in which abused woman must narrate their experiences. Spivak addresses this tendency in the context of how First World feminists must negotiate engagement with feminists from other cultures by hearing these women in their authentic voices. Using a strategy she calls the 'psycho-biography,' Spivak suggests that women from other cultures be encouraged to deliver uninterrupted narratives embracing all the cultural assumptions and discursive patterns of their native language. She argues that psycho-biographies provide insight into the complexity of the sexed subject of woman; she claims that through this technique 'you begin to see how completely heterogeneous the field of the woman elsewhere is, because there you have to focus on regulative psycho-biographies which are *very* situation and culture-specific indeed' (*The Post-Colonial Critic*, 9).

Thus, one way the abused woman's voice can be heard is through her trauma narrative, in all its possible fragmentation, anger, sadness, disconnection, frustration, etc., uttered from a variety of complex cultural, political, and economic discourses. Psycho-biographies could be used in the United States to provide a platform in which abused women can

be heard. A woman could provide a biography of her abuse, uninterrupted, unfiltered through the officer's lens. She could record her story
if she chooses, without the officer asking her questions, circumventing
her narrative trails, rearranging the details. Her words could flow un-
molested by the disruptions of legal language as well as the language of
well-meaning feminists operating in a male-dominated discourse frame.
We could perhaps understand the nature of woman battering more
fully by challenging long-held linguistic contours. This recording could
be an accompanying text to the domestic violence packet assembled by
officers, and could be heard by attorneys, judges, and social workers.
Already in many areas police officers assemble more comprehensive
domestic violence packets that include body maps and photographs to
more effectively document the abuse. Providing a tape recording or
video recording of the abused woman's narrative would be a fairly easy
next step.

   This strategy is not unproblematic; some women's advocates may
worry that one cannot control how a psycho-biography is understood,
worked on, or manipulated as it is incorporated into the legal system.
But this problem is occurring anyway; women's abuse stories are ne-
gated or filtered or twisted in the media, in the courts, in social services.
Sensitivity training for police officers and lawyers has not prevented
misrepresentations of abused women from occurring. Even women's
advocates utilize generalizations and classifications in order to enact
policy change. Therefore, the ultimate focus of the initial strategy is to
privilege the *individual* woman's voice, to provide her with the satisfaction and opportunity to express her story as she sees fit. There will
always be some unifying elements across women's abuse stories
discernable to the listener/reader, particularly those advocates for battered women working to uncover the gendered power dynamic operating within the legal system. According to Spivak, 'the task of the feminist
translator is to consider language as a clue to the workings of gendered
agency' (*The Politics of Translation*, 179), but she insists that even with
that goal, the 'translator must surrender to the text. She must solicit to
the text to show the limits of its language, because that rhetorical aspect
will point at the silence of the absolute fraying of language that the text
wards off, in its special manner' (183). Rather than adopting a feminist
response to domestic abuse that insists that women linguistically operate within patriarchal parameters, we should take a more radical perspective and provide a platform for speaking, which entails giving up
control. Our eagerness and desperation to curtail domestic violence has

made us fearful of giving up this sort of control. We want to help battered women, criminalize the abusive behaviour of batterers, and be heard by those with the power to change the system. Unfortunately, working within male-dominated frames of discourse to reach these goals has resulted in new problems, new issues. Perhaps a new approach is needed; Spivak notes (and I am, perhaps not unproblematically, arguing that we can view traumatized women as a sort of 'other'), 'Rather than imagining that women automatically have something identifiable in common, why not say, humbly and practically, my first obligation in understanding solidarity is to learn her mother tongue. You will see immediately what the differences are' (191). In other words, I am challenging previous strategies to reducing woman abuse that represented women as a collective other.

Conclusion

The site where police interview abused women is not typically regarded as an arena whereby she might experience personal empowerment, compassion, or empathy. However, very often the healing and recovery that many abused women seek involves obtaining justice by locating and choosing assistance from a variety of resources, as well as using language in empowering ways. For such a discursive shift to occur, whereby this goal can be met, officers and those who train them must encourage personal reflection, rhetorical awareness, and literary sophistication among their colleagues. Further, women's advocates must continually ask themselves whether their practices and conceptions of abused women are derived from criminal justice–based epistemologies, thus inadvertently making abuse survivors prone to objectification.

   For many abused women, their linguistic interaction with police offers an opportunity for validation, the validation of their story. In Foucault's third mode of objectification, he 'looks at those processes of self-formation in which the person is active ... isolating those techniques through which the person initiates an active self-formation ... These operations characteristically entail a process of self-understanding but one which is mediated by an external authority figure, be he confessor or psychoanalyst' (quoted in Rabinow 10–11). Abused women may look at the officer as the confessor and may be, through the veil of trauma, trying to establish a mode of self-understanding. While this phenomenon arguably falls outside the discursive realm of police work, it occurs nonetheless. And although abused women frequently encounter difficulty articulating this awareness, they are often frustratingly cognizant of how they are rendered an objective artifact during the police investigation. The organic rhythm and structure of their narratives are interrupted and obscured. As a result, their encounters with officers impede their ability to make their abuse public, an often necessary step towards healing and self-understanding.

Police representations of woman abuse, particularly in terms of how women's trauma is textually expressed in a primary legal document, essentialize women's experience and expose the problematics of feminist theory. A new approach must be advocated whereby women are provided opportunities to create their own discursive frames, beyond infantilization or objectification. While such a new strategy would assuredly complicate criminal justice's positivist framework, and by extension that of the legal arena, the current practice of essentializing the characteristics of abused women reduces her traumatic state to a caricature. To distort and abstract her identity is a negation of her humanity. It is criminal, not justice.

Works Cited

Ferraro, Kathleen J. 'Policing Women Battering,' *Social Problems* 36 (1989): 61–94.

Fisher, Stanley Z. '"Just the Facts, Ma'am": Lying and the Mission of Exculpatory Evidence in Police Reports.' *New England Law Review* 28 (1993).

Harrison, Karen [pseudonym]. Interview with the author, 15 May, 1995.

Herman, Judith. *Trauma and Recovery*. New York: Basic Books, 1997.

Hyde, Alan. *Bodies of Law*. Princeton, NJ: Princeton University Press, 1997.

Jackson, Stevi, and Jacki Jones, eds. *Contemporary Feminist Theories*. New York: New York University Press, 1998.

McElhinny, Bonnie S. '"I Don't Smile Much Anymore": Affect, Gender, and the Discourse of Pittsburgh Police Officers.' In *Language and Gender: A Reader*, ed. Jennifer Coates. Malden, MA: Blackwell, 1998.

MacKinnon, Catharine. 'Pornography: On Morality and Politics.' In MacKinnon, *Toward a Feminist Theory of the State*, 193–214. Cambridge: Harvard University Press, 1989.

———. 'Toward Feminist Jurisprudence.' In MacKinnon, *Toward a Feminist Theory of the State*, 237–49. Cambridge: Harvard University Press, 1989.

McGillivray, Anne, and Brenda Comasky. *Black Eyes All of the Time*. Toronto: University of Toronto Press, 1999.

———— *Police Department General Order.* State of Ohio, 1995.

Rabinow, Paul, ed. *The Foucault Reader.* New York: Random House, 1984.

Scarry, Elaine. *The Body in Pain: The Making and Unmaking of the World.* New York: Oxford University Press, 1985.

Smart, Carol. *Feminism and the Power of Law.* New York: Routledge, 1989.

Spivak, Gayatri Chakrovaroty. 'In a Word: Interview.' In Spivak, *Outside the Teaching Machine*, 1–23. New York: Routledge, 1993.

————. *In Other Worlds: Essays in Cultural Politics.* New York: Routledge, 1988.

————. 'The Politics of Translation,' In Spivak, *Outside the Teaching Machine*, 179–200. New York: Routledge, 1993.

————. *The Post-Colonial Critic: Interviews, Strategies, Dialogues*, ed. Sarah Harasym. New York: Routledge, 1990.

Wetlaufer, Gerald. 'Rhetori and Its Denial in Legal Discourse.' *Virgina Law Review* 76 (1990).

Chapter 8

The Language of Healing: Generic Structure, Hybridization, and Meaning Shifts in the Recovery of Battered Women

CAROL L. WINKELMANN

When Alice Clare, a white woman of Appalachian ethnicity, came to the Women's House, a shelter for battered women in an economically depressed urban area in the American upper South, she showed all the signs of living through ten years of domestic violence. Initially she was silent and withdrawn; mostly, she stayed in her room. When she did begin to interact with other women, she was hesitant in speech and behaviour. Her words belied an intense insecurity about her ability to create a life apart from her abuser. To staff and other residents, she seemed certain to return to her partner despite her physical and emotional injuries. Then Edwina came to the shelter, fleeing the abusive father of her children. By the time Alice Clare left the shelter for her sister's house in eastern Kentucky, she had made friends with Edwina as well as other residents. It was an unlikely friendship: Alice Clare, a skinny middle-aged white Appalachian stay-at-home wife without children, and Edwina, a robust young African American high-school dropout with two children who worked as a grocery clerk. With Edwina's support, Alice Clare sought legal advice in the community about her domestic situation. She came to a story-sharing group and spoke. Edwina and Alice Clare prayed together and, occasionally, they yelled at one another. They helped one another to begin to heal. Edwina's words reveal the delicacy, the compassion, with which she approached Alice Clare and, indeed, other shelter women:

> In the shelter, you have others and their feelings. What kind of feeling are we dealing with today from someone else? Their feelings as well as our

own determines your and my attitude, and how and what will be said to
that person.

With these words, Edwina discloses some of the dynamics of healing.
She has a clear sense of communal influence and energy and the deeply
collective nature of language practices. In a few words, she sketches out
the function of mutuality in communicative practices.

I was the facilitator of the story-telling circle in which these two
women became friends. Once a week, the residents and I chose a topic,
wrote, and then talked about what we wrote. The words of women like
Edwina and Alice Clare encouraged me, over a nine-year period, to
undertake an ethnographic study of that shelter language.[1] This essay
explores the language of healing of battered women in these sessions
and other activities in the shelter. My argument is that the mostly
African American and white urban Appalachian shelter women attempt to survive abuse and to heal themselves and their children by
engaging in a similar series of rhetorical or linguistic strategies and
communicative practices.[2] More specifically, during conversation the
women use hybrid language forms that can lead to changes in the
meaning of their utterances. These meaning shifts can facilitate their
recovery from the devastation of domestic violence. In my use of the
term, a hybrid language is a mix, melding, or composite of two or more
registers (or social types of language) that results from negotiating,
compromising, and creating shared meanings with other women in the
shelter.[3] A meaning shift is a conceptual change (inasmuch as we can
witness it through language use) motivated by mutuality or the desire
to communicate and manifested by hybrid language forms.

In this essay, I will look at dialogue from a session at the shelter to
illustrate hybridization and meaning shifts, focusing on the religious
language within the episode. I choose religious language because most
women in this shelter attend or have been raised in Holiness/Sanctified
or fundamentalist/evangelical church communities, that is, conservative religious traditions that distinctly affect how women perceive suffering and violence (Townes, *In a Blaze of Glory, A Troubling*; Bendroth;
Gilkes). The women's language is suffused with the semantic shadings,
metaphors, and concepts of traditional religious socialization (that is, in
addition to the linguistic markers most often recognized by linguistic
scholars – class, race/ethnicity, education, age, and so forth). Traditional religious concepts about gender roles and relations frequently
fuel the family tensions that lead to domestic violence. At the same

time, shelter women in conversation often resist or subvert traditional meanings about gender roles and relations taught by their churches in order to heal from domestic violence. Thus their religious language neatly illustrates the workings of the shared or mutual construction of meaning.

The basic significance of this study, then, is the attention to the generic structure and dynamic movement of language. The language of healing makes apparent – in a poignant and socially relevant manner – the way in which all human discourse functions to more or less explicit degree as the dynamic site of ideological action. The healing of battered women, a process involving at least three phases, often includes a shift from an acceptance of religious or other ideologies that facilitate abuse to a remediation or rejection of those ideologies. Conversation and story-telling provide the opportunity for the important work of the language of healing to take place.

In this essay, I will first offer a few words about the nature and extent of domestic violence. Next I will make some comments about my methodology. I will then explore the three phases of the generic structure of the healing process as battered women move from states of pain and suffering from physical and/or emotional abuse towards states of greater autonomy in which they develop different attitudes towards themselves, their situations, and others. Subsequently I will explore the process of hybridization as it unfolds in a story-telling episode between two shelter women and myself. I will conclude with some remarks about the universality or applicability of my findings to other survivors of domestic violence.

The Demographics of Domestic Violence

Domestic violence is one of the leading causes of injury to women in nearly every country in the world.[4] In the United States, one-third to one-half of all women will be physically assaulted in their lifetimes by their partners, many repeatedly, some to death. According to a report by the U.S. Senate Judiciary Committee, most serious crimes against women are rising at a rate significantly faster than total crimes. Yet, in 1998 (in its most recent report), the U.S. Department of Justice estimated that only half of the incidences of intimate violence are reported because of victims' fears about privacy, retaliation, or the inaction of police.

The definitions of domestic violence vary, but it involves one or more of a constellation of different forms of frequently escalating violence such as physical, sexual, psychological, emotional, or economic force or coercion in the context of intimate and/or household relationships.[5] Commonly, it involves violent actions directed at women with the intent to control, actions such as throwing objects at them, pushing, shoving, grabbing, slapping, kicking, biting, hitting with fists, beating up, and threatening with weapons. Individual women may suffer in different ways and to different degrees, but certainly they suffer the ignobility of a loss of autonomy in a relationship with a partner who seeks to control their actions through violence. In this study, I refer to the women who seek refuge in the shelter as 'battered' women, 'shelter women,' or 'survivors of domestic violence' with the express purpose of emphasizing violence against women and its consequences, yet with the understanding that not all have been physically assaulted.

Scholars and community workers contest the causes of violence against women. The various camps or schools of thought range from the dysfunctional family communicative practices to the misogynist cultural practices, particularly the obstacles to women's and girls' equal access to material resources.[6] Distribution patterns are slightly more difficult to access because of problems with reporting and compiling data. However, domestic violence cuts across every class, race/ethnicity, and age group, yet there are correlations between age, education, income, and incidences of violence. Women who have fewer resources are victimized the most by domestic violence.[7] In addition, domestic violence within the context of multicultural or race and class variables creates further survival stresses for women who are already suffering from prejudice and discrimination.[8]

Given the seriousness of violent crimes against women's well-being, it behooves us to learn more about how women use language as they move from states of suffering and isolation to situations of enhanced autonomy and self-esteem. If we are better able to comprehend the linguistic configurations of healing, we may be better prepared to accompany and assist domestic violence victims on their journey towards more wholeness and integrity.

Methodology

This essay is based on an ethnographic study of the language practices of battered women. For over nine years, I engaged as a participant-observer in many shelter activities. I participated in women's in-take sessions; hot-line counselling; group sessions for domestic violence, codependency, and parenting; house-cleaning, babysitting, and donation sorting; and literacy and art activities. I engaged in other shelter activities such as casual conversation, mealtimes, holiday festivities, and so forth. The story-telling session that I facilitated once a week has been a particularly rich opportunity to witness the language of healing. With women's permission, I collected and analysed the women's writing and I sometimes recorded sessions. Throughout the years, I engaged in conventional ethnographic research methods such as individual and group interviews and ethnographic note-taking.[9]

From the language practices of these various activities, I searched for key events, repeated patterns of speech activity, and themes of significance. Thus my study is not based on the weight of quantitative data; rather, it is based on qualitative data. For my analysis of the generic structure and the phases of healing, I offer language excerpts from the story-telling sessions, in-depth interviews, and my field journal. For the section on hybridization and meaning shifts, I use one episode of transcribed story-telling that highlights the kind of linguistic activity I am most interested in exploring: the activity of sharing and re-shaping meaning in mutually influential, dialogic ways. By means of these data, I seek to illustrate a language or process of healing that I have witnessed many times over a long period in a specific or local setting.

The Generic Structure of the Language of Healing

One way of disentangling the complexity of the language practices (i.e., the idiolects, social varieties or registers, and other cultural modes of meaning-making) of shelter women is to consider the broad and dynamic generic structure of the language of healing.[10] As a result of their shared social interaction, women in the shelter sometimes enter into new and more healthy articulations of the meaning of their battery experience. At its best, the shelter may provide an 'inter-individual territory'[11] in which new consciousness is enabled; that is, the shelter provides the opportunity for women to share their personal stories in potentially transformative conversation with other women who have their own personal stories. For the purposes of this study, I will designate the linguistic movement or trajectory from silence and isolation to increased social solidarity as a genre of *healing*.[12]

I follow Bakhtin (*Speech Genres, Dialogic Imagination* 1981) in viewing speech genres as a way of organizing cultural meanings and representing the world. Genres are sites of action, including ideological action. Further, genres are not so much rigid formal types or categories that are endlessly repeated; rather, they 'consist of orienting frameworks, interpretive procedures, and sets of expectations that are not part of discourse structure, but of the ways actors relate to and use language' (Hanks, 'Discourse Genres,' 670). The meanings of particular genres or subgenres are made against a backdrop of wider cultural systems of meanings. Hence intertextuality (linkages or types of relations) between forms of meaning-making is necessary for coherence and comprehension (Bakhtin, *Dialogic Imagination*). Social intercourse is essential for individual consciousness or subjectivity to take shape (Volosinov 12–13).

Genres have greater flexibility than other language formations (i.e., grammar, clause structures, etc.). They are functional and fluid; thus, creativity – primarily through dialogic activity – is possible, perhaps inevitable. As the notion of genre applies to my research context, however, there appear to be three distinct (but nonlinear, overlapping, and always flexible) phases (and some subphases) used by victims of domestic violence as they move from states of personal alienation to social and action-oriented accompaniment with other women (cf. Soelle; Herman). These phases are characterized by certain meaning or semantic shifts motivated by dialogic linguistic activity or the creation of hybrid language forms. These hybrids signal new sites of ideological action allowing women to move forward in the healing process towards greater autonomy or a greater sense of self-in-relation to others.[13]

The intersection (and subsequent meaning shifts) upon which I will focus here is the mix of secular and religious languages in the language of shelter women. I am interested in the dialogic activity or the action of hybridization of secular and religious languages. *My argument is that hybridization underlies the process of healing by providing the dialogic impetus or dynamic for linguistic transformation.* There is evidence in the language of some shelter women of a reappropriation or reinvention of traditional religious language in speech acts of lament and complaint, testimony and praise, and finally celebration and creative story-telling; that is, language forms that lead the way to greater (interdependent) autonomy. Interestingly and ironically, the women frequently subvert the very language practices that helped to create the crisis situation in which they now find themselves. That is, they subvert traditional religious language or sexist religious interpretations in order to invest their suffering with new meaning and to try to reorder their worlds of pain. While these new hybrid language formations show strong race, class, or other sociolinguistic markers, they also form the basis of a generic or common language of compassion that traverses the heterogeneous personal and social experience. These linguistic manoeuvres of hybridization and creativity may function to preserve women's dignity, to create communities of compassion, and to generate social change.

Three Phases of Suffering

In contemporary linguistic theory, genre consists of orienting frameworks, interpretive procedures, and sets of expectations (Hank, 'Discourse Genres'); that is, genre concerns *practice*. Language, of itself, takes its shape in part through its relation to variables of power and social distance (Leech). In the shelter, as in all communicative contexts, these power variables shape meaning. The meaning of this theory with respect to the language in the shelter *initially* is this: in practice, battered women are expected by staff to use language in certain ways in order to continue to access shelter resources. They must demonstrate self-help behaviours; otherwise, they will be suspected of malingering and their space will be ceded to other women on the lengthy waiting lists. Self-help behaviours may include job and housing searches; pursuit of criminal justice actions against abusers; engagement with medical or counselling staff; and attendance at house meetings, group sessions, and other social events. The institutional expectation of self-help behaviour, particularly performed sociality, may initially provide impetus for shelter residents to launch off on the three-phase trajectory I will describe below.[14] Whatever the initial motivation, women in the shelter often show evidence of passing through three linguistic or interpretative frameworks as they move through the intense suffering and isolation of their domestic crisis to more integrated and relational modes of being.[15] The first phase is one of silence and isolation; the second phase is one of analysis and lament; the third phase is one of agency and increased social networking or solidarity with other abused women. The phases are not engaged by all women in the shelter.[16] Nor are the phases linear or one dimensional; that is, the sufferer may re-experience earlier phases in response to new concepts or material conditions.

Phase 1: Silence and Isolation

In Soelle's model, first-phase suffering is characterized by silence, numbness, powerlessness, and isolation. The sufferer's communication is pre-verbal: it is characterized by explosive emotion, by moaning or animal-like wailing. The suffering forces the sufferer to turn inward. Autonomy of thinking, speaking, and acting is lost; behaviour is reactive. The sufferer's objectives cannot be organized because she is dominated so thoroughly by the situation. Soelle's work pre-dates yet complements the work of Elaine Scarry, author of the well-known phenomenological text *The Body in Pain*. Scarry argues that intense suffering cannot be expressed in language. Terrible pain wrecks language wholly, turning it into silence or re-rendering its expression as preverbal cries.

Women who have come to the shelter are moving beyond Phase 1 suffering. They have moved out of the isolation typical of abuse situations, often motivated by fear for themselves, their children, or even their partners. (Later they recount that they were afraid they might be killed, they might kill their partner in an act of anger or self-defence, or their children may be physically or psychologically injured.) Yet I have seen enough battered women lying motionless, catatonic-like, on common room couches or in their beds, unable or unwilling to talk about what has happened to them. In group sessions – if they are willing or able to be present at all – they do not speak. They watch and listen and often they weep. Sometimes they can be heard to cry themselves to sleep at night.

In the shelter, a Phase 1 domestic violence survivor is invited – indeed, there is subtle pressure – by staff and other residents to enter into the social stream of shelter life. When she does, her language may still be somewhat incoherent or inchoate. She shows evidence of hopelessness, meaninglessness, and depression. There may be some loss of selfhood: not only can she not easily imagine herself as a human agent apart from her partner, but she cannot easily construct or recall a self, a past, or a future outside the narrow confines of the abusive relationship. There may also be an inability or an unwillingness to perceive her own abuse as a problem of ontological, social, or structural origins; that is, she cannot easily entertain the idea that her partner is the one with the problem or that his problem might extend from social, cultural, and institutional systems. Indeed, the Phase One survivor cannot easily analyze her situation at all. She is in the grips of terrible pain, and it diminishes analytical thinking or rational discourse. The pain simply is. It is nearly all there is.

The story-telling sessions yield plenty of Phase 1 examples. The following exchange between Lynn, Mary Jo, and Pam took place during a story-telling session. The women are rehearsing together the dynamics of the suffering of Phase 1. Notice that these are recollections or reflections of the battered women's Phase 1 internal states (i.e., of mind or feeling) while they were being abused. Their capacity to share in conversation indicates that they have moved beyond this particular phase.

Lynn: We talked about that last week, that part of you that says, this is cool, this isn't cool, we numb that when you first start getting abused.

Mary Jo: Man, it feels like a dream, when am I gonna wake up? ... it feels like I'm sleeping, and when am I gonna wake up from this bad dream?

Pam: This is really depressing me right now, I'm, I'm just being honest with you ... you know, we live the nightmare, and it, it's depressing.

In a private interview, Kale also recalls Phase 1 dynamics. She says, 'One time my husband put a pillow on my face and didn't take it off until I played dead ... My husband isolated me. He knew I had no family in the area. I completely relied on him.' It would appear Kale had largely lost her agency or autonomy – or, at least, this is what Soelle's schema would suggest. In my interpretation, however, Kale uses agency, her own cunning, to survive her partner's life-threatening attack. She had to play dead to live. I believe few battered women ever relinquish their agency in its totality. To do so would be to invite injury or death. Instead, battered women must hide their own autonomy or agency, deny, or subsume it – until they are finally unable to continue to do so in the interest of their own survival. Then they leave or sometimes die.

Phase 2: Lamentation

In Soelle's view, the Phase 2 sufferer has become more aware. She can perceive her suffering as arising from a specific situation and she can analyse the situation. The pressure of suffering sensitizes her. She actually experiences her own autonomy, or sense of independent control, and she can integrate her experiences into her own sense of selfhood. Being more aware, she is able to speak, to communicate, and to express her suffering. She laments. In her expression, rationality and emotion are communicated together. She uses psalmic language, a language of praise and worship of God. In prayer, her objectives are utopian, but in day-to-day life, she seeks acceptance of her situation and its conquest through existing social structures.

In my study of shelter women, I perceive some variations in Phase 2 suffering. While the general outlines of Soelle's schema hold, there are some differences. When battered women move out of their isolation, they do not move linearly to autonomy. Instead, most women will move recursively or cyclically through periods of greater and lesser autonomy and lucidity. Previously, they hid from the public gaze. Now they move rapidly through periods in which their ability or desire for public self-assertion, autonomy, and selfhood fluctuates. They also gain autonomy by attending to relationality; that is, they must relate to others to see that they have a unique selfhood-in-relationship with others.

As Soelle argues, the form of the language of the Phase 2 sufferer is psalmic language or lament.[17] The following are examples of shelter women speaking in the language of lament:

Shasha: The Bible says the meek will inherit the earth and, ladies, we
   know this is not true!
Lora: Some men try to use the Bible to justify what they do to you!
Marianne: God shelters us women!
Janine: I can say to myself: I'm God's child. I don't need to have this
   abuse. I need a ride out of here with me and my children.

To add to Soelle's insight about the language of Phase 2: in these laments, shelter women distinguish clearly between the work of God and the workings of patriarchy. These laments name their reality, an inequitable world wherein men profit from, for example, the misuse of Scripture.

The women's language of lamentation is staple to story-telling. In acts of story-telling, women begin to reclaim their own anger, sometimes expressed as a desire for retaliatory violence against their partners for the personal, collective, or familial devastation they can now easily see that the abusive partners cause. In this phase, the survivor of domestic violence perceives the partner's behaviour, in socio-psychological terms as dysfunctional socialization, or in religious terms as an ontological issue or as personal sin. One day a woman said, 'If God were a woman, it would be wonderful! I know a lot of men would be going to hell!' The following is an excerpt from a story-telling session in which the women admit their own feelings of vengeance and anger:

Lynn: You have every right to hate this person/for what he did/I was afraid of killing somebody.

Mary Jo: Did you ever think/about burning the bed?/ I thought about that many times.

Annie: You think about/everything/you could do to 'em.

Wanda: It might be very disturbing/but/it's very normal but [I'd think] he's gonna get old and/I'd cut his goddamn throat.

In their exchange, Mary Jo, Annie, and Wanda admit to their overwhelming feeling of anger. The anger brings them together and draws them out of their sleep. It awakens them and, as they re-live their experiences together in the act of story-telling, they are able to experience the attendant feeling as righteous anger.

Rose evokes the anger she feels towards the abusive partner who beat her and molested her daughter for years. In the following passage, she recalls the anger – at one time, a murderous rage because she wanted to kill her husband for sexually abusing their daughter – to call other women out of their denial, their slumber, their avoidance of the issue of violence against women.

> I coulda been on death row/I could have/and it wasn't that far away/ because my daughter was bleeding out of her rectum/... /the only thing I could say was/Lord have mercy/you've been killing my child/then I had to look at her when she asked me/mama/she's twenty-one years old now/... /you were my mother/why didn't you know?/wake up ladies/ wake up/he bad.

Rose is able to evoke anger and then use its evocation as a call to action. She is moving into the third phase of suffering.

Phase 3: Solidarity and Action

The language of the woman in Soelle's third phase of suffering has radically changed. Unlike the Phase 1 sufferer, she is not rendered ineffective by the sheer brutality of the suffering and, unlike the Phase 2 sufferer, she is not rendered less effective by her strong reactions against it. Instead, the pressure of her suffering now results in solidarity. She can organize: that is, her objectives can be organized. She uses rational language. Finally, she experiences an autonomy of action that produces change. She controls her own action. She engages in active behaviour as she helps to shape or reshape her situation. She accepts the reality of her situation, but she seeks to conquer it through changed social or personal structures.

In my shelter work, I have noticed some variations in the basic contours set by Soelle's schema. In Phase 3 shelter women, the rational language regarding their personal situations and their own autonomy at times gives way to an imaginative, creative language with social, communal, and political dimensions. Indeed, rational language entails affective and imaginative elements. This transformation begins with the story-telling as their initial distrust of strangers and outsiders turns into trust in sister-kin, allies, and friends. The need for autonomy transforms into a recognition of the need for critical interdependence: that is, for reciprocity and mutuality between themselves and other battered women, whom they perceive as sisters or supporters. Certainly, the entire healing process is characterized by a growing recognition of healthy interdependence – the need for others. In this phase, however, a loose sense of relationality extends and deepens to a definite sense of commonality and compassion with other persons. Many third-phase women have begun to see how their individual well-being is related to the social good, or the social well-being, of all humankind. In short, the frightful first-phase loss of selfhood has transformed into a willingness to give oneself to others, to make a gift of self to others, as long as it does not compromise one's own integrity. In theological terms, it signals a widening of referentiality: women see their own suffering as intertextuality linked or related to the suffering of others.

With specific regard to their abusive partners, some Phase 3 battered women can actually feel forgiveness (that is, a desire for the well-being of their abusers), but without a need to be in relationship with them. They can feel forgiveness because they can now perceive their partner's behaviour in terms of its nature as a social depravity or a structural, systemic issue. The Phase 2 desire for conquest (a will for 'power-over' a situation) has become a desire for affinity with (a will for 'power-with') others – particularly others who suffer. Their language is less psalmic, more prophetic. Third-phase survivors of domestic violence have been able to transform fear and anger into hope and joy. In its expression, it is often cast in religious or prophetic tones. Mary says, 'One day [men] will come back to the Lord's way! In a spiritual way, God brings justice – now or later in life!'

Many shelter women will not wait. They want to help usher in social transformation now. They experience their changing self as a grounded identity, directed towards political action – however minor it may appear – for social change. After having benefited from its resources, many shelter women express a desire to work for the battered women's movement. Others attend Take Back the Night walks or other local events. A few women return to their pastoral care workers to confront them for the poor advice that, fortunately, they did not heed – advice such as admonishments to return home and try harder to make their marriages work. Nearly all shelter women express an understanding of the need to work for social, structural change. Patricia expresses the feeling concisely: 'We should have a Million Lady Walk!'[18]

The following are excerpts from story-telling sessions. Note the evidence of Phase 3 language, in particular a fuller sense of self, a sense of social connection with others, and a willingness to take action for social change:

Emma: [she is recounting the theft of money from her purse and how she took steps to address the people she believed stole her money] I was hearing and seeing the idea I had from God in what she [her friend, i.e., another shelter woman] said to me. After that, I had such a great confidence that I refused to allow myself to put a lock on my purse. I refuse to become someone I am not. I am a trusting person. I like who I am. I like being friendly. I must be gentle, but wise. The theft was a humbling experience for me. I got to share [the story of how I dealt with it] with my sister and I got to rejoice with my sister. I told her how I was strengthened by it and how I had grown and seen myself grow from the experience. And from where I was – not truly caring!

Sharon: [If I had a wish come true,] I would wish for world peace. I would wish for my kids to be educated and grow up to be very sweet and caring and young men. I would wish to be a person who can reach out and touch other people's minds. Oh Father! If all wishes could come true, bless my wishes!

Vanessa: [In five years, I want to be] working in the social work field helping others achieve their goals. Helping families stay together through struggling times, and assisting them in any way possible with the red tape in our system. To see smiles on faces, instead of desperation and no hope. [Helping] broken-spirited persons will give me joy and [make me] eager to get up to go to work.

What makes it possible for Emma, Sharon, Vanessa, and other women like them to move from states of silence or near silence to the articulation of such degrees of self-consciousness and social awareness?

Hybridization

Clearly, the healing process is phenomenally complex. In some sense, we can never fully know the psychological processes that comprise recovery from trauma. From the standpoint of language scholarship, however, we can consider some suggestive linguistic patterns in the language of battered women. Fundamentally, this evidence suggests that story-telling is a useful activity because it allows for the mixing and melding of various types of language – a process of hybridization – that may assist the healing process. First, some clarification: in order to deal with the complexity of the language of healing, I have made several working assumptions that movement through its generic structure by survivors of domestic violence is socially motivated activity that is nonlinear, multidimensional, and energized through the function of hybridization. In the next sections of my essay, I will analyze excerpts from the testimonials of battered women to support my argument that *hybridization underlies the process of healing by providing a dialogic impetus or dynamic for linguistic transformation.*

In linguistic terms, a hybrid language is a mix or melding of two or more registers or types of language. It is a process of word formation. A hybrid word has elements that come from more than one language. In linguistic philosophy and literary studies, hybridity concerns all language formation, including new combinations from within one and the same language. Indeed, in literary studies, the term is sometimes expanded to include combinations at any level of the meaning system. In my use of the term, I mean to signal differences, contradictions, or heteroglossia *within* one person's language and *between* more than one speaker's language. That is, I mean to signal combinations or evidence of stratification that derives from the mixing of voices in dialogue. My own use of the term is consonant with Bakhtin's when he makes the classic case for the heteroglossic nature of all language – the internal stratification of language into various constituent social languages that make it heteroglot, multi-voiced, multi-styled, multi-languaged (*Dialogic Imagination*, 265). The languages intermix – dialogically – and result in new concepts or new languages. 'The dialogic orientation of discourse is a phenomenon that is, of course, a property of any living discourse' (279). Below he writes:

> Thus at any given movement of its historical existence, language is heteroglot from top to bottom: it represents the co-existence of socio-ideological contradictions between the present and the past, between differing epochs of the past, between different socio-ideological groups in the present, between tendencies, schools, circles and so forth, all given a bodily form. The 'languages' of heteroglossia intersect each other in a variety of ways, forming new socially typifying 'languages.' (291)

This process is the crux of language change. Yet, in my view, some genres seem fraught with overt instances of hybridity. The language of healing is noticeably replete with instances of hybridity because, as survivors of domestic violence move from one phase to the next, they carry along instances of prior or parallel worldviews, diverse life conceptions, or articulations. And as they take part in new kinds of social activity in the shelter with new interlocutors, survivors assimilate new languages. The degree to which they are able to do so has important implications for their recovery from trauma. The crises of domestic violence (the loss of a partner, home, sometimes children and jobs) may lever open the meaning-making practices of survivors as they struggle to make sense of their destabilized situations. 'The inner dialectic quality of the sign comes out fully in the open only in times of social crises or revolutionary changes,' argues Volosinov (23).

Hence hybridity, contradictions, semantic anomalies, conceptual tensions abound: many types of languages or linguistic concepts may function side by side in the language of survivors. The contradictions are open to reflection or to question by interlocutors. Thus, the borders between concepts, the linguistic interfaces, implicitly hold the possibility of transformation and change. Hybridity and its resultant contradictions can also result from negotiating, compromising, and creating shared meanings with other women in the shelter. Slight semantic shifts may occur as the survivors transfer words and meaning from one context to the next, thus thrusting language into new forms and functions and the speakers into new linguistic territory. The destabilization of their life situation and pressure from new acquaintances (i.e., house residents, staff, and volunteers) may contribute to a *spiralling movement* of meaning shifts or language changes – from silence to lament to increased social connection or solidarity. I use the term 'spiralling' to suggest that the process is not necessarily unidirectional, linear, or permanent; rather, it is dialogic and thus not necessarily predictably or uniformly realized. Yet the dialogic activity between previous, current, or possible frames of mind about battered women's lives and experience can result in language change, the opening of an imaginative space for the realization of autonomy and self-in-(healthy)-relation: that is, healing.

Religious and Secular Language Hybridization

To illustrate the concept of hybridization and its function in the healing process of domestic violence survivors, I will focus, in one story-telling session, on one particular type of mix in the language of the battered women. Although I choose this particular intersection solely to illustrate my argument, the interplay of religious with secular languages is indeed far more frequent in the language of battered women than most social, feminist, or cultural workers have acknowledged.

By 'religious' language, I simply mean language relating to the divine or transcendent or to Christian beliefs and practices. Broadly speaking, 'secular' language is nonreligious language; however, in this discussion, I will limit my focus to distinguishable varieties such as the languages of self-help, folk wisdom, human rights, and courts/criminal justice. These types of secular languages may be conceptualized generally as languages of self-consciousness and liberation, that is, languages regarding moving out of the condition of domestic crisis and into well-being. They may be drawn from the women's own life experience or community or assimilated from the language of other resident women or staff who advise, advocate, or teach group sessions on domestic violence, drug and alcohol abuse, codependency, etc. In dealing with religious language, I will try to make qualitative differentiation between simply religious language and 'spiritual' language, that is, language that expresses a sense of self, authority, or agency above and beyond the dogma, traditionalism, or habit of religion and its institutions. Very roughly speaking, in the following exchanges secular and religious language are linguistic evidence of Phase 2 concepts; social and spiritual languages are evidence of Phase 3 concepts.

The following is excerpted[19] from a story-telling session. Notice the ways in which secular and religious mix in dynamic or dialogic ways in the exchanges:

1 *VANESSA:* I always had my faith. I say my prayers at night. I put more
2 faith in God and not in him [abuser]. Do you know how I know?
3 Because I was torn enough to get out

4 before it got too bad. I was torn about him and God helped me to get out.
5 *CHLOE:* It's different for Vanessa than for me. Vanessa came up in a loving
6 family. I had a bad life ... I had to try to believe in God. I had to try ...
7 *VANESSA:* I felt it in my heart. You have to feel it in your heart. You can't
8 do it with your head.
9 *CAROL:* what do you feel in your heart when you feel God?
10 *VANESSA:* I feel happiness in my heart. When it comes to God, it seems
11 like when I'm walking down this dark road I can see this light at the
12 end. I know there's a light ahead.
13 *CHLOE:* I don't want it to be too late before I start doing what I'm sup-
14 posed to do! In the bible, it can be so harsh!
15 *CAROL:* Do you find out about God from the Bible?
16 *CHLOE:* The Bible is very complex and real scary and other people look at
17 it as being the truth but the Bible contradicts itself.

[A short discussion of how most people think God is a male and how this
leads some men to think they are better than women. Both women disagree
with the image of God as male.]

18 *VANESSA:* [Men] do think they are better. Do you know the saying,
19 'Behind every good man, there's a woman'? It's never the other way
20 around.
21 *CHLOE:* They think they are better because of Adam and Eve ... Women
22 believe more in God. They have to. They have to take so much stuff.
23 They have to have something to hold onto. Men have each other. Men
24 stick together. They have one another.
25 *VANESSA:* But a woman doesn't have anybody. Suppose you are just out
26 there by yourself.
27 God is the only person you can believe in.
28 *CHLOE:* Me too. I don't have no girlfriends when I get into trouble ... If
29 God were a woman, it would be wonderful. I know a lot of men would
30 be going to hell!
31 *VANESSA:* Me too. I know I would be standing. I try to be a good person.
32 Carol: Does that mean God [as a man] lets men get away with stuff?
33 *VANESSA:* God lets men get away with stuff! Women pay more on earth,
34 more than men.
35 Guys don't think about it. They are not going to get their consequences 'til
36 after they die. Women get it now. But when they die, they are going
37 to get it.
38 *CHLOE:* A woman God is for women.

39 *VANESSA:* In my case, I called the police. I was the one being abused. He
40 snatched my sons. I called the police and they said he can do it because
41 he is their natural dad. That's not fair! Turn the tables. I would go to
42 jail for kidnapping them. The laws are so messed up. If a woman kills
43 a man, she gets fifteen to twenty-five years in jail. If a man kills
44 his wife,
45 he gets six years. I don't understand that! It's not fair. They don't get
46 what they deserve. We get punished a lot harder than a man.

[A short discussion about different penalties for different legal charges,
followed by a discussion of the O.J. Simpson trial. The gist of this second
discussion is twofold. First, it concerns the bias in the way whites report black
crime. Second, it concerns the way in which men are apparently able to harm
women with impunity. The foci of the critique are the media and the legal
system. Vanessa, who is an African American, and Chloe, who is Anglo,
appear to be equally dissatisfied with the outcome of the trial. The participants agree Simpson is guilty.]

47 *CHLOE:* Anyway, there's biases because of who has control. The country is
48 run by rich white men. The church too.

[A discussion about the patriarchal nature of one of the other shelter women's
church.]

49 *VANESSA:* That's why I don't belong to no church. I read the Bible. Now
50 and then I read the Bible. I feel in my heart what I have to do. I ain't
51 going by his rules or her rules. No, I can't get into that.
52 *CHLOE:* I be having a problem with the Bible all the time. Most people do,
53 but they just believe anyway. They don't admit the story is wrong ...
54 The Bible starts out with Adam and Eve. The world thinks women
55 are evil. Eve got Adam to eat the apple.
56 Everyone says women are evil. So the stories in the Bible are like that –
57 against women. It is not right.
58 *VANESSA:* [My abuser] thinks God is on his side.
59 *CAROL:* It's like a blank card to do anything.
60 *VANESSA:* There's your freedom to do anything you want to do.

In this series of exchanges, the language hybrids are clear on the rhetorical or narrative level. Chloe and Vanessa are engaging in dialogic
activity with both religious and secular content. On the level of the

clause, the secular languages can be characterized as those of folk wisdom (lines 19–20), criminal justice (lines 39–42), legal/judicial (lines 42–6 and O.J. Simpson trial discussion), popular politics (lines 47–8), popular psychology (lines 18, 33–7, and throughout), domestic violence (line 39), human rights (lines 39–57); subclausally, there are secular themes and metaphors regarding the journey or escape (lines 3–4), the moral trial (lines 5–6), and justice/punishments (42–5). Regarding the heteroglossic mix of language, however, Chloe and Vanessa both contribute from their own differing standpoints. As Chloe points out, 'It's different for Vanessa than for me. Vanessa came up in a loving big family. I had a bad life ... I had to try to believe in God' (lines 5–6). Indeed, of the two women, Vanessa is the one who (initially at least) articulates the most conventional or uncritical religious perspective. Initially, her language appears to be largely Phase 2 language; Chloe uses the most Phase 3 language. Still the tension of the secular-religious hybridity creates a spiraling or recursive effect that results in both women engaging, if momentarily, in Phase 3 worldviews.

To illustrate, I will first briefly consider the language of each woman and then discuss the ways their contributions propel the conversation forward. Notice, however, that there are traces of Phase 1 circumstances in the language of both women. They both recall a prior world – the days before they arrived at the shelter – in which they were isolated and alienated (lines 25–8). As she re-lives her Phase 1 experience, Chloe chooses the present tense: 'I don't have no girlfriends ...' In the actual present, of course, she counts Vanessa and other shelter women as her friends. In contrast, Vanessa's language is speculative: 'Suppose you are just out there by yourself ...' The chosen frame for her presentation – an imaginative world – indicates she now considers herself beyond (what I am defining as) Phase 1 circumstances; additionally, she is inviting her interlocutors, through the act of story-telling, to imagine this circumstance, to enter emphatically into it, as she rehearses a past life that no longer exists.

Vanessa's Language in Terms of Phases and Meaning Shifts

When she is not re-living her suffering, Vanessa uses Phase 2 language, initially, about religious and secular issues. Lines 1–4 reveal a somewhat uncritical religious perspective. Lines 18–20 make clear a somewhat limited though still Phase 2 awareness of her social situation. For instance, her language reveals a clear anger towards her abuser and, in lines 18–20, her view appears to be shaped solely from her own experience with him (for surely not all men think they are better than all women and 'behind' some women there are supportive men). That is, she initially does not have a full social awareness of her personal situation. Her language does not give evidence of social analysis. Yet her argument is coherent and cohesive: emotions and rationality are communicated together though her anger sometimes overwhelms her objectivity, that is, her ability to see other perspectives or possibilities.

There are additional Phase Two modalities in her language. For example, there are traces of a sense of righteousness in Vanessa's anger. Her abuser has clearly violated moral, criminal, and legal codes; yet the legal and criminal justice systems and (interestingly enough) God seem to protect men – the latter, at least, while men are on earth. While Vanessa is angry about this, her language is psalmic: it is a language of lamentation. Lamentation is composed of both complaint and praise. In Vanessa's language, in addition to the plaintive modality, there is a tone of praise and worship. When asked what she feels when she 'feels God,' she says, 'I feel happiness in my heart. When it comes to God, it seems like when I'm walking down this dark road I can see this light at the end. I know there's a light ahead!' (lines 10–12). God is praised for being or showing the light even though – she complains – the road is dark. Ultimately, she counts on God to render justice. Hence, overall, her objectives are utopian. (And why not? She cannot count on the criminal justice or the legal systems to help her.) Pragmatically, however, she accepts her situation and, despite the recalcitrance of the criminal justice or legal systems, she seeks to change her own situation through existing social structures (e.g., 'In my case, I called the police' [line 39]). More precisely: of her own accord, she does not imagine alternative or more effective social structures, but she does imagine retribution, if only in a religious sense: 'But when they [men] die, they are going to get it' (lines 36–7).

By the time Vanessa utters the last exchange of the conversation, however, she has substantially altered both her religious and secular language. In lines 33–7, Vanessa is applying in a modest way a sociocultural critique of religion. By lines 39–46, she is forming a critique of social institutions. Further, by lines 49–51, Vanessa is performing a full Phase 3 sense of her own authority in spiritual matters and, by line 60, she is performing a full critique of religion as an institution. In short, she is demonstrating some clear Phase 3 sensibilities. Her secular language has assumed a fuller social analytic; her religious language has been elaborated as more critical and more maturely spiritual. She recognizes that, when her abuser uses the Bible to justify his actions, he is giving himself an undue freedom (lines 58–60). She asserts her own authority in spiritual matters rather than relying on her abuser's authority or a church's rules or dogma: 'I feel in my heart what I have to do! I ain't going by his rules or her rules' (lines 50–1).

Chloe's Language in Terms of Phases and Meaning Shifts

Chloe displays somewhat more Phase 3 language overall in the session, particularly regarding secular matters. She evidences less anger towards men than Vanessa. Chloe more evenly balances rationality and emotionality in the conversation: it would seem she has slightly more willingness to think with equanimity about gender and gender relations. (She does believe women are more 'spiritual' than men and she thinks women are closer to God, but this is because men have a different temporal frame of reference: 'Men think for the day; women think for the future and God is their reward.') Though she has had 'a very bad life,' she appears more willing to forgive. Chloe is not paralysed by anger; she is not simply reactive. She is able to shape a perspective based on a wider view than solely her personal experience.

Ultimately, Chloe's perspective on both secular and religious matters is more fully socially analytical. She repeatedly offers a social analysis of religious matters. In line 21, she is offering a critique of dogmatic or fundamental religious views that surface in biblical interpretation. She understands (lines 23–4) that men have an advantage because they 'stick together,' with the implication being that women suffer because they do not; she understands the impact of lack of solidarity on women's lives. In lines 28–30, she is again rendering a social/cultural critique by implying that justice is a gendered concept. Chloe clearly understands (lines 47–8) that the social system (including legal, criminal, and religious systems) is dominated by wealthy white males.

Although Chloe's view is more than simply religious or religiously doctrinaire, she is initially spiritually unsure of herself or she evidences contradictions in her thinking (lines 13–14 in contrast with lines 16–17). She does not share Vanessa's initial dogmatic religious point of view, but she accepts her basic perspective and so her sensibilities fluctuate. By line 38, however, her language is, in fact, imaginative, creative, prophetic. 'A woman God is for women!' she declares, calling prophetically for a universe rectified or ordered by female justice. Surely, these are signs of a Phase 3 consciousness moving towards critical interdependence with other women. By lines 56–7, Chloe is performing a more fully mature spirituality, that is, she has assumed her own authority in matters spiritual: it is not right to use Scripture to limit or control women socially. Her statements seem to broach issues related to the meaning of life and her place in it. She has clearly broken the habit of seeking the approval of others, including men, family, and the churches. Her mystical experience is a social or communal experience. Indicating traces of political consciousness, she says, 'If God were a woman, it would be wonderful!'

Neither Chloe's nor Vanessa's sense of the need for social connection or solidarity with women is rendered, however, in explicitly political terms (i.e., in the sense of understanding the need to organize or engage in concrete actions). They do understand the problem of the lack of solidarity (lines 23–5). But they appear to seek to conquer this through changed personal or spiritual/cosmic structures rather than strictly social structures. For example, Chloe implies that if God were female, justice would be better served. Vanessa trusts only in divine efficiency: 'God is the only person you can believe in' (line 27). The two women do not offer political ideas for social change though, clearly, Vanessa and Chloe understand the need for change. Indeed, as they told me more than once in our interactions, they viewed sharing their words in this study as a contribution to the battered women's movement.

Still, within this set of exchanges, the conversation moves on a general trajectory from worldly to religious matters and from legal to sociopolitical matters. The trajectory is not unilinear. Rather, it proceeds with spiralling (or recursive) 'movements of mind' as Chloe and Vanessa return again and again to basic issues of fairness, justice, and right living interspersed with moments of their own sexism, anger, and religious dogma. The ideas advance and recede. They are rearticulated and recast. The critical point, however, is this: in the end, Chloe and Vanessa have participated in a kind of dialectic activity that results in the co-production of a more liberatory worldview (temporary though it may prove to be [cf. Berger 18–12, 32]). Perhaps neither could have arrived there alone.

Dialogism and the Spiral of Change

In relation to the curvilinear movement of the phases, there are contradictions in the worldviews of both women. For example, Vanessa does not question the discrepancy in the way God appears to divvy out justice to men as opposed to women. Other parts of the conversation (not recorded above) demonstrate both women's fundamental sexism against women though they decry the sexism of men. ('You can't trust a woman,' Vanessa says; Chloe adds: 'Women are conniving.')

Yet Chloe and Vanessa are learning from one another. They are clearly attending to relationality by listening carefully to one another, agreeing or accepting, modifying or yielding, challenging and meeting one another's challenges as they jointly construct (within the confines of this conversation at least) a mutually acceptable worldview composed of some clearly differing worldviews or languages. This creates the spiral activity and the 'energy' or impetus to influence each other's levels of perception or awareness.

Important moments in the conversation happen at specific junctures or locations. Chloe adds positively to the movement in lines 21–4 and 38. Generally speaking, in these moments, she is applying social analysis or cultural critiques to religious matters. Vanessa engages and responds, respectively, beginning in lines 25–6 and lines 39–46. It is as if the exchanges are being meshed together and a spiral motion is being created.

Notice that between lines 36–8, between lines 46–7, and certainly by the last utterance, Chloe and Vanessa are in positions of agreement and accordance: a kind of co-production made by acts of negotiations, respect, or reciprocity/mutuality. Conceived broadly, with Chloe's help, Vanessa moves from articulating a relatively uncritical religious and secular view to a more fully critical view. By the end of the conversation, she evidences more social and spiritual awareness. With Vanessa's help, Chloe moves from articulating an ambiguous or uncertain spiritual sense of self to a more fully authoritative spiritual stance. They are able to do this because the energy of each other's contributions – the dialogism – helps them to recast their initial articulations into language more self-consciously aware and mutually accommodating. In short, together they create a new world.

Interestingly, Chloe and Vanessa are able to imagine this new world because they subvert traditional formulations about religion, an institution – they imply – that unduly influences gender roles and relations. In effect, two very religious women use resistance or subversion to reorder their worlds. Through the use of hybrid language forms and ensuing changes or shifts in meaning, they render God as female and her justice as sure.

The Applicability of the Findings: Some Conclusions

Clearly, conversation, dialogue, or story-telling advances the healing process. This has been a truism in feminist thought for quite some time. Yet it is helpful to know why shared conversation or story-telling is healing so that we might better provide the conditions, the challenging or safe space, for it to happen. In this way, we can more skilfully accompany victims of violence on their way towards well-being. Through hybridization of communal language, that is, through the shifting and mixing of language, opportunities for new understandings are created. Epiphanies may happen. Linguistic transformation may occur. New languages may emerge. The dialogism or the energy of hybridization may move women to communal (rather than primarily personal or individual) frameworks of awareness.

This transformation is the essential feature of Phase 3 language. One of the many possibilities of Phase 3 sensibility is that more individualistic 'secular' language is transformed into more 'social' language.[20] As I mentioned earlier, in Phase 3, the emphasis on personal situations gives way to a new emphasis on social concepts, structures, causes, solutions. Empowerment can derive from this new understanding: individual women are subjected to domestic violence because our society condones violence against all women. As women begin to understand the many meanings of this social fact, they begin to be aware of what may have to occur before they can be truly safe, truly equal. As caretakers or concerned listeners, as neighbours, teachers, and friends, we might be more fully aware of these possibilities and accompany women as we try to make possibilities into everyday realities.

To make one final clarification, however, I do not suggest that all women in the shelter engage the linguistic trajectory I have described here.[21] I do not suggest that all battered women move through such phases of healing in the way I have described. I do not predict universals in the language of healing. Anthropologists, linguists, and sociologists study the profundity and profusion of cross-cultural variation in social behaviour and language practices, and my study is of a local setting in a particular place and time. Scholars of culture and language recognize, however, that ranges of human behaviour do cross cultures; thus, we are invited to think in terms of commonalities or strategic patterns based on similarities in social structure. I propose that many women who struggle for health and well-being, for healing, do evidence some movement along the trajectory I describe in this study. I suggest that similar linguistic patterns may very well surface cross-culturally based on universals in women's subordinate positions vis-à-vis men. To the extent that women occupy similar spaces in religious doctrine and the socio-cultural imagination, with similar constraints on behaviour, they may behave in similar ways at the strategic level I describe in this study.[22] Granting individual variation based on degree and kind of adherence to religious and gender socialization, we could expect similarities across situations or contexts in which scripture is used to relegate women to a secondary status and to police their social behaviour by any means necessary, including physical violence, which can result in women's social isolation, political alienation and personal loss of self-esteem.[23] This situation, of course, exists in innumerable loci cross-culturally. In this study, we get a glimpse of the language of healing for women in a specific community that may speak to other situations, other women, other ranges of a human language of healing.

In this particular shelter, most women are African American and white Appalachian women from Holiness/Sanctified or fundamentalist/evangelical denominations. They do share some cultural and religious practices and beliefs, including the centrality of Scripture and a conservative reckoning of gender roles. The advantage of being at the shelter for these women and for other women who seek protection from domestic violence by entering shelters is that, by virtue of the effect of the many and diverse stories (including the diversity of religious experience), the secular and religious may assume (or awaken into) fuller and felt realizations on their way to being social and spiritual quests/liberations/transformations. This is because there is more opportunity to revisit Phases 2 and 3 in community. More simply: there is more opportunity for creating intersections through the act of story-telling when there are more people willing and able to speak and listen. Story-telling is more than simply a rehearsal of past events or an exercise in emotional release; story-telling is sharing and shaping possible worlds. When we tell our stories to one another we are, metaphorically, etching a map of where we have been and where we might be in the future.

At its best, the shelter provides this opportunity. Women in crisis may have a unique and, for the first time in their adult lives, unbroken opportunity to do so – given the extent to which their abusive partners have tried, in the past, to isolate them from friends and family, from social interaction.[24]

Notes

1 Shortly, I will discuss the ethnographic methodology upon which this study was based. By story-telling and 'story-telling circle,' I do not mean to suggest that we tell stories with a typical narrative structure that involves, for example, an introduction, building climax, and resolution. I use this term in a very general sense to denote casual conversations in which the women share autobiographical details, that is, their life stories, the stories of their upbringing, marriage, and abuse, for example. 'Telling one's story' is a feminist consciousness-raising strategy of long duration. I would also like to point out that these sessions are not counselling sessions. They are get-togethers meant to provide women with a safe space to write and talk about topics of their own choice.

2 I will not analyse the language for markers of race/ethnicity or for distinctions in Holiness/Sanctified or fundamentalist/evangelical backgrounds. Though there are clear distinctions in the theologies or theodicies (that is, explanations for God's relationship to suffering) of these two denominations, I consider only a general religious language here. The two denominations, however, are currently very similar in terms of understanding gender roles and relationships. I will not focus on race/ethnicity, although African American and white battered women often face different struggles and speak accordingly.

3 Cf. Balsamo; Haraway; speech genres in Bakhtin, *Speech Genres*; and linguistic creativity in Volosinov. See also de Lauretis, *Technologies*, 'Violence.'

4 *The Human Rights Watch Global Report on Women's Human Rights* (New York: Human Rights Watch, 1995), 341. Violence against women includes physical, sexual, and psychological abuse; domestic violence is generally understood to be violence against women within family or intimate relationships.

5 For a classic discussion, see Dobash and Dobash, *Violence against Wives*.

6 See Bersani and Chen for a good discussion of the main sociological theories on family violence, including these perspectives: resource; exchange/social control; symbolic interaction perspectives; subculture of violence views; conflict perspectives; patriarchal; ecological; and general systems. See also Dobash and Dobash, 'Violence Against Women,' and Mazur Abel.

7 See the 1994 and 1996 U.S. Bureau of Justice Statistics Selected Findings documents, which summarize data produced by the Bureau of Justice, the National Crime Victimization Survey, and the FBI's Uniform Crime Re-

ports. Documents are available at http://www.ojp.usdoj.gov/bjs/pub/ press. The documents used in this essay were accessed on June 11, 1998.

8 For a sampling of the literature, see Brownell; Kenney and Brown; hooks; and Gondolf et al.

9 See Fetterman for an introduction to ethnographic methods.

10 An idiolect is an individual's use of the language, sometimes called a 'personal dialect.' A register is a social use of the language, such as scientific, religious, and so forth.

11 See Volosinov 12–13. Most scholars believe Volosinov is, in fact, M.M. Bakhtin.

12 'Healing' is the word I use to designate a linguistic movement from alienation to articulation and relationality. The designation is not intended to signal permanent or profound psychological, theological, or cognitive development, though in fact it may do so. Women in the shelter use many and various terms to name aspects of this same trajectory, including 'healing,' 'helping,' 'coming on out,' 'coming back to yourself,' 'giving it over,' 'getting through,' and 'turning it over to God.'

13 In some senses, the opposite of suffering is not pleasure so much as it is meaningful social connection or solidarity with others although, clearly, social solidarity can entail a deep sense of suffering. I do not wish to suggest that when women experience greater autonomy by being able to control their own lives without fear of violence, they no longer suffer. Certainly the meanings of suffering are culturally, religiously invested.

14 I do not wish to overstate this idea. In fact, social pressure from staff is only one motivation for participation in shelter life. Women who come to the shelter have already decided or agreed to make a fundamental, if temporary, change in their lives. The decision is often based on fear for their lives or for the lives of their children. However, a primary characteristic of their subsequent conversations with other shelter women is the compassion and empathy many women begin to feel for one another. A woman who knows she is expected to enter into the flow of shelter life, however, may initially participate without such sensibilities.

15 These phases were initially posited by Soelle to account for the experience of intense suffering, for example, of Holocaust survivors. Soelle is a feminist theologian influenced by the work of philosopher Simone Weil, especially in her development of the notion of 'affliction' (see Weil's *Waiting for God*, particularly p. 122). Soelle's framework is developed with sensitivity towards victims' spiritual dilemma; she attends to the religious imagination of victims, and for this reason her perspective is very amenable to my purpose.

Other writers have suggested stages of healing or awareness from suffering and trauma, including Judith L. Herman, Carol P. Christ (1980), and Gutierrez. Herman's model is similar to Soelle's. It involves three stages of recovery: safety, remembrance and mourning, and reconnection. Herman works with trauma survivors of various sorts, including rape and child abuse victims, and her model is a therapeutic model. I choose Soelle's model here for its simplicity and applicability, but I have adapted and amended her categories. Soelle is also concerned with suffering as a theological category and, in other phases of my work with Holiness/ Sanctified and fundamentalist/evangelical women, I am more concerned about their theological and religious language. Please note that in my use of both the words 'phase' and 'genre,' I mean for readers to hold in mind the nonlinear, flexible, and multidimensional nature of the process I describe. I am not suggesting any type of process except a fluid and curvilinear one.

16 Beyond the ken of this study are the reasons that, certainly, are as complex as the human beings that arrive at the shelter. Some women never integrate into shelter life. Some appear locked into a phase, particularly Phase 2. Some women leave the shelter within days or even hours of their arrival.

17 In theological terms, the language of lamentation includes features not only of complaint, but of praise, worship, and even divine retribution. In the Old Testament Book of Job, Job struggles with ideas of retribution in the face of his own perceived innocence (see Gutierrez, chapter 4, especially 30). These features do indeed appear in the language of shelter women. Depending on the specific context of utterance, there may be a change of tone or emphasis on one or more of the features.

18 Whether domestic violence survivors are able to engage in organized political work for social change is a different issue. Many women are struggling to survive; thus, collective or organized work for social change is beyond their immediate focus or opportunity. Most women articulate a willingness to work for social change through personal interaction or by witnessing to other women and girls. The context in which many women imagine their social change work is local, communal, interpersonal, or simply abstract. To be sure, most women – either within or outside the shelter – do not engage in political organizations. In my view, social networking or acts of solidarity between women support social change.

19 The transcript has been shortened to accommodate the length requirements of this essay. I have indicated deletions and condensations with brackets.

20 This is not to say that hybridity ends. It only suggests that individual or self-oriented secular languages have a fuller realization with emphases on

the communal or social. The speaker is more socially conscious, aware of how, as an individual, she fits into the social framework. For example, a shelter woman might continue to speak of her *desire* or *need* for a violence-free life, but she will also begin to speak about her *right* to a violence-free life and the responsibility of society to ensure it.

21 It bears repeating that my study does not offer quantitative or statistically significant numerical data. Rather, I offer ethnographically gathered, qualitative evidence (knowledge or data derived from field notes, story-telling session transcripts, in-depth interviews, and so forth) to substantiate my sense of shelter experience as I understand it.

22 See Penelope Brown for a wonderful articulation of such a position in her work on a language and gender in a Mayan community (97). I have recast segments of her articulation. In arriving at this position on language universals and applicability, I have also benefited from the work of other feminist linguists, including Penelope Eckert and Sally McConnell-Ginet, who argue for ethnographic and other interdisciplinary studies to further our understanding of social, cultural, and language universals – all with the understanding that we will never arrive at 'a detailed theory of the general principles and parameters of gender and language interactions. ' Instead we hope to 'get a gripe on the ranges of human language, thought, and social life' (454).

23 Recall that the three phases of the healing process were first used by Dorothee Soelle to describe the behaviour of Holocaust survivors. These phases clearly have wider applicability to other categories of trauma survivors (cf., for example, Herman for similar categories). The religious components of these battered women's language have a more restricted applicability.

24 See Winkelmann for further discussion. The names of women quoted in this essay are pseudonyms; their words are used with permission.

Works Cited

Abel, Eileen Mazur. 'Psychosocial Treatments for Battered Women: A Review of Empirical Research.' *Research on Social Work Practice* 10.1 (2000): 55–77.
———— *The Dialogic Imagination*. Trans. Michael Holquist and Caryl Emerson, ed. Michael Holquist. Austin: University of Texas Press, 1981.
Bakhtin, M.M. *Speech Genres and Other Late Essays*. Trans. Vern W. McGee, ed. Caryl Emerson and Michael Holquist. Austin: University of Texas Press, 1986.

Balsamo, Anne. *Technologies of the Gendered Body: Reading Cyborg Women.* Durham: Duke University Press, 1996.

Bendroth, Margaret Lamberts. *Fundamentalism and Gender, 1875 to the Present.* New Haven, CT: Yale University Press, 1993.

Berger, Peter L. *The Sacred Canopy: Elements of a Sociological Theory of Religion.* Garden City, NY: Doubleday, 1969.

Bersani, Carl A., and Huey-Tsyh Chen. 'Sociological Perspectives in Family Violence.' In *Handbook of Family Violence*, ed. V.B. Van Hasselt, 57–86. New York: Plenum, 1988.

Brown, Penelope. 'How and Why Are Women More Polite: Some Evidence from a Mayan Community.' In *Language and Gender*, ed. Jennifer Coates, 81–99. Oxford: Blackwell, 1998.

Brownell, Patricia. 'Multicultural Practice and Domestic Violence.' In *Multicultural Perspectives in Working With Families*, ed. Elaine P. Congress, 217–35. New York: Springer, 1997.

Christ, Carol P., *Diving Deep and Surfacing: Women Writers on Spiritual Quest.* Boston: Beacon, 1980.

de Lauretis, Teresa. *Technologies of Gender: Essays on Theory, Film, and Fiction.* Bloomington: Indiana University Press, 1987.

———— 'The Violence of Rhetoric: Considerations on Representation and Gender.' In *The Violence of Representation: Literature and the History of Violence*, ed. Nancy Armstrong and Leonard Tennenhouse, 239–58. New York: Routledge, 1989.

Dobash, R. Emerson, and Russell P. Dobash. 'Violence against Women.' In *Gender Violence: Interdisciplinary Perspectives*, ed. Laura L. O'Toole and Jessica R. Schiffman, 266–78. New York: New York University Press, 1997.

———— *Violence against Wives: A Case against the Patriarchy.* New York: Free Press, 1979.

Eckert, Penelope, and Sally McConnell-Ginet. 'Think Practically and Look Locally: Language and Gender as Community-Based Practice. In *The Women and Language Debate*, ed. Camille Roman, Suzanne Juhasz, and Cristanne Miller, 432–60. Brunswick, NJ: Rutgers University Press, 1994.

Fetterman, David M. *Ethnography: Step by Step.* 2nd ed. Thousand Oaks, CA: Sage, 1998.

Gilkes, Cheryl Townsend. '"Together and in Harness": Women's Traditions in the Sanctified Church.' In *Black Women in America: Social Science Perspectives*, ed. Micheline R. Malson, Elisabeth Mudimbe-Boyi, Jean F. O'Barr, and Mary Wyer, 223–44. Chicago: University of Chicago Press, 1990.

Gondolf, Edward W., Ellen Fisher, and J. Richard McFerron. 'Racial Differ-

ences among Shelter Residents: A Comparison of Anglo, Black, and His-
panic Battered.' *Journal of Family Violence* 39.3 (1988): 48–49.

Gutierrez, Gustavo. *On Job: God-Talk and the Suffering of the Innocent.*
Maryknoll, NY: Orbis, 1987.

Hanks, William F. 'Discourse Genres in a Theory of Practice.' *American Eth-
nologist* 14 (1987): 668–92.

————— *Language and Communicative Practices.* Boulder, CO: Westview, 1996.

————— 'Language Form and Communicative Practices.' In *Rethinking Linguistic Relativity*, ed. John J. Gumpertz and Stephen C. Levinson, 232–70. Cambridge: Cambridge University Press, 1996.

————— 'Text and Textuality.' *Annual Review of Anthropology* 18 (1989): 95–127.

Haraway, Donna J. 'A Cyborg Manifesto: Science, Technology, and Socialist-
Feminism in the Late Twentieth Century.' In Haraway, *Simians, Cyborgs, and
Women: The Reinvention of Nature*, 149–81. New York: Routledge, 1991.

Herman, Judith Lewis. *Trauma and Recovery.* New York: Basic, 1992.

hooks, bell. 'Violence in Intimate Relationships.' In hooks, *Talking Back: Thinking Feminist/Thinking Black*, 84–91. Boston: South End, 1989.

Kenney, Catherine T., and Karen R. Brown. *Report from the Front Lines: The
Impact of Violence on Poor Women.* New York: National Organization of
Women Legal Defense and Education Fund, 1996.

Leech, Geoffrey N. *Explorations in Semantics and Pragmatics.* Amsterdam: John
Benjamins, 1980.

Scarry, Elaine. *The Body in Pain: The Making and Unmaking of the World.* New
York: Oxford University Press, 1985.

Soelle, Dorothee. *Suffering.* Trans. Everett R. Katlin. Philadelphia: Fortress, 1975.

Townes, Emilie M. *In a Blaze of Glory: Womanist Spirituality as Social Witness.*
Nashville, TN: Abingdon, 1995.

—————, ed. *A Troubling in My Soul: Womanist Perspectives on Evil and Suffering.*
Maryknoll, NY: Orbis, 1993.

U.S. Department of Justice. 'Murder by Intimates Declined 36 Percent since
1976; Decrease Greater for Male than for Female Victims.' (1998). Available
at http://www.ojp.usdoj.gov/bjs/pub/press/vi.pr.

Senate Judiciary Committee. 'Facts about Violence Against Women.' http://
www.inform.umd.edu/EdRes/To.../genderIssues/violence+Women /facts.

Volosinov, V.N. *Marxism and the Philosophy of Language.* Trans. Ladislav
Matejka and I.R. Titunik. Cambridge: Harvard University Press, 1986.

Weil, Simone. *Waiting for God.* Trans. Emma Craufurd with Introduction by
Leslie A. Fiedler. New York: G.P. Putnam, 1951.

Winkelmann, Carol L. *The Language of Battered Women: A Rhetorical Analysis of
Personal Theologies.* Albany, NY: State University of New York Press, 2004.

Conclusion

CHRISTINE SHEARER-CREMEAN
AND CAROL L. WINKELMANN

Survivor rhetoric is complex, multi-layered, dialogic, and situated discourse. When researchers, academics, women's advocates, social workers, and other care providers fail to recognize the dynamic, fluid, and often contradictory nature of language in context, they risk creating a falsely linear or universalizing perspective on personal healing and social change. One consequence of the tendency to conceptualize language in static terms is to delegitimize the lived experience of survivors. Another consequence is the tendency of professionals, academics, and other providers to become isolated and entrenched in their separate specialties, disciplines, and communities of interest. Static discipline-anchored paradigms cannot create the epistemological and political bridges needed for social change.

Progressive social change to eliminate violence against women and girl children calls for inter-agency, cross-community, interdisciplinary, and indeed global response. Countering the problem of violence against women requires approaches that do not make singular, monolithic, or hegemonic assumptions, even about the seemingly self-evident concepts of violence and patriarchy. Solutions must take up the challenges of the situational and the particular, and simultaneously reveal and advance the interconnections, the bridges, between even seemingly disparate discourses competing to represent women and the violence against them within the economic, social, cultural, and political spheres. Contradictions and conflict in representation cannot be ignored or dismissed, for ignored contradictions hide power inequities and privilege some sectors of society over others. As feminist scholars working towards identifying multiple truths about the nature of gender violence, we believe that we can mark out spaces of power inequality and imbalance through sustained analysis of linguistic evidence – as ultimately elusive as that endeavour may be.

The recognition of the unique, along with the re-imagining of what has been assumed to be universal, make it possible to develop a more adequate and holistic approach to the problem of violence against women. When an episode of violence or oppression is made manifest linguistically in different discursive sites or locations, it does not remain intact and unchanged. Indeed, an episode may not even be named and labelled as violence or oppression unless it finds itself in a certain community with certain cultural assumptions. Thus, the concerns of experts or advocates in different locations may not coincide; indeed, the concerns of Western feminists and non-Western feminists frequently fail to coincide. For instance, the practice of clitoridectomy is typically regarded by Western feminists as violent, but many non-Western feminists recognize the practice as extraordinarily complex and culturally bound. Non-Western feminists do not necessarily claim that clitoridectomy is not violent or inhumane; rather, they balk at the reductive, reactionary, and simplistic nature of Western feminists' critique.

Further, some feminists tend to make assumptions about problems and solutions that – for others – do not seem cogent or appropriate. Contemporary debates over the Islamic practice of women's veiling, which Western women generally decry as oppressive, are a case in point. Yet the practices of Islam currently are only the most visible aspect of the debates about the situation and status of women within the public or global forum. Muslim scholars, both Western and non-Western, tread through a linguistic minefield when they make choices about terms such as 'patriarchal' and 'sexual inequality' or the use of even the oppositional terms 'Western' and 'non-Western,' which seem to pose a hyper-separation between the West and Islam (Barlas xii–xiii; Wadud xviii). Yet, as the writers of this volume show, interdisciplinary and intercommunity languages often do not neatly coincide.

Perceptions, and thus language, are always culturally, socially, and communally influenced. The nature of language is conditioned by the conventions and regulations of communities. Yet the answers to a particular situation or problem – such as violence against women and girl children – are localized and holistic, though still informed by ever-widening circles of discourse. A holistic approach involves an integration of many different perspectives that maintain their own vitality, orchestrated to work together towards a shared goal. Holistic solutions do not erase difference; rather, they carefully orchestrate different perspectives to work towards social change. The United Nations documents developed in preparation for and in the aftermath of discussions at the 1995 Fourth World Conference on Women in Beijing, China, exemplify such an approach. These documents encourage policy changes that put legal, political, religious, health, and other overlapping cultural practitioners in dialogue with one another (*Beijing Declaration*, *Strategies*).

By engaging in a sustained analysis of situated language use, the writers of this anthology make distinct contributions towards holistic approaches to violence against women, and they do so by looking at the complexities that arise when victims move from community to community as they try to survive and heal. They deal with the journeys of Western women along different axes of time and space, journeys from childhood sexual abuse to adult self-definition, spiritual, sexual, and political. The contributors examine the linguistic difficulties that arise as women take those journeys.

Elana Newman argued that mainstream, male-oriented therapeutic language cannot capture the huge obstacles a victim faces when she is trying to create a cohesive, healing narrative. An adequate therapeutic response necessitates unpacking the socio- and psycho-cultural context of abuse. Christine Shearer-Cremean contended that an empirical rendition of a woman's trauma will never adequately represent her lived experience. Police discourse renders women as body-objects; therefore, a woman can never be the subject of her own abuse story unless enabled to speak for herself, unhampered, however disorderly and disruptive such a narrative might be. Such a practice, though, would be threatening to the interests represented in the multiple discourse sites that such evidence would traverse, interests that are either open and obvious (like those of the perpetrator) or hidden and covert (like those of representatives of a patriarchal social order). The strategy of introducing multiple narratives into the legal context challenges the firmly entrenched epistemological framework currently controlling women's representation in the judicial system.

Carrie Baker took up this theme as well with her emphasis on how the battered women's defence was designed to empower abused women and more accurately represent the nature of the violence they wielded on their abusers. Baker showed that well-intentioned strategies, designed to help battered women, can backfire by representing those women as if without agency or subjectivity. Indeed, feminist legal scholars continue to struggle with the implications of the battered women's syndrome. Although generally regarded as an outdated or problematic concept within the field of feminist law, it is still used occasionally as a legal strategy.

Abused women and articulations of episodes of violence cannot be merely 'misrepresented' in judicial frameworks; the inevitable slippage of words and meaning as episodes of gender violence traverse discourse systems does not only transpire in nonfeminist or secular frameworks. Holmes and Ristock discussed the issue of how even feminist discourse often limits conceptions of abuse. In their research, they challenged feminist readings of lesbian battering, at the conclusion of their paper referencing Bat Ami Bar On, who argues for a 'nuanced feminist rethinking of the relationship between women and violence ... in a manner that necessarily problematizes the neat, clean distinctions that some feminist paradigmatic understandings of violence assume' (4). Ristock and Holmes illustrate both the danger of creating false dichotomies and the importance of keeping language central in developing more comprehensive, more effective strategies for change.

These are not merely problems identified by scholars and theorists. The linguistic complexity is also evident in the disconnect that a survivor often struggles with between her experience and the array of discourse systems she negotiates in her attempt to re-establish her life and well-being. An examination of the inherently dynamic language of abused women – language necessarily malleable as it becomes situated in social service, legal, therapeutic, religious, and criminal justice contexts – is the basis from which new solutions will spring. That language dynamism and its attendant difficulties must first be marked out and articulated before more effective solutions can be found.

Accordingly, Brenda Daley's essay problematized facile articulations of the healing process. In lockstep, linear theories of survivor healing, story-telling is both the process and the solution. The memoirs of writers such as Kathryn Harrison and Linda Katherine Cutting should help them to heal; however, the reception of their memoirs in hostile or indifferent communities hinders the process. Only when the survivor undertakes political action – though she herself decides what the political action may be – can healing actually be said to have begun. This concern is shared by Judith Lewis Herman, whose work inspires many in the battered women's movement. One benefit a survivor cannot count upon, however, is a certain reception of her story in the public forum, so fraught it is with language complexity and multiple points of view.

Unsurprisingly, then, as we conclude this anthology and look to the future, we wish to emphasize repeatedly the importance of multiple perspectives and careful attention to language. One of our overarching concerns is that solutions or approaches grapple with the process of organically integrating many perspectives. Thus, we use the term 'holistic' to begin dealing with the complexities of managing multiple approaches. Admittedly, 'holistic' was made a cliché by overuse in the 1990s. We would like, however, to harken back to a central semantic feature of the term, that is, the notion of relations of parts to wholes. By using the term, we mean to suggest that attention should be given to the functional relations between strands of the whole of discourses about gender violence. We believe that progressive discourses can retain their integrity while being informed by the words of women and the goal of accompanying them. There should be an attempt at systematic coordination between such discourses. At the same time, participants must realize that there will always be shifts of meaning as episodes of gender violence are recognized and articulated in the many, or at least currently increasing, discursive systems that deal with it.

Hence we suggest a process by which strategizing is informed by the local and the particular. This means listening to abused women; disentangling the power mechanisms at work in race, ethnicity, age, and other sociological factors that determine the experience of gender violence; and interrogating the language of all interested parties claiming to speak for and intervening in the problem of violence against women. A similar approach is used by Ruth M. Mann in her study *Who Owns Domestic Abuse: The Local Politics of a Social Problem*. Mann describes how a committee of community activists worked towards establishing a battered women's shelter in Ontario, Canada. She found that activists for the Domestic Violence Abuse Committee – and their opponents – discussed unique factors like the township's rates of poverty, abuse, and alcohol abuse, as well as childhood physical and sexual abuse that was suffered by future perpetrators. As Mann listened to the narratives of abused women, surveyed the community regarding what *they* perceived to be the causes of violence, and participated in workshops with township members, she came to understand that community members and abused women inhabited directive roles in the establishment of the shelter, roles established at the local language level rather than through statistics, police or social worker reports, or the sole testimony of professionals. The language of the community, including the language of the abused women within it, was an essential part of weaving together solutions to violence, the result being that the shelter plan was not devised solely by outsiders who would have known little else but to impose a system on the community. Indeed, although the authors in this volume do not assume that the perspectives or solutions posed by local communities will always be unproblematic, or should be unquestioned, we do believe that the perspectives of local communities should never be neglected or ignored.

Like Mann, all contributors to this volume question the language of others claiming to speak for abused women, listen to abused women's words, and deliberately interrogate linguistic renditions of abuse. These central concerns with language, its inherent instability, and the problems it will always pose inform our ideas of localized, holistic approaches to social change. If we listen to abused women speak, we are more able to identify the strands of discourse or themes of significance for them, and thus develop more effective local and holistic strategies. Three of our contributors have shown this process at play.

Winkelmann, Weinbaum, and Colton describe and examine the manner in which abused women negotiate their relationships with religious communities, imagined or constructed. These three scholars did not begin their investigations of abused women's language with a focus on religious discourse; instead, the theme emerged through the analysis. In their findings, religious discourse functioned as a network of interpretation: first, as it was imposed by abusers in order to justify their violence, and second, as used by abused women as they tried to make sense of their suffering. Further complexities and contradictions arise as the analysis expands to the wider communities of religious practice. As these three essayists show, religion cannot be regarded in simple or reductive terms as the institutional cause for women's oppression, as some Western feminists have regarded it.

Religious discourse functions in many competing ways as it traverses speakers and discursive sites. Weinbaum demonstrated that a religious conversion can provide a discursive framework that liberates the abused woman from male dominance. She argues in her case study that the interpretative frame of reference offered to Dorit through Catholicism for many years prevented her from freeing herself from physical, emotional, and sexual abuse. Through Dorit's conversion and relocation to Israel, she finds language – housed within Jewish and, regrettably, anti-Arab, anti-Muslim networks of interpretation – to express her anger and sadness and to justify her need for vengeance. Weinbaum notes that this strategy is also (mis)directed at Palestinians – an unfortunate but attendant consequence of Dorit's conversion experience coupled with her abuse history. In Dorit's case, the complex interaction of culture, society, and particularly religion gives rise to her desire to embrace another epistemological system, one she deems more suitable for her self-expression. Rather than liberating herself from the confines of a systematic network of interpretation, Dorit finds comfort in exchanging one system for another. Clearly, the exchange was an uncritical and thus problematic one.

Moving from a linguistic to a material rhetorical analysis, Cathy Colton examined how Catholic teaching and language – which Charlotte Fedders sought out in an attempt to understand her abuse and at the same time relieve it – functioned to imprison Fedders in an abusive relationship. She found it necessary to throw off the perceived shackles of institutionalized religion in order to leave her violent marriage, finding solidarity through her women's book group. Further, Colton argued that an expanding definition of what we mean by 'language' is in order through her analysis of how the physical body possesses a textual role. A woman's body is a text through and upon which she and others make meaning. Violence is a rhetoric to be examined, critiqued, dismantled.

Last, Carol Winkelmann's study of the language in a shelter for battered women clarified, on a micro-level, the shifting, hybrid nature of language as it unfolds in context. She shows how different threads of discourse – specifically religious and secular feminist discourse – intertwine in shelter talk and enable the creation of new, perhaps previously unavailable worldviews. It is critical to be able to identify themes of significance in an attempt to imagine or design strategies for change. Winkelmann's essay highlights the importance of not just hybridity but story-telling in the healing process. Through the process of story-telling – so thoroughly dialogic in its essence – abused women are able to etch a map of who they were and are and who they might become in the future. Though they cannot guarantee outcomes, they can collectively imagine their way to new solutions for the problems and challenges of life as survivors.

Writ large, this is the challenge and the accomplishment of global conversations or international conferences on the status of women and girl children. Indeed, we draw inspiration from the remarkable work accomplished at the Beijing Conference in 1995 by women from all over the globe. Their accomplishments are captured in United Nations documents, published before and after the conference, encouraging the interrogation – by local governments, agencies, religious leaders, educators, and so forth – of traditional or customary practices that are harmful or detrimental to women and girl children. For example, the local community members interrogate religious expression to discern whether or not it is actually the basis for discrimination against women and girl children (*Beijing Declaration*, 149–50).

Those who care about the well-being of women and girl children might begin similarly by looking at their own localities, their own governmental and religious institutions, and their own cultural practices. In concert with others in the community and in touch with global discussions, they must define, redefine, and define again the problem and changing conditions of violence and, in particular, the ways in which violated women themselves articulate the problem.

This volume deals with some concerns of Western women; however, transnational and cross-cultural discussions – fundamentalist or progressive – will reveal commonalities and differences across culture. Thus, we identify international studies, informed by feminist perspectives, as a critical forum and lens through which to encourage and critique such dialogue. Many feminists have already contributed to this project, feminists such as Chandra Talpade Mohanty (2003), Nawal El Saadawi, and Gayatri Spivak. (For another fine example, see Lay, Monk, and Rosenfelt, *Encompassing Gender: Integration International Studies and Women's Studies.*) We support such a trajectory for further work specifically on survivor rhetoric in its global variations.

We, the writers of this volume, attempt here to contribute to the struggle of women world wide by offering up what we know best: our understanding of local sites of struggle, the voices of battered women themselves as they struggle to survive, and the importance of pragmatic solutions in the struggle for women's human rights. We wish to stay grounded in the concerns of battered women as they express those concerns, at the same time as we hope to become involved in ever-widening circles of conversation about social change; that is, we wish to attend carefully to survivor rhetoric as it situates and re-situates itself across discourse systems. Finally, we wish to remain ever self-reflexive about theory and methods as we engage continually in dialogue with concerned others. We invite you, the reader, to do the same.

Works Cited

Barlas, Asma. *'Believing Women' in Islam: Unreading Patriarchal Interpretations of the Qur'an.* Austin: University of Texas Press, 2002.

Bar On, Bat Ami. Introduction to Hypatia: Special Issue on Women and Violence, *Hypatia* 11.4 (1996): 1–4.

El Saadawi, Nawal. *The Nawal El Saadawi Reader*. New York: Zed, 1997.

Lay, Mary M., Janice Monk, and Deborah S. Rosenfelt. *Encompassing Gender: Integrating International Studies and Women's Studies*. New York: Feminist Press at the City University of New York, 2002.

Mann, Ruth M. *Who Owns Domestic Abuse? The Local Politics of a Social Problem*. Toronto: University of Toronto Press, 2000.

Mohanty, Chandra Talpade. *Feminism without Borders: Decolonizing Theory, Practicing Solidarity*. Durham: Duke University Press, 2003.

Spivak, Gayatri Chakravorty. 'Can the Subaltern Speak?' In *Marxism and the Interpretation of Culture*, ed. Cary Nelson and Lawrence Grossberg, 271–313. Urbana: University of Illinois Press, 1988.

United Nations. *The Beijing Declaration and The Platform for Action*. New York: Department of Public Information 1996.

United Nations. *Strategies for Confronting Domestic Violence: A Resource Manual*. New York: Centre for Social Development and Humanitarian Affairs, 1993.

Wadud, Amina. *Qur'an and Woman: Rereading the Sacred Text from a Woman's Perspective*. New York: Oxford University Press, 1999.

Contributors

Carrie N. Baker, JD, PhD, is an assistant professor of sociology and anthropology and director of women's studies at Berry College in Rome, Georgia. Her research interests include women's legal status in the United States, women's political activism, and feminist legal and political theory. Her dissertation, 'Sex, Power, and Politics: The Origins of Sexual Harassment Policy in the United States,' traces the emergence and development of the issue of sexual harassment out of the second wave of the women's movement. She has published several articles on sexual harassment in educational and workplace environments.

Cathy Colton is a member of the English faculty at the College of Lake County in Grayslake, Illinois, where she teaches composition, basic writing, twentieth-century American literature, and women's literature. She has contributed essays to a rhetoric textbook and published an article on Alice Walker's womanist rhetoric in a collection of essays on Walker. Her current research project is on women who fight back, an exploration of popular movies, novels, and music in which abused women kill their abusers.

Brenda Daly, professor of English and women's studies at Iowa State University, is currently working on *Deep Learning: An Aging Feminist's Continuing Education* and *Lost Albums: Photographs of a Fifties Family.* Two earlier books are entitled *Authoring a Life: A Woman's Survival in and through Literary Studies* (1998) and *Lavish Self-Divisions: The Novels of Joyce Carol Oates* (1996). She has written numerous articles on contemporary women writers and on feminist pedagogy, and co-edited the collection *Narrating Mothers: Theorizing Maternal Subjectivities* (1991). Daly is the editor of the *NWSA Journal* and teaches literary theory and such interdisciplinary courses as 'Trauma, Memory, Narrative, and Healing' and 'Women and Madness.' In 2001, Daly was named the Louis Thompson Distinguished Undergraduate Teacher at Iowa State, and in 2003 she received a Research Excellence Award from the College of Liberal Arts and Sciences.

Cindy Holmes is a community-based feminist educator, researcher, and organizer in Vancouver, British Columbia. She completed her master's degree in sociology and equity studies in education at OISE/ University of Toronto, where she researched education about lesbian abuse. She is currently the program manager of the BC Association of Specialized Victim Assistance and Counseling Programs and the Coordinator of the Safe Choices project, a community education project about abuse in queer relationships. In addition, she works with community groups in the areas of violence against women, anti-oppression education, and program evaluation and research.

Elana Newman, an associate professor of psychology at the University of Tulsa, Oklahoma, studies the meaning, aftermath, and treatment of psychological trauma. Her research has focused on gender and trauma, assessment of trauma-related difficulties, the ethical conduct of trauma-related research involving human participants, juvenile justice and trauma, and treatment of post-traumatic stress disorder. Her current work focuses on the intersection of journalism and traumatic stress studies, with a particular emphasis on ways to enhance media coverage of trauma, conflict, and tragedy from the perspectives of journalists, people directly covered in the news, and the general public.

Janice L. Ristock, coordinator and professor of women's studies at the University of Manitoba, is the author of *No More Secrets: Violence in Lesbian Relationships* (2002). She co-authored, with Joan Pennell, *Community Research as Empowerment: Feminist Links, Postmodern Interruptions* (1996) and co-edited, with Catherine Taylor, *Inside the Academy and Out: Lesbian/Gay/Queer Studies and Social Action* (1998). She is a founding member and past president of the Canadian Lesbian and Gay Studies Association. She continues to do anti-heteronormative work with feminist and lesbian community groups as well as program evaluations and anti-violence work.

Christine Shearer-Cremean received her PhD in rhetoric and writing from Bowling Green State University, Ohio, in 1997. She is an assistant professor at Black Hills State University in Spearfish, South Dakota, and the author of 'Body as Text: A Rhetorical Analysis of Police Reports about Conjugal Violence against Women,' forthcoming in *PreText: A Journal of Composition Theory*. Her research interests are in the areas of material rhetoric, trauma studies, and women's rhetoric.

Batya Weinbaum received her PhD in American studies from the University of Massachusetts at Amherst in 1996. Her most recent book is *Islands of Women and Amazons: Representations and Realities* (1999). The piece that appears here is part of a series of articles on oral history with women in Palestine/Israel, to be published in a forthcoming book. She is the founder and editor of *Femspec*, an interdisciplinary journal.

Carol L. Winkelmann is an associate professor at Xavier University, Cincinnati, Ohio. She teaches language/linguistics courses, including a gender studies/peace studies course on women and violence and a course on women and sacred literature. She has written articles on women, religion, and education and on critical pedagogy. Winkelmann's book, *The Language of Battered Women: A Rhetorical Analysis of Personal Theologies* (2004), examines the language of Holiness/Sanctified and fundamentalist/evangelical shelter women in the American upper South. Winkelmann's current research concerns literacy practices and the situation of Buddhist women in northern India.